# The Despiritualized Church

by
Rev. Keith Bender

**OZARK**
MOUNTAIN
PUBLISHING

**Library of Congress Cataloging-in-Publication Data**
Bender, Keith. 1927 -
"The Despiritualized Church" by Rev. Keith Bender
What the church is really supposed to be and what Jesus was really attempting to teach .
1. Church   2. Jesus' Teachings   3. Bible
I. Bender, Kieth 1927 - II. Title

Library of Congress Catalog Number: 2008938649
ISBN: 978-1-886940-52-9
Cover Art and Layout by www.enki3d.com
Book Design: Julia Degan
Book Set in: Times New Roman, Lucid Calligraphy

Published by

PO Box 754
Huntsville, AR 72740

www.ozarkmt.com
Printed in the United States of America

# Table of Contents

**Part One        Spirituality or Churchianity**

| | | |
|---|---|---|
| 1 | Religion and Spirituality | 3 |
| 2 | Churchianity | 9 |
| 3 | The Devolution of the Church | 15 |
| 4 | Later Developments of the Church | 21 |
| 5 | Our Right to Choose Without Fear | 27 |

**Part Two        Misunderstandings and Misapplications**

| | | |
|---|---|---|
| 6 | Yes - God Still Talks To Us | 33 |
| 7 | Dreams: Inspired Intuition | 41 |
| 8 | The Ambiguity of Truth | 51 |
| 9 | The Truth Within | 59 |
| 10 | Jesus: The Christed Man/Woman | 65 |
| 11 | Mary Magdalene | 75 |
| 12 | Adam, Eve and Soul Mates | 79 |
| 13 | Soul, Spirit Guides, and Little People | 91 |
| 14 | Two Trees in the Garden | 99 |
| 15 | Karma - What You Sow, You Shall Also Reap | 109 |
| 16 | Reincarnation | 119 |
| 17 | It's In The Bible | 127 |
| 18 | The Tides of Life | 133 |
| 19 | Of Life and Death | 139 |
| 20 | Destiny and Fate | 149 |
| 21 | Destiny and Free Will | 155 |
| 22 | Misunderstandings | 159 |
| 23 | Lucifer | 169 |
| 24 | Creative Evolution | 175 |
| 25 | Prayer | 183 |
| 26 | Meditation | 191 |
| 27 | Guilt and Shame | 197 |
| 28 | Ten Commitments | 205 |
| 29 | Good Intentions | 211 |
| 30 | Death: Why We Resist It | 215 |

| 31 | Sex and Homosexuality | 221 |
| 32 | Faith and Doubt | 229 |
| 33 | Forgiveness and Grace | 235 |
| 34 | Marriage | 239 |
| 35 | Creativity and Co-Creation | 245 |
| 36 | I Am and Co-Creation | 251 |

**Part Three    The New Age of Spirituality**

| 37 | The Winds of Change | 261 |
| 38 | The End Times | 267 |
| 39 | The New Age of Responsibility | 275 |
| 40 | The New Church | 282 |
| 41 | What Lies Ahead | 289 |
| 42 | The Dawn of a Rising Sun | 295 |
| 43 | Coda | 301 |

| Author Page | 303 |

# NOTES FROM THE AUTHOR

My book, *The Despiritualized Church: What Went Wrong, and What Must Change,* is the result of a difficult examination of truth and how it is misunderstood and misapplied in the Christian churches of today. What I have come to realize is that our churches no longer represent what Jesus meant them to be when he attempted to embed universal love and forgiveness in our hearts and minds. As the Church grew in power and arrogance, it bastardized his original teachings and subsequently despiritualized itself and its offspring, which includes virtually all the mainstream Christian churches and various cults. Few churches today any longer serve as beacons of light illuminating the way to spiritual understanding and reunification with God. They have instead, to the neglect of spirituality, become material institutions of conceit and self-empowerment by fostering misleading doctrines and dogma. In wrongful socio-economic interpretations of scripture, they have led their followers into sinkholes of misapplied humanism.

I am not against religion per se, but I am fiercely against what the Church has done to the pure teachings of Jesus the Christ by turning them into anti-spiritual renditions of what Jesus taught and exemplified in his life. I have a fervent belief in his teachings, and I have an indestructible connection to the spiritual essence of what Jesus exemplified in his life and in his relationship to Father/Mother God – the same connection that he tried to help all of us understand and accept as our birthright; that which is the right and heritage of all God's children.

Contrary to popular opinion, Christianity was not established by Jesus. It is a religion that is in many ways, the

i

antithesis of spirituality. It was created not by him, but by the apostles and other converts over the centuries that came after him. Jesus had nothing to do with the formation of the materialized religion we follow now with all its rules and regulations, dos and don'ts, and stratified belief system. Christianity is a man-made institution, a religion that has all but tied us to a condition of slavish obedience to the Church's dictates – not to God who gave us free will, but to the Church that has taken it away!, and all of which is based and perpetuated on a foundation of fear. The Church has come not to represent love, but its opposite: fear. In its time it became void of the spiritual essence of freedom and self-responsibility. That is not what Jesus wanted to establish when he walked the earth.

A new Church is being established in this New Millennium. Its foundation is universal love, forgiveness, freedom, unity and responsibility. It will include respect and acceptance of all men, including that of self, and communal responsibility to care for others – not to be their custodians, but to do what is in our power to assist them to become self-sufficient and self-responsible for their spiritual growth. God has set into motion that which cannot be stopped. It will eventually result in a world of men and women living in freedom and equality, abundance and creativity for all. And it doesn't matter who is for it or against it; the urge of freedom and self-expression will prevail. It can be delayed, but it will not be stopped.

I am certain that the readers of *The Despiritualized Church* will find it interesting and provocative – if so, well and good, for that is what it is meant to be – to start people thinking, and to understand that what we have been conditioned to believe is not necessarily the truth. With this new way of seeing, we can open our minds and hearts to a new and joyous one-on-one communion with our Creator. Then and only then, will we lose fear and gain the love, peace and abundance that has been withheld from us for so long.

In the New Millennium the things of man-mind: religions and churches, our many and varied socio-economic institutions, and others that are not in accord with responsibility, truth, and unconditional love, will undergo a healing that will rearrange priorities, removing those that are at odds with God's will, and nullify any that can't adjust to the attributes of the New Millennium. Morals and values will readjust to truth. The sins of the fathers, which are really sins of the Church, will be recognized for what they are – most notably sins against the word of Jesus and against those of us who look to the Church for spiritual guidance that has not been forthcoming. Their errors will be recognized and acknowledged, impelling severe amendments to basic dogma and doctrine that can bring the Church back to the original and pure teachings of Jesus, unaffected or influenced by past or future conjurations of man-mind.

*The Despiritualized Church* is not intended to be another scholarly treatise of Church history and theology, full of references and footnotes. It is opposed to a restrictive scholarly method of analysis, favoring instead, a balancing of research with inspiration and intuition. Research was a necessary part of this book, but so also was direct intuitive reception and inspiration from a higher source – the Universal Mind. It is written for the ignorant of pedantic theology, and for the entrapped who live in timid acceptance of Church conditioning. It can enable all to see with clearer vision what the Church has come to stand for and what it has done to us. In pertinent chapters, the book examines the misunderstandings and misapplications of truth as evidenced in church dogma and doctrine. Its intent is to educate the men and women of confusion and doubt in terms understandable to them, as to what their conditioned beliefs center on and from what it is derived. In this manner, it looks at the various doctrines of belief and conduct as practiced by the Church in a way that will inform them of the truth, and reveal to them the lies and deceits that have been holding them prisoner to programs of misinformation and stultifying rules and regulations. Only truth will set them free.

It is to be understood that Jesus is not superior to us, or greater than us, for we are all children of the one God, inheriting the same gifts and potentials. The differences lie in how we have used or abused our inheritance, and how it has established our personal stage of spiritual evolution. Jesus was able to express greater abilities because he achieved greater spiritual development and became Christed. That is our destiny also. We all have the same Christ spirit within, developed in greater or lesser degrees as is our wont. Didn't he say that greater things than he did we can do also? And didn't he also say: *Know ye not that ye are gods?* It is only our unbelief, schooled in ignorance that holds us back from our inheritance and inevitable unity with our Father/Mother God.

Our personal Christ child lies within in the manger of gestation, waiting to be birthed with understanding, then to be nurtured and developed into the magnificent child of God that is our birthright and destiny. In our maturity we will recognize and accept our divinity and oneness with God as the natural order of things and become christed as Jesus was christed, co-creators with God in unity and love.

# PART ONE

# SPIRITUALITY
# OR
# CHURCHIANITY

# RELIGION AND SPIRITUALITY

In the far, distant past, man in his most elementary form was not a very intelligent person, lacking most of the refinements of reason and creativity. But he did have a gift of intuition – a direct link to God that we are just beginning to reconnect to. It is the ability to receive from Universal Mind on an intuitive level, simply by going within to the Source. It is an ability that was given to us at creation, but which has since atrophied through disuse. We set it aside in favor of reason, and have lost our awareness that it is an innate part of us that can be reactivated.

In time, emerging intelligence modified the purity of man's soul expression and eroded the sanctity of our communion with God, creating a separation of spirit and mind. Words took on a reality of their own and created a schism between rational mind and God-mind, resulting in a spiritual disconnect. In the interim between then and now, reason became man's god, ruling his thoughts and actions thereby superceding intuition, placing intuition and the truth of inner knowing in the back seat. Reason became the dominant factor in man's life. In the continuation of it, the inner essence of spirituality was replaced with an outer expression of man-originated and oriented concepts of religion. It became void of the spiritual essence of our Godly reality.

There is a difference between religion and spirituality. Religion is an outer expression of an inner core of spirit. And as such it is a mental, rational, legalistic expression that too often lacks the essence of spirituality, which is our innate equality and oneness with God. This materialistic expression of spirituality is not a development of recent years; it began closely following Jesus' resurrection and persists in that insistence today, manifesting in a crisis of faith in Christians and the church. It was spawned in the early church when Paul realized that the fledgling church of Jesus needed a more organized structure if it were to Christianize the world, as he thought Jesus wanted. It was nurtured during the years when the scattered congregations had grown large enough that it was felt necessary by the elders to organize the scattered groups into cohesive dioceses under the control of regional directors, or bishops.

The church was soon regimented under the guidance and control of the bishops and gradually the original teachings were formalized into dogma, doctrines, tenets, rules and regulations and all the stultifying things bred from them. All these were invented by the church hierarchy, following one another lock step in succession as the need arose. It resulted in an expression of faith and worship that was at variance with the spiritual intention of Jesus' mission. It became a religion of man, established not by Jesus, but by men of ecclesiastical power. It continued to expand as the church grew in power, gaining ultimate control over the lives and spiritual expressions of its members.

The spiritual church of Jesus became an inflexible institution of religion – a man made entity that lost its original purity and intent and became mired in power and self-serving activities, and whose existence was dependent on the continued suppression of its members. Its power base was unsubstantiated fear instituted with the conjured concepts of original sin, damnation, punishment and other culpable doctrines. The restrictions and demands placed on the followers of the church became so bad that it brought on a period of total suppression of spiritual inquiry and freedom of human endeavor in the Middle and Dark Ages, affecting every expression of man, including the arts and sciences.

The period of extreme deprivation and debasement of human spirituality lasted for well over 1,000 years, from about 450 AD to the middle 1400s. Here and there, it is still evident in various Christian churches. It was the cause of the Dark Ages, a period of the lowest debasement and depravity of religion during the Middle Ages. It was an extreme degradation of mind and thought that began to end only with the advent of reason and a reawakening of spirituality. The change emerged at the end of the Middle Ages with the appreciation and expression of left brain logic and right brain creativity, a period of time known as the Renaissance that occurred roughly around 1450 AD.

The Dark Ages marked a time of ignorance, superstition, social and material chaos and repression of human spirituality. It was a time of spiritual darkness, void of the light of truth; it was a time when the Catholic Church exerted pernicious influence and control over human thought and activity. It was the womb of the Inquisition, during which suspected heretics and dissenters were subjected to imprisonment and torture of the vilest nature, all under the guise of love – its ostensible purpose was to save the souls of the sinners. But that required confession of their supposed sin, whether guilty or not. If they refused, they were tortured until they confessed. Some of the means of torture were to burn the victims alive, some were tied to the rack and pulled apart, and others were impaled on spikes, or squeezed to death until confession was wrought out of them. Jews were even locked into ovens and baked alive. It didn't matter if the people were innocent or not, if they were accused of heresy, that was enough. Only confession of real or imagined sins could save them. Even so, innocent people were tortured, crippled and scarred for the rest of their lives, or if they were fortunate, they died a quick death.

That was the universal, or catholic church that *man* built; now spelled with a capitol "C". It was a church that was based on a religion of conditions, fear, and loss of freedom. It was not and is not, the church that Jesus said he wanted. The oppression by the Catholic Church still continues today, although in a modified form that doesn't include physical imprisonment and torture. But fear of eternal damnation for anybody that deviates from Church doctrine is still viable and coercive. Although not openly acknowledged by the members of the Church, it is nevertheless an insidious, influencing factor in their lives. It inhibits freedom of expression and inquiry of the truth that God says will set us free.

There is a difference between religion and spirituality. Although they are considered by most to be one and the same, they are too often antagonists. Religion can be inspiring and uplifting when it is grounded in true spirituality, but too often it is not. And it can be good for people when it is expressed in unconditional love and freedom. But again, too often it is not. Religion is especially valuable for people whose understanding of God and spirituality is minimal and under-developed. But religion has come to be expressed as *churchianity*, a vehicle that often involves the suppression of spiritual inquiry with a misuse of power and prestige.

Religion is a system of expressing one's belief in a manner established not by God and not by Jesus, but by man in a formalized, ritualistic program of rituals, rules and regulations, none of which were taught or established by Jesus. We think we have a fair idea of what religion is, but do we? Because we see through the glass darkly there is little understanding or appreciation of what should be its spiritual base. Although we should because spirituality should be the core of religion, whereas in practice it is not. If religion doesn't have its roots firmly planted in expressions of spirit as its foundation of faith and its reason for worship, it is nothing but sounding brass and tinkling cymbals, sounds without substance in misleading, stultifying and stupefying expressions of man-mind. Religions emphasize humanism, social activities, personal and psychological counseling, size of congregations and the shape of the church building, soup kitchens, welfare and charity. Most of that can be wonderful, Godly, and needed, but the primary emphasis in almost all Christian churches is exclusively on these things, and little or no attention is offered for the spiritual welfare and edification of man. There is only token guidance and instruction that helps the individual members gain communion with God on a personal basis and become one with Him as Jesus taught and exemplified in his life. There are some religions and churches that express the true spirituality of faith and love, but their numbers are few.

Our essential and primary purpose in life is not to serve man, but to find our way back home and become one with God in love and creativity, which is our birthright. But religion does not emphasize that. Although it emphasizes the necessary concomitants of spirituality, such as charity and compassion, which are the *application* of the love we should always express as children of God, they do not show the way – they are not the path – they are only the desirable expressions of living our faith.

True religion on the other hand, can be expressed by lying in the shade of a spreading tree on a warm summer's day with thoughts of peace and tranquility. True religion could be going fishing, communing with the essence of God instead of sitting on a hard bench in Church on a Sunday morning, fighting to stay awake. True religion could be strolling on a wooded trail breathing in the fragrance of a bright summer day, or being spiritually refreshed while walking in a warm spring rain. Or it could be doing dishes with a song in your heart. True religion is nothing but the expression of one's spirit in graceful moments of peace and tranquility, or in moments of despair while maintaining faith and gratitude in the power of love, giving thanks for the wondrous gift of life. It is communion with God on the level of feeling and intuition, which is the language of the soul. True religion is a never-ending essence of love and peace.

Spirituality is the true religion – the knowing of God's presence and that we are one with Him. Spirituality is a system of principles that express who and what we are. It is self-empowerment with a direct link through feeling and intuition with our higher selves. It is a one-on-one communion with Father/Mother God, and of being a co-creator with the Grand Creator, the Source of all.

Spirituality is self-expression in exploring the unknown. It is the right to question preconceived ideas and conditioning, free of restraint and fear of what could be. It is our right to say "no" to God without fear, and still receive His approval and blessings. It is the freedom to fail without remonstrance or punishment. Spirituality is the right to cast off the rules, regulations and restrains of organized religion and formal worship that have long held us to the limitations of ignorance and incompleteness. It is the unrestricted freedom to be ourselves in whatever manner we choose, in all our grandeur as children of God. It is the knowing that we are one with Him. True spirituality is nothing but love in action.

## 2

# CHURCHIANITY

Mankind was created with an indwelling intelligence of spirit with all the qualities of God, the innate ability to reason, visualize, organize and create, but above all, to love. But the effective use of these abilities did not come easily for he lacked the necessary tools to be able to use them wisely and effectively, which was language plus an under-girding of prior experience with which to innovate and create. When he eventually developed his innate intelligence, it was a miraculous achievement, but it had its downside. He began to compare what he was beginning to observe through his physical senses with what he had always before accepted as reality through his intuitive feelings –the voice of his higher, or universal mind. As he learned to reason, he started to question, then to rationalize and that led to doubt, and doubt led to disbelief and finally to rejection. Words took on a virtual reality of their own and commenced to separate his rational mind from his God-mind creating a spiritual disconnect. He created a world of illusion in which he found himself entrapped, believing that illusion was truth.

In the passing millennia, comprising hundreds of thousands of years, mankind went through cycles of growth and regression, creation and destruction, and spiritual cycles of love and fear, including times of the most horrendous satanic expressions of hatred and cruelty. We are familiar with Noah's flood when mankind was so debased and immoral that God flooded the Earth, at which time only a handful of people survived to recreate and repopulate the Earth. But that may not have been the only time that God wiped the slate clean and started over. There is ample evidence that worldwide cataclysms occurred at other times in localized parts of the world. So it appears that mankind has had difficulty in accepting and retaining the high spiritual qualities of love, which is the essence of God.

Periodically, at the most down-times of man, God has sent spiritual avatars, masters and prophets to reawaken man to his true spiritual heritage. There have been many, a few of whom were Zoroaster, Buddha, Mohammed, Moses, Mani and Confucius. And then two thousand years ago, Jesus, who called attention to God's Church – the Temple of God within man, firmly rooted in love and forgiveness. His church was not an edifice of marble and glass, but a spiritual entity of love and truth, conceived by the intelligence of Spirit and universal love. Its foundation was not steel and cement, but the timelessness and irrefutability of God's Truth and eternal presence; it was a spiritual church of knowledge, understanding, love, wisdom, and an awareness of our oneness with the essence of God.

Jesus taught that we are God's children and, as such, equal to our spiritual Father/Mother just as Joe and Susie are equal to their material father and mother. In this we are the rightful heirs of God's goodness, power and creativity. In everything we think, desire and do, we are one with God and co-creators with Him. This was the essence of Christ's teachings, but along the way, the original teachings deteriorated into entrenched deviations of Truth.

As the power of the defenders of the faith grew, their control of the Church became unbreakable. Their proclamation that man is born in sin and is unworthy and incapable of salvation except through Jesus, which in practice meant through the Church, compelled them to create faux truths, including restrictions of conduct and regimentation of worship in order to hold the loyalty of their congregation.

Sin is merely a temporary self-created separation from God. But the Church's concept of sin as a mortal transgression was used as an expedient by the Church to enforce compliance to their demands. There is no Godly judgment for so-called sinners

– none except as they may unwisely judge themselves; hence there is no punishment and no hell from which to be saved. The Church reasoned that should it be known that there is neither hell nor punishment, fear of their authority would be lessened and the Church would lose its tight control of its members. Therefore, if the Church was to retain its power, it was necessary for it to redesign truth to fit its own ends. They had to control the minds of the masses. To make them subservient to the Church, they used sin and fear of eternal damnation to assert and maintain their control.

That's what happened centuries ago when the Church developed and imposed false religious concepts and dogma to fit the framework of their self-serving purposes. Through lies and the imposition of intimidation and fear, they were able to enforce obedience. With the threat of eternal damnation hanging over their heads like Damocles' sword, the followers of the faith submitted to the will of the Church. It became heretical to think for oneself and deviate in any manner from approved doctrine. In the process, they surrendered their right of free will and became subservient vassals of the Church, unable to freely reason for themselves and unable to follow the dictates of their hearts and souls that were crying out for expression.

Religion as a material expression of spirituality, finds security in form. Man loves order and becomes confused when something is not in its expected place in the proper order and scheme. As we like to be able to identify things by our senses, spirituality is not solid enough for us; it lacks structure. So we materialize the spiritual essence of religion in buildings, priests, dogma, and ritual – and in this we gain comfort. We resist change because it upsets our sense of order and predictability. So we cling to the comfort of the expected thrust on us by the servants of the Church. We accept their conditions no matter how restrictive they are of our freewill and our individuality, all so that we don't have to experience the unexpected and the discomfort of uncertainty.

We have surrendered our birthright of freedom to comfort, and we accept the known and the reasonable over the amorphous reality of spirit and Truth. In the process, we churchify religion. In time, our restructuring of religion creates a de-spiritualization of faith and worship. The institution of man becomes an illusion of reality, expressed as the Church with its many conditions, demands, threats, punishments and fear. It is fear that binds us to the Church, rather than love. We have forgotten our true spiritual inheritance of freedom and power. We are no longer aware that we are God's children born in love and freedom, with the rights of inheritance of all that He is. We don't realize that as brothers and sisters of Jesus, *we are equal to him in every way!* The difference is that he has achieved a level of Mastery far above our developed ability, but we are working at it. Didn't he tell us when he performed miracles, *"Greater things than these you can do?"* He would not have said that if we didn't have the same potential of mastery that he demonstrated, and it would not have been said if we were not also the children of God with the same rights of inheritance and potentials that he demonstrated.

It is helpful to realize that religion is the product, not of God-mind, but of man-mind, and is therefore suspect and unreliable. So it is not necessarily spiritual. In individual cases it may be, but too often it develops into *Churchianity*, lacking the essential qualities of the higher values and true essence of God: self-responsibility, freedom, understanding, power, peace and love. The various interpretations of truth exemplified in the many churches developed by the many religions of man are of man. And every utterance that comes forth from every religion is either the conjuration of man-mind, or it is filtered through man-mind and is therefore unreliable and suspect. This includes all the world's religions: the Hindus, Buddhists, Zoroastrians, Bahaists, Mormons, Catholics, Protestants, Manicheanists, Shintoists, Muslims and the thousand others. The only reliable source of Truth is God, and the only dependable channel to His truth is within our own beings – the Temple of God. It is available in one-to-one communion to all who should want it enough to humble themselves to seek it.

The Church developed a religion of error and compromise, and even at times of terror and torture in order to enforce its authority. In the years of growing Church power, its effects increasingly separated Christians from God. Fear induced by conditioning and brainwashing replaced love and became a satanic ruler influencing and crippling the natural expressions of love and man's innate equality with his creator.

Churches, Catholic and Protestant alike, have become insular bastions of humanism, barren islands in the cosmic ocean of spiritual needs. Preachers and priests teach as they were taught, as they were taught, as they were taught, lock step, ad infinitum, all the way back 2000 years, and far beyond that. As the years rolled by, opinions, politics, self-serving desires, simple stupidity, and even good intentions altered the original, basic understandings of truth, universal love, unity and forgiveness. Language was changed and misinterpreted, meanings took on new definitions, misunderstandings arose and we're now at the point in the devolution of Christianity that we're no longer certain what Jesus originally meant.

So it must be asked, is religion spiritual? Does religion meet these criteria of truth? Are the churches spiritual, and do they encourage the free pursuit of spiritual expression? The answers depend on the belief systems of the individual and the churches, both the neighborhood church and the universal church, and on their purpose and motivation.

What say you?

# 3

# THE DEVOLUTION
# OF THE CHURCH

The Catholic Church that ultimately emerged from the early years of discord and jockeying for power within and without its area of control was neither planned nor encouraged by Jesus. It is doubtful that he would recognize his church today as the church he intended to establish in our minds and hearts. Jesus taught unity and the principle that all men can personally commune with God.

Rather than being based on love, it developed, and continues today, a variation of legalism originally established by Moses, albeit in modified form. Resting on a foundation of fear, it resulted in a church of contradiction becoming continuous battles of duality, of opposites that resulted in a victory for deception and fear in the defeat of Truth and Love. It was a loss of spirituality and freedom so stupendous that the church gained absolute power over its fearful members. With the inclusion of dogma and doctrines of its own making, it effectively removed God from any direct connection and personal involvement with Christians. The church took it upon itself to tell people what to believe and how to worship. It thus negated man's inherent right to worship in their own way devoid of coercion, reason or ritual, and it thereby reversed the natural upwelling of love that would infuse them with the presence of God.

In a reversal of the Garden of Eden when God expelled man from His Garden, the church took over and *expelled God* from meaningful participation in the spiritual lives of Christians.

It took over 1500 years from the time of Jesus to Martin Luther for the Christian world to begin to repair its severed communion with God. That period of isolation is known as the Middle and Dark Ages – a time when the church cut off God from personal relationships with its believers. It was a time when the church was its own master, devising expressions of politics, judgment and salvation, worship, and power bases according to its finite reasoning, all done without the benefit and guidance of the Infinite.

The Church was originally established on universal love, but over hundreds of years, it gradually changed with the imposition of what the Church believed was best, not for man's spiritual development, but for a de-spiritualized system of a material religion that developed for the benefit of the few. It established a system of dogma that was every bit as demanding and coercive as the Mosaic Law it was supposed to supersede with love and forgiveness.

The emphasis of the Catholic Church is slewed toward self-interest and the preservation of its power, more than with any concern for the needs of the people. This is best exemplified in the Inquisition of centuries ago, and in the example of the church today, in the way it has shown greater concern for the church's reputation than with the emotional and spiritual welfare of its innocents who were victims of priestly pedophilia. In its emphasis on the material over the spiritual side of the duality represented by the Tree of Good and Evil, the church has eaten the fruit of the tree and is beginning to find it bitter.

Altogether, the church won a pyrrhic victory when it achieved material supremacy over spirituality for it had to use fear to capture the obedience of the people. Whereas with love, it would have realized loyalty born of respect and devotion to a common cause of love. The church professes that God is unconditional love, but it exercises love with conditions – love that is framed with limitations set up by the church. It speaks of

16

God's grace, yet enforces a system of law with conditional grace. It espouses free will that can be exercised only in a narrow field of limited expression – just enough to make an inhibited use within the limitations of church doctrine.

In Catholicism, there is no freedom for one to go to God on one's own volition. Forgiveness is an integral part of church dogma, but it can be achieved only through the intermediaries of the church: the priests and bishops and others of priestly power. The church then has conjured a role for itself of judge, jury, and executioner and provides no opportunity for appeal to the High Source of Justice. The church accuses and excuses, judges and dispenses punishment as it is inclined to do. Without the forgiveness of the church, there is no other hope for salvation. So fear dominates and replaces freewill and love.

Unfortunately, in the Church's victory in its war of duality, it resulted in a de-spiritualized religion that effectively destroyed free will and responsibility. The Church won dominance of the minds of its members and has maintained it with its control of dogma and doctrine with its subsidiary rules and regulations.

World religions have seen a succession of Avatars, Saviors, Masters, Prophets and Teachers as long as man has been on this Earth. They have appeared whenever there was a need to restore the people to the path of spiritual unity with their God. Each one gave to the people of their time what was most needed for their spiritual revitalization and advancement.

Moses established the rule of Law and obedience. Through him, God gave to the world the Ten Commandments and although they were difficult to follow in strict obedience, they were at least believed to be attainable. But over the centuries, the number of laws multiplied from the original ten to staggering numbers, of sub laws when each succeeding generation of priests continued to add more "dos and don'ts" to the list. It resulted in a conglomeration of rules, regulations and laws that were impossible to obey in their entirety. Something had to give and it was naturally, obedience.

Jesus' ministry brought unconditional, universal Love and forgiveness to the world. But after 2000 years, it too has not succeeded in its intent. Not because of unnatural requirements, but because the founding church has been unable to extricate itself from its web of conflicting laws and false dogma. The church has established creeds, doctrines, tenets, repressive rules and its own list of "do's and don'ts," very few of which were formulated by Jesus. The love it preaches is conditional, requiring unswerving obedience to all requirements of the church, with the resultant erasure of free will. It negates love by instilling fear of damnation. All these enforce compliance to the demands of the church. Those who obey get assurance of salvation; those who don't, well.....

Jesus' teachings certainly never required any kind of judgment or penance for salvation. One can find in the Bible many references to Jesus' forgiveness of sinners, but where in the Bible is there a reference to punishment meted out by Jesus? Jesus gave to all men and women: love, forgiveness, and freedom to be themselves. The church's use of threats and intimidation overrode love and freedom, thereby binding the loyalty of the congregations to an institution made not by God, nor by Jesus, but by man. It created servile obedience and loyalty to persons and to a material edifice of stone and icons, rather than to one of Spirit, Love and Truth. Its success was accomplished through love's opposite – fear.

The Church was, and still is, afraid of independent spiritual growth and development because growth requires change, and change is predicated on the freedom to choose. If the change turned out to be at odds with the position of the Church, the deviation would provoke immediate reaction. It doesn't take much imagination to realize that few would dare such a chance if the results could mean something as serious as imprisonment, torture, excommunication or eternal damnation. The Church doesn't use the extreme methods in these days, but the threat of excommunication and damnation of sinners is still real and viable.

Contrary to what the various religious sects teach, God does not judge, not even when the Book of Life is opened at the time of death. The book is real, but not in the sense of a hard covered and bound volume with page after page of sins and mistakes. The book is written on the skeins of time and space and is called the "Akashic Records". These records include every minuscule event, condition or situation of a soul's journey through its many lives.

When the soul transits from the physical realm to the spiritual realm, the records are read by that same soul, and all the things encountered or experienced in that particular life are revealed, both the positive and the negative. At that moment, every soul will review its own life in full recall of every word spoken in anger or peace, and every thought and desire and every action. It all takes place in a brief instant of time. From this *review,* soul will understand that what it did or did not do, was or was not conducive to its spiritual growth. It will be read not in horror or with guilt, but with calm acceptance of mistakes made and progress achieved. It is similar to an artist who surveys his painting in progress, evaluating what has been done to see where corrections should be made and what could be done to improve the finished work. Then he or she will pick up the brush and continue with the development of the work. In like manner, soul will understand that all things can be corrected. It will then have the opportunity to do what is needed to change anything that holds it back in its spiritual development. The events are revealed so that soul can see in its physical experience where a particular thing was helpful or hurtful to itself or to others. In the awareness that the review provides, it can be understood what needs to be worked on in a subsequent life. The review is not a judgment where there is condemnation or guilt or punishment; it is for edification and greater understanding and spiritual growth.

Every man and woman will, in their time, realize that judgment comes not from God, but from man. At no time does God ever judge or punish. When there is punishment, it is inflicted by man or the church, not by God. Occasionally, an individual will punish himself and the source of the punishment then is from within his own self. Punishment is never necessary, never recommended, and certainly never required, and if inflicted on oneself, it is stupid. If therefore, God does not judge and neither does He punish, what authority does the church have to judge and impose punishment on God's children?

God cannot punish because He is Love. What is the church then? Is it an instrument of Truth and love, or does it mislead by false teachings and fear? Does it instill a respect for God that is based on gratitude, mutual respect and loving devotion, or on suspicion, guilt and judgment? Does it base its actions on the Golden Rule, or does it follow its own guidance and subvert the rule by doing unto others what it, the Church, believes is best? And of what is done, is it done in love without conditions, or in self-righteous interference? Think back to the Inquisition – what was the motive of the Church then? In other words, was the church then, and is the church of today, ruled by a theology of unconditional love, forgiveness and freedom, or by a philosophy that Church knows what is best, and the ends justify the means?

4

# LATER DEVELOPMENTS
# OF THE CHURCH

Religions are man-made systems of faith and worship that may or may not be true representations of God's intent. One can find religions in every corner of the world that have at their core an unmistakable essence of God's love and infallible spirit in His participation in the lives of men. But one can also find religions with a heavy emphasis of materiality rather than spirit, such as certain churches of the mind or science. And too, there are religions that worship Satan – the personification of evil and not of love. There is something for everyone – a thousand to pick from. Whatever religion it is, or whatever church best represents what the individual feels drawn to, it is believed by its followers that through allegiance to its peculiar dogma, and living it in strict obedience and active participation in its rites and rituals, they will be saved. For Christians, the Church has made salvation as easy as falling off a log. They don't have to change, just believe and accept Jesus into their hearts and get a free ride to heaven.

There are aboriginal religions scattered around the world, some that innately understand and practice in innocent purity their personal relationship with their Creator. They are found in the Australian outback, in the hills of the Borneo rainforest, in the Amazon River Basin, in the jungles of Africa, on the islands of the Pacific, in the ice covered lands of the Arctic, and on the plains and hills of the Americas. Of all these, perhaps the most telling example of pure spirituality is that of the "Real People" of the Australian aborigines. They have no formal organization, no methodology, no rituals or lists of requirements, no written records or books or manuals or hymnals, and no need of any in order to exercise their intuitive understanding of God's love and participation in their lives. They are born in love and live in trust. Everything they think and do is a hymn of praise to God. They live in a land that is inhospitable to any but them. They find water where there is none and food when none is at hand. God is in them, and of them, and with them, guiding, loving, protecting and providing for them. They are living examples of man living in oneness with their Creator and Provider.

There are those who say organized religion is necessary. By this, they support the regimented hierarchy of churches that determine for people what they are capable of understanding, what they are permitted or able to know of Truth, what they should believe, what is good and what is not good for them, and how to express their faith. Nothing is left for their followers to do, but to attend church and obey, confess their sins and receive absolution or forgiveness.

It is important to understand that religion and church are co-derivative and co-dependent. Religion and church are intertwined, being both the creator and the creation of each other, which are essentially man-made institutions with formalized systems of belief and worship – the conjurations of theological deviations from truth.

The roots of the major world religions are found in the teachings and examples of spiritual masters or avatars, but the theological foundations of religion are formed not by a Master, but by the hierarchy of the church that followed him. Religion and church therefore, are essentially man-made institutions that have developed formalized systems of worship independent of their master or avatar. They are organized, regimented, and rigid, dogmatic expressions of faith. Their foundations and their future rely on the perpetuation and maintenance of each other.

Today's churches are composed largely of people of sincerity and good intent, desiring to know God and to serve Him and their fellow man in love and compassion. In spite of mistakes and misinformation, there is a need and a place for churches as structured in our present culture, for they provide a means for their members to find a degree of solace and comfort. It gives them a buttress from the hardships of life and a sense of belonging to a God of love. It offers companionship, opportunities to learn selflessness and expressions of compassion, and it offers encouragement and hope. In its rituals, it may provide a sense of mystery – the attraction of belonging to something greater than limited understanding offers, and more loving and forgiving than what has been known and experienced. But rarely does the church offer anything other than a superficial explanation of the mysteries, although the knowledge is available to any who wish to pursue it. As a result, preachers and priests are relegated to the inferior positions of shepherds rather than facilitators, social workers rather than teachers, who structure and control the lives and thoughts of their followers.

Unfortunately, they offer little of the deeper truths of God and life, and how man can come to know the God that lives within them and how they can grow to become one with Him. Their beliefs center on the outer trappings of faith – the rituals and regulations that essentially revolve around sin and punishment – the expressions of faith that are predicated on false understandings and misinformed teachings of God's Truth. Theologians of whatever church are conditioned to believe the parental Catholic Church's exposition of original sin and that man is born in sin and is inherently evil. They don't understand that a child of God, of a God who is Love, cannot be evil. They may do evil, they may see and hear evil, but that doesn't make them evil. In their hearts, in their souls, in the very reality of their Spirit as a heart-cell of God, they are Love, even if they don't know it and even if their fellow men convince them of its opposite. They are of the same stuff as God because they are His children – how could they be otherwise?

In uncertainty, people accept in their hearts a God, not of love and forgiveness, but one of anger and punishment, based on their conditioned beliefs of sin and damnation. In spite of their desire to know the God of Love and a life of freedom, conditioned beliefs hold them to a life of timidity and fear, rendering them unable to throw off their misconceptions and be true to their spiritual selves.

When Jesus taught, he called attention to the Church *within* man; a church not built of stone walls and stone hearts, but of spirit and love; a church not of overflowing collection plates, but of overflowing love and forgiveness – a church not of separation, but of unity.

When Paul assumed a position of leadership in the fledgling church, he believed the church Jesus intended would not be achieved without a more cohesive organization, which at that time was a loose collection of believers with little or no structure at all. So he promoted the establishment of the material church in which the informal congregations of disjointed groups would gain strength and cohesion in a more formal organization. In the beginning, it was helpful for it enabled a growing number of people to benefit from Jesus' ministry. It served a good purpose by kindling a light of truth and understanding in the common man, those not yet advanced enough in spirit to receive the full benefit of spiritual knowledge without a formalized religion of dogma to guide them. But the Church eventually became a monster because of the changes and additions it made to what Jesus taught, resulting in the de-spiritualization of the Church and of man. It largely remains so today.

Following the resurrection of Jesus, his followers who were scattered throughout the Mediterranean area, met in small groups of informal congregations and discussed Jesus' teachings with the apostles, and later with the successive leaders. But as the congregations grew, the informal approach was regimented and the scattered churches appointed bishops as leaders of their group. It didn't take long for their worship to become formalized and ritualized. False doctrines were developed and achieved respectability and were adopted as true teachings of Jesus; things that he never promulgated and which he never intended, such as hell, damnation, confession and penance. As the universal (catholic) church grew in power, so did its leaders. As some bishops were more enamored of power and the trappings of office than they were of freedom and truth, a system of obedience and worship was developed largely to assure the continuity of their power. In short, they created a religion that was largely not in accord with Jesus' intention, and it came to be called Christianity.

A belief system was promulgated among the early Christians that dramatically changed the intent of Christ's teachings. In the passing of the years, the bishops, in the nature of man, "improved" upon his teachings. In time, these became programmed dogma of laws, doctrines, creeds and tenets supposedly established by Jesus or the apostles, but which in reality, were conjured and enforced by the bishops of the Catholic Church to promote and sustain their own idiosyncratic beliefs, self-centered desires and activated wills. In their own minds, they believed they were chosen to interpret God's word and had the authority to impose their will on the Church and its members. But in order to solidify their positions of authority, they had to justify and enforce their power. Thus, over the passage of years, it became necessary to develop a system of worship and obedience that was to embrace concepts of original sin, judgment and punishment, of hell and damnation, and the many other claims and actions of erroneous interpretations of Jesus' teachings. In many ways, religion separated the people from their original condition of unity with God, and the Church became materialized and consequently, despiritualized.

To ensure that their flock receives salvation from sin, which was an invention of the Church, various rules and requirements were instituted, which, if scrupulously followed, assures salvation. They make it plain that due to man's inherent sinful nature that resulted from the disobedience of Adam and Eve, God doesn't hear them and thus it created an almost irreparable schism that destroys personal relationships with Mother/Father God. They don't explain that God is to be found

25

within and accessible to every man, woman and child; to do that would undermine their power and control.

In order for the Church to defend the conjured claims that were used to authenticate their developing systems of worship and programs of obedience, it became necessary to proclaim that man had to earn salvation through rituals and obedience to the dictates of the Church. This included self-flagellation and mortification through privation and sacrifice. Most importantly, it meant that mankind had to give up the right of exercising free will without restraint, unless we were willing to suffer condemnation and punishment without hope of salvation.

# 5

# OUR RIGHT TO CHOOSE WITHOUT FEAR

The emphasis of Christian religion is on sin and being saved from it. But the question remains, what do we have to be saved from? We need to ask ourselves a few questions. Do we need to be saved from doing the very things God wanted us to do when He gave us free will? To exercise the freedom to be what we wish, to do what we wish, when we wish, and how we wish – to make mistakes, to learn from them and to correct them? And if in the using of this wondrous gift, we use it in what seems to be to our detriment, or to the seeming disadvantage of others, would God punish us for our error? Would we punish our children if they make a mistake when they use the freedom we give them to help them grow materially and spiritually? Is God any less loving and forgiving than we are? No. Like any good parent, He would help us see our error and give us His unfailing love and encouragement to try again to correct our error – then again and again if it's needed until we accomplish its purpose.

God wants us to use the free will that He gave us, and to use it with confidence so we can choose and make mistakes without fear of punishment, and to eventually learn to exercise our will in synchronous harmony with His. But we have been taught that our free will is only free when it is used according to the will of the Church; to be used basically to determine which of two destinations we want for our soul's ultimate fate. In other words we have but two choices: heaven or hell. What kind of choice is that?

It is only in the process of choosing and experiencing, succeeding and failing that we shall come to remember our oneness and equality with God. But in our unquestioning obedience to the Church, it has assumed a false authority as a necessary intermediary to God. Lacking the freedom to choose according to our desires, we long ago abdicated our royal sonship with God, and surrendered the opportunities that life affords us to think, desire, create, err, or even love in freedom without fear of censorship and punishment. In all Truth, we are God's children just as Jesus is, and we are one with God just as Jesus is. The difference is that we are not yet wholly developed enough spiritually and are not yet aware of, or in acceptance of, our oneness with God as Jesus demonstrated he was. When we are, we too will walk on water, heal the sick, raise the dead, and move mountains.

If there is nothing from which to be saved, fear of authority would be lessened and the Church would therefore lose its iron fisted control of its members. If it would retain its power, it would have to design truth to fit its own ends. That is what it did centuries ago when it developed and imposed false religious concepts and dogma to fit the framework of their self-serving purposes. Through lies and the imposition of intimidation and fear, they substituted illusion for truth.

During this time, it became apparent that in order to retain their personal power, and the power of the Church in the politics of the land, adjustments had to be made in the Church's belief system. Sin and hell were conjured and stressed to instill both fear and unquestioning obedience. Because their dogma stated that man was unfit and unworthy to go directly to God for forgiveness of sins due to their inherited sin resulting from the fall of Adam and Eve, an intermediary was required and forgiveness could be achieved only through that office. With man being unable to communicate directly with God, the Church conveniently provided the needed intermediaries – their priests who alone had the sacred anointment to act in behalf of the supposed sinner. But one wonders, since the Bible stresses that the Temple of God is within, why would man need an intermediary? When God is within us already, securely ensconced in His temple and eager to commune with us, to talk with us, to laugh with us, to love with us and to be one with us, why can't we go to Him directly without the need of outside assistance from a minister or priest?

As sin is merely a self-created and temporary separation from God, there is no judgment except as the "sinner" may judge himself. In this light, there is nothing, neither punishment nor a hell, from which to be saved. Why then, if we are God's children and able to go to Him directly, would we need an intermediary, since God is within us already and as close as a thought?

In order to enforce compliance with the laws of the Church, punishment was threatened for sinful acts. The threat of hell hanging over every thought and act instilled both fear and obedience. Since everyone believed they had sinned at some time in their life, it was necessary that the Church provide a means of escape, or salvation as they call it. Therefore, ritualized forms of worship and obedience to a long list of requirements, and self-flagellation through privation and sacrifice were instituted and rigidly enforced. The believers of the faith were locked into subservience. So one thing led to another and, in time, the Church became regimentized, formalized, materialized, socialized and fossilized. The inevitable result was the de-spiritualization of man and the Church, and the humanizing of God by recreating Him in man's image to become merely a Superman, albeit one of power and wisdom, but like man, one also of anger, judgment, and weakness.

To discourage anyone from going within to the Source for forgiveness, thereby bypassing the Church, it was essential to create a means of keeping the congregants dependent on the good will of the Church. That was accomplished with the creation of salvation through confession and penance. This forced a dependence on the priesthood because only a priest was able to perform the necessary ritual, as he alone had the divine authority to give absolution. He did that through the implementation of certain procedures of contrition and confession – punishment that resulted in forgiveness. With that kind of fear-based belief, it is apparent that without the Church and the priest as an intermediary, a sinner would believe that he didn't have the chance of a snowball in hell would have of being saved.

It should be realized that religion, as expressed by the Church, is the product not of God, but of man, and is therefore suspect and unreliable. So it is not necessarily spiritual. In individual cases it may be, but too often it develops into churchianity. This includes not just Christianity, but all the world's religions. In this, we are kindred brothers and sisters all under the umbrella of One God.

No master, no avatar, no savior or prophet, including Jesus, ever preached religious concepts, nor did they establish any religions. They taught only Truth, and lived it by example. They demonstrated the innate spirituality of man and our oneness with the One God. The only pure source, the only reliable source of Truth is God within, and it is available on a one-to-one communion to all who should want it enough to humble themselves to ask for it.

The Church controls through fear, but that control is slowly slipping away. There is a resurrection taking place, a rebirth of truth bringing with it the fresh air of renewal and restoration to original roots. Jesus' intent is now being reasserted and reestablished in churches across the land, finding expression in the minds and hearts of those longing to breathe the air of freedom, and live free in unity and communion with God.

PART TWO

# MISUNDERSTANDINGS
# AND
# MISAPPLICATIONS

# YES – GOD STILL TALKS TO US

There was a time about 2000 years ago and extending far beyond that, when it was not unusual for God to talk to people. When He did, people listened. The Bible is full of His conversations with people of all kinds: shepherds, carpenters, philosophers, fishermen – people such as Moses, Jesus, Mary, Paul, Abraham, Noah, Jonah and countless others. There are many more in other world religions: Buddha, Confucius, Zoroaster, and Mohammed to name only four. Sometimes His voice was unmistakable like rolling thunder, other times it would come through like a silken whisper of feeling, or an unmistakable inner knowing – intuition.

But most often God spoke to people in dreams. There was Joseph, Daniel, Jacob, Abraham, Peter, Nicodemus and others. But that was centuries ago, and it is commonly accepted now by clergy and parishioners that He doesn't talk to us like that anymore. It is an interesting coincidence that He stopped talking about the time when the Church created the doctrine of Original Sin and its related doctrines and dogma. The result of that was to make us believe that we are born in sin and unworthy of hearing God, and the Church became our intermediary to Him. But the Church, was then and continues to be wrong, because God does speak to us.

Paradoxically the Church teaches that we should listen to our voice of conscience and not go against it; yet if we do listen to the still small voice, and apply what we hear, we will be censored if it is contrary to the rules of the Church. In other words, do it, but don't do it – a classic catch twenty-two. That's only lip service to truth, and what the Church does allow us to have is often based on deceit and misrepresentation of truth.

Why don't we hear Him when He speaks to us? It's because we believe what we have been taught and we stopped listening because of the fear that has been instilled in us. We have been taught that we are inherently evil, born in sin and live in sin, and if we do this or do that, or if we don't do this or do that, all as the Church prescribes, we will die in sin. We have been conditioned to believe that God will not talk to us. But if He does and if we should hear Him, we must deny our senses because if it can't be God, then it must be the devil – a conjured entity of evil having no basis in fact or support in the teachings of Jesus. Our minds are closed to any possibility that the voice we hear just may be God, or maybe His angels trying to break through our wall of fear and disbelief.

We no longer give credence to the voice of God or His angels when they try to speak to us, which they do through our feelings, intuition, dreams and visions, and for a few, even in one-to-one communication. God has never stopped trying to break through our resistance. He is not a quitter – it is we who are the quitters. The problem then is not with God, but with us. He still speaks to us, but even if we should listen we don't hear – what He says doesn't register. Why? Mostly because of unbelief and fear, so when we do hear his temperate voice, we tend to reject it because of that fear. We have a conditioned rejection of anything that doesn't come to us through the Church. So it's put down as imagination, or wishful thinking, or unbalanced mentality. Or it could be vanity: "I don't need God – I'm doing very well on my own, thank you," or, "I make my own decisions," or perhaps, "Only the gullible or those that are not very bright hear Him." But whatever our reasons, we close our minds to any possibility that it could really be God, or perhaps our spirit guides or angels trying to communicate with us.

It's interesting that we ask for help, and then refuse it because it doesn't come to us through our five senses, packaged as we would like it to be. It's our conditioning that when we are repeatedly told the same thing countless times, it eventually becomes acceptable. From the moment we first suckle our mother's breast, our grounding begins with the corrections and admonishments that the little things we do in error or disobedience are wrong, even that we are bad, and God doesn't like that. So after repeated warnings, we begin to think that "God doesn't like me." Our lives are rooted in fear. We are taught the children's prayer: *Now I lay me down to sleep, I pray the Lord my soul to keep. If I should die before I wake, I pray the Lord my soul to take.* Fear! We are taught to fear God! This is absurd for fear is the opposite of Love. We are taught to fear God who is nothing but LOVE.

Our parents unwittingly continue to encourage, or at the least, condone the Church's indoctrination of fear and guilt, reinforcing our growing belief that we are sinners, guilty of original sin and not worthy to hear God. As they were taught by their parents and teachers, so they teach their children. We are shackled to an aura of guilt that we have learned to live with. It doesn't take long for an immature child to believe and never to question the programmed duplicities of their mentors and the church. Our lives are encoded with fear. The conditioning that begins in childhood continues, and is compounded by well-meaning Sunday school teachers and the exhortations from the pulpit that God is vengeful, demanding, and easily provoked. There is little attempt to balance our negative conditioning with the Love of God. But that is what we must do if we are to ever gain peace and harmony in our lives – or in the world. It comes with the truth that God says will set us free. Although the church should lead the way, they have done the opposite; rather than liberating us from our fears, they have compounded them.

It's fascinating that we pray so sincerely and religiously, yet at the same time negate our intent with fear and doubt. Some will pray devotedly while on their knees, maybe for hours, talking, begging, crying, or thanking God for favors granted. So busy talking, they don't have time to listen. They get so boxed in with their fears and personal needs, they build an impregnable wall around their conditioned beliefs that not even Joshua could break down with all his trumpets and the shouting of multitudes.

Too often, prayers are merely rote, mechanical repetitions of the same words and actions. The Tibetans spin their prayer wheels, and every time the little ball on the end of a string attached to a hollow cylinder whirls around, the cylinder rotates and the prayer inscribed on it, or contained within the cylinder, is offered up to God. The Lord's Prayer of Christians is not much different, nor is the Rosary, for both are usually thoughtless, repetitive utterances given without thought of what the inner meanings are – just mechanical repetitions with little or no personal involvement. What do these kinds of prayer mean to the one who offers them? Do they mean anything to God when there is nothing of the heart and soul in the prayers? Many children's prayers, the Lord's Prayer or the Our Father prayer, the rosary, are similarly repetitious and can be equally meaningless when uttered without sincere intent or awareness of what is really meant. They are only words uttered, or beads fingered, or cylinders rotated – all religiously repeated actions without meaningful purpose. When the heart's intent is not involved in prayer, it is simply a mechanical repetition of utterances of one sort or another with little power or effectiveness. Yet even so, there is some value in them, for they can contain at the least, hope. God hears the intent, and no matter what is said or how it is said, with sincere intent the prayer reaches God, although it may be with little power.

We continue to talk to God, but with feelings of inadequacy and inequality. But we don't listen. Should God talk back to us, we react in disbelief or fear, because we can't imagine that God would ever converse with us. But He does. If it is revealed to another person that we heard God, we are suspected of having a few loose marbles, or worse, we could be suspected of being a charlatan, a false prophet, or self-delusional. How sad it is that we are so conditioned to unbelief that we are closed to God's interaction with us. He does talk to us, but in ways we are mostly unaware of. But with effort and desire we can learn to hear Him.

Why should we not hear Him? He lives within us in His temple, and doesn't it say in the Bible, "Know ye not that ye are Gods?" We are God and God is us, within us, and part of us. How our lives would change if we understood that, and accepted it as the truth it is, and use it as the cornerstone of our relationship with God. When He talks, we should listen as the ancients did with belief and understanding.

The question remains, how does He talk to us? The ways are numerous. Most are so simple and unobtrusive we don't recognize His voice when He does speak. Some of the ways are through feelings, intuitions, dreams, visions, and meditation. There are other ways so subtle and understated as to pass us by unnoticed. You may hear Him in a comment made by one person to another as you walk by them; it may be the headline of a newspaper or a magazine article; it could be a Freudian slip of the tongue; perhaps something on TV that pricks your ears – a word, a phrase, a sentence or a picture that may seem at the time to be totally unrelated to your needs or interests, yet pertinent. What ever it is, if it resonates with you, pay heed for there could be a message for you. God does talk to us.

It could be the words of a song; especially a song that keeps running through your mind and you can't get rid of it. If you look at the words and hear what they're saying, chances are you will find a message aimed directly at you. It may be the title or a phrase, even a pun but with a distinct meaning for you. It is especially pertinent when you awake from a sleep or a nap with a song in your head. You will notice that as soon as you are aware of the lyrics and find a message in them, the annoying song will usually disappear.

It may come through in synchronicity – a fortuitous set of circumstances or coincidence of events that seem to be meaningfully related. They are events that happen that are odd or unusual at unexpected times, which seem to strangely coordinate together, seeming coincidences that aren't coincidental at all, but purposefully coordinated.

But whatever it may be, if it causes even a momentary flicker of notice, it could be trying to get your attention – perhaps a reminder of something that happened recently, or long ago that could be relevant to the current situation, or something that may happen. Pay attention to it for it could be a message to you from your higher self, or from God.

When we are open to receiving, and don't casually brush aside seemingly unrelated and irrelevant things and start paying attention to them, we can hear God's angels, our spirit guides, or our higher selves speaking to us, giving us what we have prayed for. It may be an answer before a question is asked, or perhaps a direction or guidance before an awareness of need. Contrary to church teachings, we are worthy of hearing God. The main reason we don't is conditioned unbelief. If you set that aside and stand back and open your mind – you will hear Him. We have been wrongly taught, and it is up to us to seek and know the truth, and in that, gain our freedom from the tyranny of self and false dogma.

There are many ways of contacting God and His messengers. There is prayer, which is talking to God, and meditation, which is listening to Him. We've never been taught to listen. We don't even listen to each other. When listening is practiced diligently and with pure intent, the time will come when there may be a one to one communication, conversing with God as you would with a friend. And that is one of the keys to successful communication. As difficult as it may be to believe, God wants a rapport based on friendship. There are also mediums, psychics, seers, prophets and others. But great care should be taken when consulting one of these for many are self-anointed and untrustworthy. But greater than all of these is intuition, for it is the flow of information from the highest spiritual realm of the Universal Mind – God Mind, coming directly to you. Intuition is a knowing, a certainty of truth. It is the voice of the Higher mind – the connection between your conscious mind to the Source – the Source of all truth: God.

Psychics or mediums can be very effective, but they are not wholly reliable because they receive information in symbols that they then have to interpret, and that is problematic and uncertain. Intuitives are more reliable than any of these because they receive knowledge directly from the Universal Mind with the use of far fewer symbols, and there is less chance to mistakenly misinterpret what is received.

By going within in silence to your higher mind, you are establishing a connection with God. All that is required to do this is to trust and be silent. Believe in your hunches, your urges, your fleeting thoughts and feelings and give them credence. It takes courage. Because we are so dependent on rational thinking and reason; we have to learn to trust our inner voice when it speaks to us. When intuition talks, it is like a knowing thought. It is not a disembodied voice of an unseen spirit or devil; it is our own higher mind relaying to us what is for our highest and greatest good, be it understanding, direction or inspiration. A kissing cousin of intuition is feelings, for it is the language of the soul. They both come from within and are in direct contact with the higher mind and the Source of all. When feeling is combined with knowledge, it equates to wisdom.

Creation is an intuitive moment of an "Aha" experience when realization bursts forth from the higher mind. Intuition is the vehicle for that spark of creativity and inspiration, and comes not from man-mind, or the conscious mind, but from the super-conscious, the higher realm of mind. The rational brain which is too often miscalled the "mind", is but an organic computer knowing only which hole the square peg fits in, and is not in by itself, creative. If it is properly trained and controlled, it is the tool of the mind.

Inspiration comes not from reason but through intuition. Therefore reason does not precede, but follows inspiration. Let intuition guide and control us; let it be our teacher, our mentor, and our connecting link to the Source of all knowledge both known and unknown. Science, the church, the arts and teachers can only inspire us; they aren't able to connect us to God. Trust your inner guidance to do that for you, for it is the connecting link that enables us to commune with Him. We have been told that that is impossible because we are sinners, but that it wrong. We have been hobbled in our spiritual growth because of these false teachings. How sad that is; but how wonderful it is to know the truth and follow our inner intuition to freedom. Cut off the cacophony of doubt and in the stillness of receptivity, hear the many voices of God whispering to you.

# 7

# DREAMS: INSPIRED INTUITION

For the first fifteen hundred years after Christ, the Bible was not available to the general public. It was written in Latin, the language of the Romans. It remained the official and only language of the Church until the 15th Century with the advent of the Renaissance. It was able to be read and understood only by the clergy and a few educated laity. Except for these elite, it was a forgotten language. The masses received from the Bible what the Church felt was in their best interests, that and that only, which in practice, meant what was best for the Church.

With the advent of the Renaissance following centuries of darkness, during which God had been effectively expelled by the Church from any meaningful participation in the lives of the people, it was possible for God to once again touch the hearts of struggling mankind. With the breakout of resurging independent thinking, held underfoot by the Church for 1500 years, mankind rediscovered the philosophies of the ancient Greeks and Romans. They began to think and reason for themselves and threw off the stifling cloak of Catholic dogmatism. Martin Luther challenged the power of the Church when he tacked his Ninety-Nine Theses to his church door and fomented the Protestant Reformation; Gutenberg invented the printing press and the Bible became available to others outside the Church; Michelangelo created unspeakably beautiful marble sculptures and painted the Sistine Chapel ceiling while lying on his back; Leonard daVinci, painted equally beautiful paintings, and invented machines not thought of before or during his time – only recently did science catch up with his visions and build some of them – the tank which helped change warfare in the later centuries, the helicopter, parachutes, water screws and many others. Copernicus, Galileo, Newton, Raphael, Titian and other artists of the Renaissance changed man's understanding of the world and themselves.

Out of the deep darkness of the Middle Ages, God's light was rekindled and shone brightly on mankind. Science flourished again; culture and the arts and music highlighted the glories of God; reason and good will resurfaced; and a new mankind emerged. Freed from the tyranny of excessive ecclesiastical control, Christians were able to break away from the rigidity of the totalitarian Church, on which until then, they were totally dependent for their spiritual guidance and salvation.

But even during the terrible time of the Dark Ages, God continued to speak to man, but man was no longer listening. He spoke in ways that were not understood or appreciated at the time, and are still not fully acknowledged and acceptable even in our enlightened age. We are speaking here of dreams. For us as children of God, dreams are our most common means of communicating with Him. It has always been so, and it is so today.

In the early years of the Church, dreams were not considered unusual or without value. They were accepted as revelations from God. But in time with the advance of reason and the stultifying interference of the Church, dreams were discouraged and ultimately considered as having no value, or worse, as consorting with the devil. The loss of daily communication with spirit proved to be as debilitating to man's spiritual growth as shortness of breath would be to our physical health. The Church facilitated this development by insisting that God no longer talks to ordinary lay people in any manner, and that He speaks to us only through selected intermediaries of the Church. It wouldn't do if man were to start listening to God instead of to them.

Dreams are the language of spirit guides, angels and God speaking to us. Of all the ways God or spirit talks to us, dreams are the most common because everyone has them. Science has proven that sleep with dreams is vital to our mental and physical health. Insufficient or inadequate dreams can result in harmful mental and emotional aberrations. There are many ways God talks to us, but of them all, dreams are the most recognized. They are God's forgotten language. They are the voice of spirit and higher mind, the language of truth clothed in symbols most of us don't understand, but then neither do we try. And we could if we tried. Our attitudes toward dreams, range from being interesting, to confusing, to perplexing, and hard if not impossible to understand. Some are flattering, some are frightening, some are encouraging or correcting, but all are languages of truth that attempt to call attention to something in one's life. Thoughts, actions, problems, maybe desires that need to be seen for what they are. They are often prophetic, and they are also often revelatory of past lives. When these are understood we are armed with tools that enable us to assume greater control of what and who we are. When they are understood to be pertinent to one's life, and thusly applied to the situation indicated in the dream, great changes and greater control are possible.

Dreams have always been God's most effective means of speaking to us. Records of this go back millennia, as far back as Noah. Biblical history is replete with dreams of people of all strata of society and persuasions. A few of the most notable personages of the Old Testament were Noah, Abraham, Jacob, Ezekiel, Daniel, and Solomon. In the New Testament, some were Mary, Joseph, John, Peter, Paul and many others. These Biblical personages represent God's ability to enter into human consciousness, bypassing reason.

You can't intellectualize God; you can't reason your way to any understanding or relationship with Him. It can only be experienced, and dreams are a way to accomplish this. Dreams are expressed in feelings, and feelings are the language of the

43

soul. In our feelings we can experience the love and presence of God, helping us to realize our oneness with Him.

God communicates with us in many ways. Among them are feelings, intuition, and visions. But we have traditionally paid little attention to feelings, less attention to intuition, and none to visions for they are considered "day dreams" and of no value, or at the worst, of the devil. But one cannot ignore or escape a vivid dream, be it one of terror or one of beauty. They beg to be understood.

What were once accepted as normal communications with God are today, things of suspicion and gullibility and of little or no value. We no longer trust our intuitive abilities, relying instead on logic and empirical reasoning. We are dependent on our senses and rational faculties, and everything that comes to us must be accepted or supported by one or more of these. But there are other ways to receive the subjective influences that affect our awareness. Among them are clairvoyance and clairaudience, prescience, feelings and synchronicity. Messages can come to anyone, at anytime, or anyplace, whether unsought or prayed for. The more alert one is to the unnoticed things, the greater is our receptivity in hearing spirit when it speaks to us.

Underlying all receptivity is our intuitive faculty. It is through intuition that we receive dreams, visions and the other means of communication from God and the higher spiritual realms. When it is adequately developed we can receive knowledge directly in words. It is as though they are spoken, but without sound and without need of symbols or any kind of hidden or esoteric language. There is no need of translation for the message is clear and concise.

Western culture has emphasized objective reasoning and minimized subjective inspiration, resulting in an imbalance. We have substituted the objective, rational mind, for the truths as evidenced in subjective reality. We have exchanged spiritual experiences and inspiration for religious liturgies and dogma, and have adopted formalized worship of ritual and creeds, replacing the spontaneous upwelling of spirit emanating from the higher source of spiritual knowledge – the soul. We labor in the grip of the rational mind and the tyranny of intellectualism, and in the process we lost the liberty we once had in communication with God and the spiritual realm.

In many ways we have dispensed with dreams as revelations of God, relegating them to the trash bin of gullibility, superstition and outmoded beliefs. We are now an "enlightened" people, who condescendingly appreciate the needs of the early Christians who we think of as ignorant and impressionable, as needing "irrational" experiences such as dreams to keep them in harmony with their faith.

The New Testament for the most part consists of stories passed down from mouth to mouth over hundreds of years or more, then compiled and adopted as the inspired and infallible word of God. It is commonly accepted that revelations stopped with the New Testament, and are no longer relevant or needed due to our sophistication and greater wisdom. Any revelations or instructions from God that may be needed are now channeled through an anointed intermediary. In the Catholic Church, it is the Bishop of Rome – the Pope whose word on these matters is infallible as he once declared, and must not be questioned

We live in a world of duality. As a culture, we have allowed reason to grow out of control, no longer balanced with feeling, or with revelation. Modern man is mentally and emotionally sick and needs healing and rebalancing with the revelations and meaning of life that only God can give, and which rational consciousness can't provide. But we have lost our belief that it can be done. We need a return to the faith that expressed Jesus' intentions before reason and dogma gained control of our beliefs, and inhibited free will.

We need to give credence to the ever-presence of God. It doesn't matter if the churches have decided that dreams, or *inspired intuitions* as Carl Jung described them, are no longer relevant or needed, because their opinion cannot change the fact that God is still with us and continues to speak to us daily in our visions and nightly dreams. We have only to open our eyes to see, and ears to hear, to receive the word of God.

It is only in the last few decades that consideration has been given to dreams and their practical value. Until Sigmund Freud investigated dreams and assigned meaning and value to them they were neglected for centuries. Karl Jung and Gerhard Adler carried the investigation further, until dreams are now indispensable diagnostic tools for the understanding and treatment of many mental and emotional problems.

Their therapeutic value is not limited to mental and emotional applications, and is not confined to psychologists and psychiatrists. They are equally valuable to laymen as well. They have a far greater usefulness than just diagnosis; they are tools for everyone to use. In a sense, a dream is nothing but self talking to self – the higher self or universal mind talking to the conscious self. It is not our lower mind talking to us in the veiled language of symbols. The messages and revelations are from our subconscious or higher mind, and often from the universal mind that channels its intentions to us through our subconscious, to the conscious mind and revealed to us in dreams.

When one wishes to converse with the Source of truth and Infinite Wisdom, it is necessary to understand the language of dreams – symbols and feelings. In time one will hear intuitively, receiving the message in clarity and in direct reception bypassing any need for symbols. Dreams can be one's residing physician, one's spiritual guru, or mentor, advisor, teacher in every aspect of life, even our stockbroker. Advice is available for all components of life, in all areas of life: social, physical, emotional, creative or business. And it is free, given to all without condition or expectation.

One is not limited to only passive receptions of messages in dreams; it is possible to initiate dreams on topics of concern by simply requesting a dream before falling asleep, for advice or guidance on a particular thing. And even during the dream, one can be aware that he is dreaming, making it possible to redirect the course of the dream to satisfy the conscious will. Those are *lucid* dreams during which the dreamer can direct the dream while dreaming, to rewrite the script as it unfolds and take control of the flow of events. Should it be desired for example, to receive a more detailed examination or understanding of a thing or event while dreaming, you can do it by simply willing the dream to give you what you want – such as a better design for the gadget you have been laboring on for over a year. Or if you wish to fly using only your flapping arms to cruise around the neighborhood, or sit on the topmost pinnacle of Mount Everest, you can do that too. Of course you should be aware that if you choose to have only happy, satisfying dreams day after day, that's what you will get – but, in doing that you will temporarily close the door to receiving from universal mind what it knows you most need at the time.

A good technique for receiving general help in a dream is to request it in this manner: *"I ask that your advice and guidance come through to wherever it is needed the most, and in a form that I will fully remember and clearly understand. Thank you."* For specific guidance, including healing while asleep, insert the request for the help you need in the above phrase, just after the words "advice and guidance."

Dreams are often playbacks of the recorded events of our lives. They may discuss something that happened in the day preceding the dream, giving advice of encouragement, correction, new information, explanations, and whatever will be helpful for our material and spiritual progress. But they are not limited to a rehash of yesterday's or yesteryear's events. They are concerned with the total being – physical, mental, emotional and spiritual bodies, not only with current concerns, but also with what is yet to be.

The persons we are now, are influenced by our past, whether it was in a past life, or in our current life. And we can also be influenced by the future, since there is no time as we know it, and all that is, exists in an ever-present now. As time is

47

non-existent, it can truthfully be said that the future has written the past, and the past can also write the future. A seed is planted in everything we do, and that seed will sprout and mature in a resulting condition of good or bad. When we become aware of what the seed was that we planted, whether recently or in the long ago, understanding can be achieved and a course of action can be determined and followed enabling the current situation or condition to be resolved. Dreams will help us by showing us a past life during which the seed was created and planted, enabling us to better understand a current situation or problem exemplified in its fruit, and resolve it.

A spiritual process forms the basis of our dreams. Our dream's primary concerns are with our spiritual growth and our physical and emotional welfare. Everything we think, feel, say, do, create and radiate are grist for evaluation because they manifest in our lives for good or bad. Our higher mind, our angels and spirit guides look at all these things and offer help for our greater understanding of what's going on and what we can do about it. But dreams are not only about us, they are also about our relationships with other people, and most especially of Mother/Father God.

There is a very practical side to dream interpretation in that dreams will often focus on pressing needs of the body. They will tell you if what you are doing is harmful and should be corrected or changed; they will suggest the cause of excessive acidity in your stomach and how to correct it; they may warn you that a particular physical exercise is harmful, or conversely, that exercise should be practiced more rigorously.

They will give advice on practical matters, on business ventures, on social events, personal relationships, and job opportunities. They will warn you that the brakes on your car are about to fail and need replacing. They will warn you of upcoming situations that you should be aware of, or prepare for – a problem with your boss, or a coming change in the stock market that needs attention. They will give you understanding that an attitude in an earlier life has carried over into this one and is the cause of a current problem. You can gain an understanding of yourself – what you are, why you are as you are, why you are experiencing the things that are interfering with the joy of living – their root causes. Or conversely, why you have the innate ability to achieve great things in life, also of why you have failed to live up to your potentials.

Dreams have access to all knowledge and through the medium of the subconscious, they can relay God's wisdom to you. God does indeed speak to us, and nothing is withheld if it's for the highest and greatest good and well-being of all concerned. It is to our benefit to listen and hear what He says. A trained psychoanalyst or priest is not needed to explain these revelations; we can do it our self.

The greatest reward in understanding dreams is in the feeling and the knowing that we are never alone, and that God is always with us because He lives within us, and speaks to us in our dreams. He is an ever-present reality in the knowing that He walks by our side. Dreams are the assurance of a constant companion that is a viable part of us, always here and always available to give what is needed at the moment, be it love, guidance, correction, or friendship… or peace and more love

God speaks to us. He always has. He always will. We only need to listen, hear, understand, and apply what we are given.

# 8

# THE AMBIGUITY OF TRUTH

Pilate asked Jesus, "What is truth?"

Truth... what is it? Why is it necessary to ask? Truth has been so pounded, hammered, and twisted out of shape by those who find it expedient to alter or evade the truth to suit their particular agendas, it is often unrecognizable. Although it remains an important and essential part of our lives, what we are told is often unreliable, sometimes a sham. Although it may be acknowledged, it's often accepted with an element of distrust. It used to be not too long ago, that truth seemed a reliable barometer of our culture's values and mores. But the veracity of public statements, of scientific claims, and the probity of our journalists, politicians, corporate officers, teachers, and the clergy are now suspect. Once-respected persons and institutions are showing evidence of a galloping corruption of truth, or at the best, willful but misleading deceits and misrepresentations of truth.

Neither in the days of Jesus 2000 years ago when he strode the earth, nor in our own time, is there a consensus on the definition of truth. Neither in the millenniums past, or in the days of now, were there, or will there ever be agreement, because we are people of a dual nature, living in a material realm of positives and negatives – in a realm of duality where everything has its opposite: day and night, love and fear, and true and false.

Truth is not a constant in our dual world because all things exist in a state of flux. We live with truths du jour – flexible truths that are defined by what is accepted as the reality of the day. In such a state, truth is unreliable for it fluctuates with the given of the moment, and with the ever-changing understanding of what we want truth to be, forcing it to harmonize with disharmony.

In Webster's New world College Dictionary, it is stated that truth can be considered *"as a particular belief or teaching regarded by the speaker as the true one."* Note that the definition uses the words: *"regarded by the speaker,"* indicating the unreliability of *subjective belief* that is based less on fact and more on wishes and feelings. Consider the claims of yesteryear when it was declared that the sun revolved around the earth; or when it was proved by the laws of aerodynamics that a bumblebee cannot fly. Those were misconceptions of material truth – the truth that lies in the biases and limitations of knowledge. Unassailable Truth, the Truth that sets man free, is found in the Universal Mind – God Mind.

Our values are deteriorating; it is advisable to examine every utterance, claim and pronouncement for signs of deception. Has it always been this way, only to become more visible due to the mass media's rabid investigation and reporting of public statements, especially those of politically opposite persuasions? When a past President of the United States attempted to evade the truth by deceiving Congress and the people of the United States, he manipulated the nuance of words to suit his own ends and was allowed to get by with it. Worse yet, was when his political supporters and the public accepted his evasions, rationalizing his dishonesty and excusing his distortions of the truth by saying, "We all lie; we all do these things. Besides the important thing is the economy, stupid." So there is reason to wonder. More importance was placed on the economy than on respect for the integrity of the person and the office of the Presidency. All lost in that farce of exploratory justice when he was under oath: the President, the congress, and by condoning it, we the people. The integrity of individuals and the nation was tossed into the trash bin of the public's corrupted values and morals. We must ask ourselves: Where do we stand? What are our values? What is truth, and pursue the answers with diligence and full responsibility to us and to others.

There are two truths: one that we use and abuse, convenient and unreliable everyday truth; and the other is the truth that only a few are aware of – the Truth of God. To understand that there is a difference and what God's Truth is, these two must be considered apart from each other. One is changeable and inconstant and the other is constant and unchangeable, always the same, always reliable. It is the Word of God.

The most noticeable and reprehensible acts of immorality and lack of truth and probity in our society and culture, have been exposed in our institutions of religion when deceits, pedophilia, blasphemies, greed, and illegalities of many sorts among the various systems of faith and worship were caught in the spotlight of truth. It came to light with the exposition of some Protestant televangelists who were caught in acts of blatant immorality, greed and deceit. But the most noticeable and grievous was the exposure of pedophilia in the Catholic Church. It attained the apex of moral dissolution in the discovery that priests had sexually abused many hundreds, perhaps thousands of innocent boys and some girls.

It was made even worse when it came out that the Church hierarchy long knew of the immoral acts without doing anything meaningful and lasting to stop it. The Church's priests, monsignors, arch-bishops, bishops and cardinals just looked on, repeatedly condoning the pedophilic actions of their priests and doing little to prevent further abuse. Although there is no concrete evidence that the Pope was also aware of the satanic actions being perpetrated and condoned by the Church hierarchy, it is hard to believe that he was unaware. The most they did to address the situation was to sometimes give a few of the offending priests some counseling and transfers to different parishes. That was often done with no mention to the new diocese or parish of the transferred priests' pedophilia, or if they did, the offending priests were still put in positions of trust with children under their care. So the door was kept open for repeated violations of innocent children. New policies for disclosures of violations have been forced upon the Church, but only time will tell if there has been a fundamental change of attitude within the Church hierarchy.

The Church has shown little or no concern for the welfare of the traumatized children. Their primary concern has been the Church, and the damage that would accrue to them if what was going on behind their crumbling walls of moral sanctity was exposed. Their concern was not for children; it was for the reputation and the welfare of the Church and priesthood. Their concern was not for the innocent, but for the guilty. They took no chances of allowing anything to tarnish their unearned reputation of high moral integrity and probity, by keeping deviant behaviors hidden behind the frayed curtain of feigned piety. But like the Tower of Babel, their cathedrals of power and self-aggrandizement are showing signs of interior rot and conditions of self-destruction.

As in all things, what goes around comes around. The Church is reaping the fruit of its sowings. It's too early to evaluate the long-term damage that the exposures will eventually have on the Church, but it will conceivably result in a total restructuring of its systems of belief and worship. It will require some deep soul searching, with a great deal of humility and honesty that it doesn't seem to have in any abundance.

There will have to be a humble reassessment of the despiritualizing effects it has had on its parishioners for close to 2000 years, and of the humanizing image it has created of God, making Him a fearful superman of anger and vengeance. It is an image made possible by the Church's unauthorized assumption of spiritual authority, and its presumption of spiritual superiority over mankind and other religions. In both instances they were the result of the creation of things that were not of God, nor of Jesus, but things of their own conjurations. The effect was to put God in second place and mankind in servile obedience to the Church. It achieved control over the minds and lives of its parishioners by its coercive use of fear and its opposition to the exercise of free choice, outlawing the God-given freedom to choose their personal path to God and method of worship

It will require the Church, and all churches to re-examine the long-held beliefs of centuries, and re-examine them in a state of humility and honesty, basing their revised understanding on what Jesus taught – in the spirit and intent of love and forgiveness, rather than on the good intentions of his apostles, and miscellaneous followers. It will be necessary to go to the source of Jesus' teachings, some of which are recorded in the Dead Sea Scrolls and other scrolls, parchments and books located around the world, such as Tibet, Persia and Egypt. Some are readily available, some are not, and some are kept hidden in the secretive vaults of the Vatican archives, safely away from the prying eyes of free-thinking people. They are kept hidden from the world in fear of the cleansing and purifying effect that the truth would have on the people and the Church. Consider for a moment why they are kept hidden. Didn't God tell us that the Truth would set us free? Then what does the Church have that needs to be hidden? And why? It is the knowledge of the Church's duplicity of what it did to the pure intent of Jesus' mission, and its staggering and blasphemous history. The knowledge could very well destroy the Church as it is known to the world. But the Truth will out. It is only a matter of time.

The various systems of religion will have to set aside their conditioned beliefs that are based on the writings of Paul and other New Testament writers and go to the uncorrupted words of Jesus as it is found at the Ultimate Source of truth, the throne of God. It is the Source not found in the mouths of man or in books but in the higher mind – the Universal Mind of truth and knowledge. Should the churches do this, they will see themselves as God sees them in brutal clarity. The wise among them will realize that what they find is the truth that sets them free, and they will be eternally grateful. The fearful, the self-servers will find disagreement and defend the status quo regardless of consequences.

But the religious institutions have shown a deep reluctance to take this necessary step to purity and realign with the teachings of Jesus. For instance, it has taken legal action for the Catholic Church to publicly recognize that it has a problem with priestly immorality. In addition, it has proclaimed that any interpretation of God's intent is revealed through the Pope only, for only he is able to receive and reveal God's uncorrupted word. In this, they say the Pope is infallible. But since it was the Pope in a Papal Encyclical that had issued the proclamation of Papal infallibility – his infallibility, it doesn't seem likely that he will ever reveal the truth that could cause irreparable harm to his Church and his reputation. It will therefore, be necessary for the priests of the Church to step out in courage and faith in God's love for protection against the ever-present threats of heresy and excommunication. It must be realized that excommunication separates one from the Church of man only; it is not in any form, expulsion from God's Church, which is what they want us to believe. The only way for truth to ever be revealed without being forced into compliance by secular law, is for the priests of the Church to do what is right for all men, and not for the Church only, limited to self-preservation. The resistance they have shown is understandable, but unpardonable, so it will likely occur only under the coercion of law and public opinion if the facts are to ever be illuminated with the light of truth.

There will have to be a re-evaluation of dogma. The doctrines of original sin and its progeny such as confession, absolution, penance, hell and others, will have to be re-examined and realigned with God's truth as it was revealed in the words and works of Jesus. For example, where does Jesus warn of damnation, judgment, hell, original sin, and the many other doctrines of the Church? Who formulated these doctrines? Who developed their rules, regulations and rituals, and who determined the Pope's infallibility? Jesus did none of that. The process was begun by Paul, developed by the apostles, formalized by bishops, then changed, revised, added to, altered or removed by succeeding bishops over the movement of the years, until the New Testament reflected what the bishops of the Church wanted – and what they wanted were supports and props to maintain their power and false façade of sanctity. The Church's inclusion and interpretation of the material in the New Testament, and their derived dogma, are based less on the unadulterated word of Jesus, and more on the conjured doctrines of man-mind. The reconstructed churches will have to be based on a religion of spirit, rather than on a religion of man.

In time, the truth will prevail and the time for that change is upon us. It cannot be put off any longer. It is inescapable, for it is God's will. What the Church is not willing to undertake on its own, will be thrust upon them, and it has already happened with the exposure of the Church's duplicity and self-serving dishonesty regarding their pedophilic priests.

It takes motivation and persistent determination to succeed in a search for truth, whether political, scientific or spiritual. When there is not enough interest in the pursuit to put up with little setbacks, disappointments, or errors of judgment, and deemed not worth the discomfort of persistence, defeat is assured. Those who are not dedicated enough in their pursuit of truth to continue in the face of misunderstandings, false impressions, lies, and self-serving interests of others, will in time give up and live out their lives in bondage to their ignorance in whatever area they are seeking truth.

Freedom rests on a foundation of truth – this is the rock that Jesus wanted to build his church on.

# 9

# THE TRUTH WITHIN

Through our developed expertise in mental gymnastics, men have argued and ever will over what is true and what is not – just as they did in Jesus' day. When Jesus was interrogated by Pilate, he commented, *"...Came I into the world, that I should bear witness unto the truth. Everyone that is of the truth, heareth my voice."* Pilate then asked, *"What is truth?"* Jesus didn't answer, leaving it up to Pilate to seek the truth for himself.

In this, it is symbolic of the necessity for everyone to seek and find truth for themselves. The question is still being asked today, and will continue to be asked although the answer is available at any time for anyone willing and dedicated enough to go within to the Source, where it lies waiting for its revelation. For truth to be fully appreciated there must be an individual search requiring effort and unquestioned desire. Truth will be found in the religions of man only in truncated and opinionated forms, for it is filtered through the minds of man, and their understanding is confused by limitations of misinformation and prejudices. Most lack the awareness that truth lies within themselves. The various religions believe that the truth is up there, or out there, or in their books, and of course they all claim that it is in their own dogmas and theologies as conjured by their respective church.

In spite of God's statements that His temple is within and that we are sons and daughters of God, we are unaware that the Source of all truth is located within our own beings, in our minds and hearts. Truth must be dug out, examined, then rejected or applied if acceptable. The seeker is not left alone during his search; there are spirit guides with him at all times, often referred to as angels or guardian angels who guide, protect and encourage him until the goal is reached.

So where is truth in all this? It is in our minds – our higher minds, and it's available when it is sought. Unfortunately, when it is found and brought to light, it's too often misunderstood, influenced and manipulated by current misunderstandings and opinions based on the knowledge of the day, and on wishful thinking of misinformed, misled and misleading religious or theological pundits.

It's difficult for some to believe that unadulterated truth is attainable, but it is. However, each individual must find and evaluate it for themself, basing the conclusions on personal evaluations and intuitive insight. Whether one accepts another's beliefs or not, it is often valuable to consider them because different beliefs could be helpful to develop one's own concept of truth. If nothing else, it is the feeling of "No that's not it", and continues in a step-by-step elimination of what is not, eventually leading one to what is.

It must be remembered however, that the understanding and opinions of others may be like a child's, derived from immature and conditioned concepts. In this, truth is unique to the individual, and because it is unique, it is not unusual for it to be incompatible with the beliefs of others, or with one's own opinions and beliefs. God's truth will be revealed to all who seek it, but only when the seeker is willing to set aside the reasoned beliefs of others and his own inclined thinking as well. He must be willing to step out of religion's straightjacket of conformity and comfort, and set out on a courageous quest regardless of where it may lead, or what it may uncover. The seeker must go beyond the boundaries of conditioned beliefs, reaching into the unknown where truth is to be found gift-wrapped in illusions of the minds. It is only necessary to remove the wrappings to reveal the gift within. It helps to remember that truth is a gift of freedom.

Truth is the path of freewill and creation. Any creation, if it's not based on truth, will either be stillborn or it will self-destruct. If the search for truth is done in sincerity, humility and persistence, it will be revealed. When it is realized that Truth is not to be researched but discovered, then the goal becomes reachable and it will be attained. It will be found that it is not somewhere out there but within, in the minds and hearts of every living person. Some of it may be found in theology and mythology, or in anthropology and geology, and in sociology and the many other 'ologies of science and thought, also common sense and even in an occasional Sunday sermon. There is some truth in each, but it will not be found in its entirety in any one of them. The source of truth is to be found in our higher mind where God placed it at the time of creation. He established the opportunity and the channel whereby we can connect to the Universal Mind. It has been said with a great deal of irony, that if God chose to hide from man, He would hide within man because that's the last place we would look for Him. As God has said, *"Ye are the temple of the living God;"* and again, *"I will dwell in them, and walk in them, and I will be their God, and they shall be my people."* Both refer to God and His truth lying dormant within each of us.

The problem with the pilgrim is how to go about the search. How are Joe and Jane Jaberwocki going to discover the route to the inner sanctity of their minds – to the source of knowledge and truth that was placed there awaiting its discovery? How will they know how to proceed, and how will they learn to listen to the still small voice, or see the inner on again off again beacon of white light that guides them out of their accustomed darkness into the all encompassing light of love? Who will show them the way? Who will teach them? Who will strike the first light for their journey through the dark tunnel of conditions and self-serving opinions and prejudices? Is there anybody or anything? Yes – the spirit within. It is ignited by desire, and nurtured by intent. That is God's plan, His promise, and His will.

What does it require? A few things like desire, sincerity, openness, dedication, persistence and a willingness to set self aside and listen to the still small voice, and enough humility to recognize truth when it's presented will make a good start. But it will also require a readiness to let attitudes and opinions change should it all make sense. All these will help; all are necessary. But first, one must ask for it persistently and with pure intent.

To sum it up, the greatest need is pure intent and the willingness to humble oneself enough to admit ignorance and the need for God's guidance. There must be a willingness to set aside ingrained attitudes, philosophies, opinions, reasoning and all the conjurations of man-mind, and allow truth to emerge like a butterfly from its cocoon of transformation into the light of God. Of equal importance is trust. Even if one doesn't know what's happening, where he or she is headed, or what may lie around the corner, one must learn to trust. The sooner that's developed, the easier it gets; a power greater than self will give all that is needed: guidance, encouragement, strength, love, courage – whatever is necessary to succeed. God wills that no man shall fail. If something is lacking, ask and it shall be given.

When seeking truth, it is not so much a search for it, as it is a process of discovery, a process of revelation to recognize what is already possessed – the knowledge that is tucked away in the unused recesses of the mind and forgotten in time. Truth is a sleeping princess waiting in the upper room for the kiss of desire to awaken it. It sleeps peacefully, covered with the dust of forgetfulness, waiting in patience to be awakened, enlivened and used. The seeker has to have the courage to climb the tower to the upper room of the mind, dig in and poke around in the dark and musty corners where the spooks of timidity and fear dwell until he finds what he seeks. When truth is found, it's only necessary to acknowledge it and claim it. It's there, and will in time be discovered, but it's the seeker's responsibility to find it and possess it. It won't be done for them.

The process of discovery begins in the newborn child with its first breath. It continues in the ensuing everyday experiences of love and laughter, of sharing and caring, of loss and gain. It's found in the very life that is lived, whether it's lived gloriously or vaingloriously. All that is needed is to go within in silence, setting the rumblings of self aside and listen for the soft voice of truth, and then meditate on what is revealed. In short, it's necessary to evaluate experiences, learn from them and apply what is revealed to one's daily activities. In this manner, truth may be acquired and understood. In the silence enveloping the mind while ruminating gently on a thought, perhaps immersed in a tub of warm water, or lying in the shade of an apple tree on a hot afternoon, suddenly an apple falls: EUREKA! I UNDERSTAND!

Life provides unlimited opportunities for the individual to learn and discover what is important and what is not, and then to develop what is of value and make it a part of one's being. What may appear to be devastating, unimportant or stultifying to one's growth should be accepted with gratitude for the lessons that can be learned from it. It's a process of experience, gratitude, and release, letting the energy of the experience return to God.

Life is a process of experimentation and adjustment – a process of discovery that is obtained through a developing ability to see without prejudice. It provides the means whereby we can learn to know God and our relationship with Him. For some, illumination comes quickly, for others it may take awhile, but for all, opportunities are repeated over and over again until understanding is grasped and becomes part of the reality. Dedication and persistence are required. Like fishermen, those who persist in spite of obstacles, unexpected snags and broken lines, the Big Fish will be caught; pure intent will be rewarded with success.

When one is willing, a way will be found. Help and assistance are always available and immediate in the promises of God. He has given us a symbol of this. It's seen in the sky after a storm when the sun breaks through the clouds, spreading across the cloudy sky an arc of many colors for all to see. It stands in glory, a symbol of His promise that we are not alone, and that He is with us, loving, guiding and protecting us every moment of our lives.

The truth is! It cannot be denied. God's truth is undeniable, unassailable, constant, and available. It is our incomplete or inadequate understanding of His truth that makes it seem unreliable and changeable. We see through a glass darkly for our focus is on ourselves, and we find it difficult to see the reality outside the illusions of conditioning and vanity. One only has to want it and ask to be shown the way to its discovery, and when one is ready, it will be revealed. One will not need to ask, what is truth? One will need only to go within to the upper realm of the mind and uncover what is there, patiently waiting to be awakened and used.

When it becomes a part of us, then God's promise is fulfilled. The truth will have set us free, free to be ourselves and free to be one with God and all of life.

# 10

## *JESUS:*

## *THE CHRISTED MAN/WOMAN*

We have made Jesus a man of many faces. What he is to one may be quite different than what he is to another. He is in truth what he said he was, but over the seasons the Church has changed what he said and what he meant. It has made him a man at odds with his reality. So now we don't know what he said, and if we know that, we don't know what he meant. The Church has stretched and maimed his teachings to the point that his true message is lost in labyrinthine theology. We are not certain of who or what he was, although it's pretended we do. Was he born of a virgin? Was he God incarnate? Was he the Christ? Was he a master? Was he the messiah that was promised to man? Was he truly a man with all the characteristics and traits of man, with the same desires, needs, temptations and fears as the rest of us? Was he the son of man, or the son of God – or both? What was his mission? Did his mission succeed?

The Church has made a pseudo religion of what Jesus taught and it is called Christianity. But there is a problem: the Church has betrayed its roots so that it has come to accept its deceits as truth and its illusions as reality. The truth is available, but it is concealed in the nefarious deceptions and the self-serving intentions of the parental Church. Just as the sins of the parents are passed down from generation to generation, so too has the Church passed its seeds of deception to the many sects and churches that were spawned from it. But the truth of what Jesus taught is being revealed today, and in the glaring light of exposure, betrays their duplicities.

In the early years the Church paid credence to the teachings of Jesus, but within a few centuries, his message was subverted. The pure essence of his teachings of love, non-judgment and forgiveness were bastardized and used as tools to manipulate and control the minds and hearts of Christians. His message of universal love and equality became dogmatic rituals of materialism, separatism and fear. The expressions of unconditional love and responsibility he taught were twisted out of shape, and through clever use of "catch twenty twos," they were used to create conflict and dependence on the Church.

The needs of the Church changed as the political climate both within and without the hallowed chambers of their magnificent cathedrals changed. Just as truth is variable according to the needs of the moment, changing with the vagaries of knowledge and need, our concept of Jesus has also varied with the differing interpretations of theology. Just as Jesus was spirit 2000 years ago, so is he spirit today. But he was then a flesh body as well, manifesting a highly spiritualized essence of being. He was not born as the Christ; he became Christed. He was born of woman just as we are born of woman. He experienced the joys, tribulations and the temptations of life as he was growing into his maturity – not much different from what we experience – *except*, he was an old soul highly developed, a master that volunteered to reincarnate to experience life in a physical body so that he could help the rest of us, the lost and confused, to find our way.

His life as Jesus was not the first time he helped mankind, relaying to us messages of truth and understanding. He had lived before in other lives and other climes, just as we have lived before. In his many lives, he experienced all aspects of his dual nature – all the expressions of good and evil, and one by one he overcame and perfected each aspect of his flesh nature and became a master. This is the same process that we experienced in the days and lifetimes past, and which we are continuing to experience today. In this role he reincarnated many times in the various roles as avatar, teacher, or prophet, each time to help mankind know the truth and to find their way back to the Source of All. In each incarnation, as he gave to others guidance, healing, hope, and understanding, so did he receive the increase and grew ever closer to Mother/Father God, ever growing in perfection becoming the Christ.

It is believed that Jesus was a perfected being. He was not. He was closer to perfection than most others, but he was a pilgrim and student also, having achieved a mastery of many things, but he was not the perfected being that theology says he is. Didn't he say that he came to learn obedience? He was a master among others, a prophet among many, and he became the Christ as others had before him, and as some have become after him. Jesus is one of many in the Christ Mind; there were also Buddha, Mohammed, Lao Tzu, Baha-ulla, Krishna, Zoroaster and others – and some unknown to history. His life was for the purpose of showing us that we are all equal, and that it is our destiny to be what he is; and do what he did. As he said, "What I have done, you may do also, only greater." He lived among us to show us through the example of his life, the path to become what he demonstrated: a spiritualized being in a body of flesh that achieved Christhood. And so, too, in some future time, shall we become Christed sons and daughters of God, balanced as God is balanced in both male and female attributes.

Please keep in mind that Jesus was in reality unified and balanced in masculine and female qualities. As a human, he exhibited this balance, being both gentle and forceful, thoughtful and intuitive, calm and angry, patient and assertive, expressing nothing to the extreme. He was a son/daughter of God, moderate in all things except for his love of Father/Mother – in his love he was focused and unwavering.

Jesus did not come to save our souls for the simple reason that we don't need to *be* saved. There is nothing to be saved from! We are already saved, saved before we were born! We are here not to save our souls, but to develop our souls, to work on

67

the things that deter our spiritual growth, and also on those things that encourage and facilitate our spiritual development into unity with the All. To fully understand Jesus, we have to understand that our destiny is to become what he was and is. We cannot fully appreciate the meaning of his life and mission if we fail to understand that he was showing us how we too can become Christed and one with the Father/Mother God.

Jesus did not establish a religion; he did not establish Christianity with its dogma and misleading doctrines and creeds. Jesus lived to show the possibilities of being human with traits of male and female qualities in balance and harmony. What he did, all men can do, and what he is, all souls *shall* be. He brought love – unconditional, universal love and forgiveness, but it is hard to find that emphasized in Church dogma, for everything is veiled with conditions, expectations and subservience. Jesus stands for forgiveness; the Church stands for judgment and retribution. It is a Church of fear and it separates; love of Jesus unites.

The purpose of life is to bring into balance those things of opposition in us and achieve harmony and unity with all aspects of our being. When that happens, we will then realize our oneness with God and that we, as well as Jesus, are divine beings. In a sense, each of us is a Jesus child, an embryonic Christ to be. His life was to show us how to achieve our destined maturity. We live in flesh so that we can practice learning to live as God; Jesus lived in flesh to show how we can do it. Jesus is not our savior; he is our spiritual master, our teacher, our guide, our brother and our friend. He is not to be worshiped but revered and respected, and if we are wise, we will follow in his footsteps.

He experienced all the things that any man experiences in life – hunger, pain, sorrow, love, joy, laughter, temptations and all the other vicissitudes and pleasures of life. He was tried and tested; he was shamed; he was ridiculed and cursed; he was hated; he was loved, and he was tortured, and yet in all this, he loved unconditionally and universally. By living his love, he showed by his examples and precepts how we too should live. He exhibited long-suffering and forbearance, patience and impatience, and anger and forgiveness. He was a soul in a flesh body, and knew the things all men know of trials and temptations.

Theology and the Church have made a creature of Jesus that is not in accord with the real person. They have made him God Almighty, the Grand Creator, the Source of All; they made him not *a* god, but *The* God – the creator of all that is. They have made him not one *with* God, but God Itself. Jesus never said that he was God; he said these things: *I and my father are one; I am the* son *of God; Believest thou not that I am* in *the Father, and the father* in *me?* All these words of Jesus and others do not say that he is God, the Supreme Lord and Creator; they speak of his special relationship with Father/Mother God; a relationship that he assured us we have also. Jesus is not God; he is God in experience and in expression, he is God in love and unity. In the words of today, Jesus is God in DNA – the same building blocks of physicality and spirituality that we have – it is what he did with this that makes him the Christ.

Jesus was sent by God to show us the way. He laid out a pathway for us in the examples of his love and works, which if we follow, we will gain unity with all creation. He was saying that God is in him and by extension, in us also. Does it not say, *Ye are Gods*, and also, the *temple of God is within.* Jesus refers to the fact that God lives within each and every one of us and that we live in Him also. And more than that, he is saying that we are Gods! It is this realization that will lead us to our wholeness with Source of All. Words, creeds, and protestations of faith will not do it. Only unconditional, universal love and forgiveness, the hallmarks of a person that expresses in living love, will do it.

There are other statements made by Jesus such as, *He that believeth on me shall have everlasting life. I am that bread of life.* Also: *This is the bread that cometh down from heaven, that a man may eat thereof, and not die…* And, *I am the living bread.* The Church takes these statements and professes that if we simply accept Jesus in our hearts, and obey all their conjured rules and requirements, we shall be saved. The Bible makes it clear in the many statements made by Jesus that the words water and bread are clearly metaphors for the *word* of God. In these statements, Jesus makes it clear that he speaks of the *word.* Simply believing in Jesus is not enough. We must eat of the *word* of God; we must consume it and let it be our nourishment and our salvation, our strength and our guidance. He says it is the *word* that he represents which shall harmonize, or balance, our dual nature of good and evil. It is therefore necessary that we believe and follow in his footsteps and meet him on the cross. We will find in the cross the anchor point of grace, which is our release from materiality, our means of escape from our many lives of duality when all will become unified with spirit in living love. Then, in our maturity we will be like-kind with Jesus, a true brother, Christed and one with God.

The cross is an enigma in our understanding of what Jesus was, and what he really did for us. His death on the cross opened the way for living love to show us the path home. To understand the cross and what the crucifixion represents, it is necessary to identify with its symbolism. We must comprehend that, before it is possible to understand what the crucifixion did for all of mankind. It is also necessary to know that Jesus did not die on the cross for Jews only. He died for all of mankind and all religions heretofore existent. Jesus came with grace, to heal the separation of man and God and the conditions of duality and abandonment. Unfortunately, rather than bringing the polarity of opposites together in balance and unity, the Church increased the separation.

The cross is a composite of two things – the horizontal arm of our dual nature, and the vertical arm of God's living love. The horizontal arm represents our duality, the separation of man and God and our resultant feelings of abandonment. It is the experiences of life in all their manifestations of good and evil. It is echoed by the other two crosses on the hill, one on each side of

Jesus, which in the two thieves, represent the positive and negative aspects of our duality: one expressed regret and asked Jesus to remember him, and the other one spurned Jesus, suffered in pain and died without hope.

The vertical arm of the cross is the living love that came down from God into the body of Jesus, and through him, into all of mankind who live in the duality of our unbalanced natures. The cross maintains the vertical connection with God, and where it crosses the horizontal arm of our duality, it establishes a balancing point of good and evil. It is at this nexus where it establishes an anchor point of grace where all things of disunity are brought into harmony. It brings into unity all the good and evil which we have expressed at different times in our many lives, and brings us into harmony with the oneness of all. This is the grace of unity. All disharmony and imbalance and the disunity of positives and negatives of our being, are brought into the unity of the Now. The past is Now; the future is Now; the present is the all of life, and in this we live in total harmony and peace of unity with the Oneness of the All. When we are in this position – at the point where we balance our dual nature with living love, we shall find our release and the path home.

Jesus was human as we all are, but there was a difference: his entire life was wrapped within the presence of God. He never knew a moment in his life without the ever presence of God encasing him in His love. There was never a moment of separation, until when hanging on the cross, God removed Himself. Nailed to the cross, with his arms outstretched on the horizontal arms of good and evil, the dual nature of man, Jesus experienced for the first time in his life the horror of isolation and abandonment, and the pain of disunity and separation from God that man has felt and endured for all his many lifetimes. It is understandable, how in his anguish he cried out, *My God, my God, why hast thou forsaken me?*

That's what Jesus did for us. He had to experience that separation, for only in that would he be able to anchor the living love that would be the means whereby mankind could be released from the disunity of self and separation from God. The point where the vertical arm of living love comes down from God and dissects the arm of duality is the anchoring point of grace.

Vertical rays of light that emanate from Jesus on the cross lead up to God; they are the pathways that we can travel on and return to the love of Mother/Father God. Our goal is to remember that we are love, and balance our dual nature. Love is the all of all; it is the unity of opposites and the balancing and harmonizing of our dual nature in the oneness of God's love. When we align ourselves with that radiant light, the balance point of our dual nature appears and the doorway of grace opens and our path home is clear. This point is where grace anchors to the cross of materiality and illusion. All we need to do is turn around in our minds, and see that our past and present are but illusions of the duality we live in, and that time is collapsed into an ever-present Now. It doesn't matter what our past was, or what lies ahead.

The important thing is that we live, breathe and move in a unified moment of non-time, with no concern for what we have been or will be. The reason is simple: nothing can or will affect us except as we allow it. In other words, we can be a new person free of all the karma, or the things we have sown in our past, and undo all the errors, mistakes and pitfalls we brought with us into our present life and create a new Now life; we can recreate a new future that has already been gestated by our thoughts, wishes and desires, and also erase or delete a future of conditions and situations that we would rather not experience. And by doing this we will create a different Now life.

It is similar to what we experience in our dreams that seems so real while we are dreaming, but which also are but illusions of daily reality. Dreams have no past, no future, only a Now in which everything unfolds as it will, free of time restrictions or pre-established conditions or destinies. Keep in mind that we are able to take control of the dream while dreaming, called "lucid" dreaming, and to change the course and details of what we will experience in the dream. So there really is little difference between a Now time in our sleep and a Now time in our daily awakened life. When we get to this understanding we will realize that life is a treasure to cherish, and reconnect to God.

When we return to love, we will no longer have to deal with negativity and separation. It can be realized from this that our re-connection depends on a lot more than just saying, "I believe," or, "I accept Jesus into my heart," and expect a reserved seat on the Heavenly Express. He didn't do it for us, and he won't. We must do it for ourselves; we must take up our own cross and balance our duality and align ourselves with the vertical rays of God's white light. When Jesus ascended, he didn't leave us bereft of his help. His sacrifice established the means whereby we who follow, can balance our dual nature and find peace. He showed us how to do it. He did not do it for us! That is our responsibility and our joy!

The Garden of Eden exists now: in it are the same two trees. As there is no time, that event is occurring now in our past, now in our future, and now in our present – all simultaneously. We eat of the apple just as Adam and Eve are eating of it, and assume a life of duality just as they are doing. It is not a sin and never was. Jesus came not to save us from a non-existent original sin, but to show us the way to freedom and to establish the anchor point of Grace in the center of the cross, freeing us from lives of duality.

# 11

# MARY MAGDALENE

Mary Magdalene was a woman not of her time. She was a woman of strength, power, mental and spiritual attainment that was unequaled by any others. She has been described as a whore, and was so proclaimed by Pope Gregory the Great in the late 6th century when he pronounced, for expediencies sake, that she was the repentant prostitute who washed Jesus' feet with her tears. That lie has stood unchallenged for fifteen hundred years. But the truth is now emerging.

Mary was Jesus' wife and was with him before his time of ministry, and with him during his time of teaching, miracles and suffering, and at the last supper. She was with him in tears at his crucifixion suffering equally with him, and rejoiced with him at his resurrection. She was one of the chosen – the 13th disciple who Jesus loved.

Her story is an interesting one, a strange one only because the truth of her relationship with Jesus has been veiled from our understanding for so many hundreds of years. The discovery of the Nag Hammadi texts in1947, the unearthing of the Gospel of Mary in the late nineteenth century, and other items from the Gnostic text Pistia Sophia and some from the Manichaean Psalms of Heracleides, all point to a close relationship of human love with Jesus – a relationship as man and wife.

In-depth research of ancient texts, those of both orthodox and Gnostic persuasions, reveal a woman that belies and puts to shame all the false conjectures of what and who she was, of what she represented and how she fit into Jesus' mission. She was an inseparable companion, but much more than that. The records show a woman of deep intelligence and high spiritual attainment.

She was an active participant in Jesus' ministry, assisting him in all ways giving him support intellectually, emotionally, spiritually and physically. And following his resurrection, she continued their dual ministry but apart from the apostles, carrying his teachings of gender equality and expression to other lands and repressed peoples. Part of her agreement with Jesus was that she would go to the underworld where souls existed in hopelessness in their self-created illusion of hell, forgetting that they were lovable. They were unaware of their divinity, and believing the illusions of their fears and separation, they lived within themselves, lost in a sea of suffering and separation from the Source. She brought to the lost souls who had forgotten their divine heritage of union with the source, the love and the light that is the promise of the rresurrection of all sentient beings.

Mary was Jesus' helpmate, confidant and mentor, equal in status and importance with him while sharing his mission. Their mission was singular, yet dual in that while they shared a single purpose while he was active in his part of their assignment, she continued her phase of the mission without him after he had risen. Her mission was two-fold: one was to be with Jesus during his ministry, and following his resurrection, to continue what he had started.

She was married to Jesus before the time of his baptism and the beginning of his ministry. She was with him throughout his trials and tests, and with him when he performed his miracles. She was his equal, mentally and spiritually, and as Jesus often counseled and mentored her, so too did Mary mentor Jesus with her great wisdom. He relied on her counseling, over that of the twelve disciples, which did not sit well with them, for they were of the old school where women should be seen and not heard.

In that time, women were regarded as having low intelligence, spiritually inferior, and incapable of reason and abstract analysis. They were considered mere chattels unworthy of respect, held under by the rigid and debilitating constrictions imposed on them by men. They were valued for the most part as servants and for bearing children. So it is understandable that the disciples resented Mary's intimacy with Jesus, and his deep respect for her. They were jealous and showed great resentment and contempt.

With the antipathy that the disciples had for her, it made it impossible to work with them, and when Paul took over the leadership of the fledgling church, he too, holding the same cultural attitudes of male superiority and inferiority of the female, felt disrespect for her, and helped make it impossible for her to work with them in truth and harmony.

Her lifetime with Jesus was all about the balance of duality – the polar opposites of life in a material world. God's plan is to merge these disparate qualities in all expressions and manifestations of creation: animal, vegetable and mineral, so that all will know its completeness and its own ability to create and procreate. In this context, it is the responsibility of mankind to recognize and equalize the divinity of the feminine with the divine masculine. His message and hers always had the underlying principle of balance of the male and female duality in us. This is the true reflection of Mother/Father God – all in one in the balance of unity and intent. It is to be known in the proof that all aspects of divine creation are one with the Source.

When Mary embarked on her own journey of faith, it was necessary to leave the apostles to continue her phase of the ministry. She has not been heard of since because of the apostle's antipathy towards her, and also because of the Biblical revisionists who wrote too little, or nothing at all of her in the years following. The only records of her life and activities are the incomplete and misleading references to her that were not removed from the Bible, and also the texts recently revealed that were unknown to anyone but those who purposely kept them hidden for their own purposes. She was veiled from our eyes and understanding for fifteen hundred years, unknown to the world for what she was. But now in the opening years of the 2nd millennium AD, the veil is being lifted, and she is becoming recognized as whom she was and what she represented – a messenger of God in her own right who fulfilled her original assignment with, then apart from Jesus. Upon the second coming of Jesus, she and he united in spirit, will continue their dual mission, not as saviors, but as light bearers and way-showers to our ultimate reunion with God, giving to all of us the love and the living light of Mother/Father God.

# 12

# ADAM, EVE AND SOUL MATES

We as souls in ages past, before being birthed in human form, chose the opportunity offered to us to become co-creators with God, to know good and evil, and unite with Him in all ways. To accomplish this, we chose to live in a world of duality – consisting of an outer world of materiality, and an inner world of spirituality, in which we accepted the duality of life with all its conflicts and discomforts. We chose to take on a dual nature where all is uncertain and leave the realm of security wherein we were, in our original state, one in God, but not ourselves. We became dual with the acceptance of polar opposites within our being: attitudes, emotions, opinions – all the things that make man what he is. As part of our learning process to become one with God, we had to experience the opposites we encounter in life and learn to harmonize and balance them in a unity of love, and thus accomplish our goal to reunite with God in a wholeness of love and co-creativity.

We elected to experience the conditions of separation from God so that our life experiences could be met without remembrance of our divine nature. Our spirit bodies that were in the beginning, balanced in a unity of oneness with God, being both male *and* female, were divided to become two separate entities, male *or* female. Some souls chose to undergo this experience; others elected to forego it and remain in their divine state as angels in the loving embrace of God, never to know privation, hunger, fear, pain, or evil in any form or manner. But neither would they ever be able to express creativity, or *appreciate* the grandness of love in all its glory and become one as God is one in the wholeness of love.

To fully appreciate love or anything, it is necessary to know its opposite and that can be known only through experiences of duality. Nothing can ever be appreciated until there is something with which to compare it. One can never appreciate light until the dark has been experienced; one can never feel compassion until indifference and hostility has been experienced. How can one appreciate love if love is all he has ever known? You must eat hamburger to appreciate steak; you must experience ill health, to appreciate good health; and you must experience the bad to appreciate the good. To appreciate love one has to experience non-love, or its opposite, hate and fear. Our dual nature provides us with the opportunities to experience those opposites.

This is the reason God created man. It was to enable Him to experience through us, through our feelings and emotions the grandness of love. And it could be accomplished only vicariously through us – mankind. Yes, God is love and always has been love. But He didn't know Himself, and was able to experience what He is only by experiencing the opposites of love through us. In this manner, He has been able to experience, to know and to appreciate His totality; this is why He needs us.

To experience our dual nature and become one with God, not just as we were in the beginning of creation when we were angels without power and creativity. We chose to separate ourselves from Father/Mother God, from the unity of our divine self – separating the masculine and feminine qualities of our angelic being. We separated our androgynous self into two parts, and in the separation we became masculine or feminine: we became man or woman – two beings instead of the man/woman we once were, united in a single body.

In our separateness, we each live in a perpetual sense of incompleteness yearning for a love we don't understand; a love to make us whole once again. Pinning our hopes that aren't understood, on a lover that is only a vague conception, but unconsciously sought. Until that union occurs, there will always be a feeling of incompleteness and loss – a need for something that can't be defined or expressed. But the point has been reached in mankind's spiritual evolution when the reunion of our separated selves, is upon us, bringing with it love and creativity and a completeness that is beyond knowing except for those who are experiencing it. When that occurs, we will be united once again with our other halves, our soul mates, in a union of love and wholeness, and in a triune with God.

Since God purposed a world of duality for man's spiritual growth, it was necessary that man experience duality in its various forms of manifestation. It was the soul's mission in its many incarnations, to explore and express all aspects of its dual nature – both the good and the bad, and learn to balance them in harmony, thereby becoming one as God is one, in unity and a wholeness of completion; this would necessarily include the positive and negative attributes of the male and female polarities.

The masculine and feminine qualities so essential to the exploration and expression of our dual natures, can be experienced and developed to their full potential only if they are independent of their polar counterpart. Hence, it was necessary to separate the negative and positive qualities inherent in the wholeness of Adam/Eve. That was done by removing the negative portion of Adam, creating a woman that embodied qualities complementary to those of Adam. The separation was necessary because the unique characteristics of the male and the female entities could be explored and fully experienced only in separation, independent of the other.

Man was created in the image of Father/Mother God, neither male nor female, but both in one. It was a gestalt of complementary qualities: the spiritual Adam/Eve before the separation in which he/she became Adam and Eve.

Genesis 1: 26 - 27 *And God said, Let us make man in our image, after our likeness… So God created man in his own image, in the image of God created he him; male and female created he them.*

*Genesis 2: 21-22 And the Lord God caused a deep sleep to fall upon Adam, and he slept: and He took one of his ribs. And closed up the flesh instead thereof; and the rib, which the Lord God had taken from man, made He a woman, and brought her unto the man.*

The purpose of man's dual nature is to provide opportunities to experience all forms of expression in every area of life, including male and female sexuality. When the separation occurred, the antecedent unity of positive/negative qualities of Adam/Eve became individuated as Adam *and* Eve, or, as man and woman. Each was then able to express its individual characteristics in the dualistic framework of our three-dimensional world, becoming the symbolic progenitors of the human race, passing on to us their inherent natures of duality.

After the physical decoupling of the male/female principles in Adam, the primal unity of oneness that was Adam/Eve was further severed by time and space. Possessing only half of their full potential, Adam and Eve yet believed in their illusions of duality that they were each whole and complete. They and their offspring, us, forgetful of what we once were, even forgetting our innate divinity, went our own ways as prodigal sons and daughters. Yet the separation of the soul into male and female counterparts did not completely erase our true nature from our subconscious memories. There remains within each of us a formless memory, a subconscious yearning to reunite with our other half, our soul mate, although it is seldom identified or understood for what it is.

The purpose of the separation was for each to explore and develop their dual nature. The male was to balance his masculine qualities of power and aggression, for example, with the feminine qualities of gentleness and peace; and for the woman, her passivity and spirituality were to be balanced with, let us say, masculine qualities of self-assertion and materiality. In all things, the male and female entities have to achieve a balance with their polar opposites; balancing and uniting their male and female attributes and thus becoming whole and complete as they were before the separation. When an imbalance occurs in either the male or the female bodies, the results can be conditions of inequality, which is not beneficial but destructive in the long run to an individual's or a group's welfare.

Adam and Eve, it could be said, were the original prodigal son and daughter, and like them, we too have left our garden with the free will God gave us, to experience all that life can offer. In our many lives, we have wallowed in depravity and exalted in goodness, we have been evil and saintly, and we have tasted the bitter and the sweet. We are prodigal sons and daughters who have set aside our birthright for the pleasures of flesh and the freedom to explore life in its many hues and tastes. We have lost awareness of our divinity and the inheritance that is awaiting our return to our true home. We confuse illusion with reality. Disoriented in the maze of our illusions we are unable to find our way back to square one – the starting point where we began our odyssey around the game-board of life.

In our belief that what we are and what we have is our only reality, we accept a world of illusion as one of truth. Yet it is our destiny to regain what was lost, to reunite with our other half, our soul mate, and return home to our Mother/Father God in a unity of love and creativity. We will then realize our oneness with each other and God – becoming a triune of three-in-one in love and creativity.

To understand the world we live in and our place in it, we must go back in time to the beginning before the separation. Adam was an androgynous spirit created in the image of God, neither male nor female, but both in one as God is both in one, balanced without polarity. Then the spiritual body of Adam was separated into two individuated spirits, male and female, as Adam and Eve, in an unnatural division of positives and negatives. In their spirit forms they each ate of the tree of knowledge of good and evil. Upon eating the fruit of the tree, they became aware of their unnatural state of flesh bodies.

*Genesis 3:21-23 Unto Adam also and to his wife did the Lord God make coats of skins, and clothed them. And the Lord God said, Behold, the man is become as one of us, to know good and evil: and now, lest he put forth his hand, and take also of the tree of life, and eat, and live for ever: Therefore the Lord God sent him forth from the garden of Eden, to till the ground from whence he was taken.*

In their dual condition of separateness, they showed shame and guilt for the first time. Thus began man's journey in a dual world, expressed in unending battles in their own beings, battles between the dual illusions of good and evil.

God encased their spirit bodies in coats of skin, which are the layers of skin on human bodies of flesh, and from thence they knew the duality of human existence in all its beauty and pain. From thereon we have expressed in our beings, the dual natures of our distant parents as our own, in conditions and situations of opposition, which is the duality of material existence and the substance of our lives. Thus was established for our benefit, a world of duality – a world of life in polarized forms.

The Church proclaims that eating from the tree of knowledge was an act of evil, where in actuality it was a blessing from God to us, for in our conditions of duality we can become like God in wholeness and creativity. That could not be done without experiences of choice. Without the opposites of duality, there could be no choice, for what choices would there be? And without choice, there would be no way that free will could be experienced, and without free will and choice, we would never be able to develop ourselves and our creativity to become one with God. It can be seen from this, that the so-called *Fall*, which was, according to the Church, the act of Original Sin, was in reality a gift of love from God to us, the opportunity that enables us to not only find our way back to Him, but to return in a condition of equality, as sons and daughters of Father/Mother God.

This is the reason why we should be grateful for all things, and accept what happens to us without complaint. As the Bible admonishes us, we should *not* resist evil in whatever form it may appear. We should instead accept everything in gratitude, for in all things there is a lesson. Learn what we can from it, whether we understand or not, and let it go. Do not err – don't hang on to something that is not for your highest and best.

Since God purposed a world of duality for man's spiritual growth, it was necessary that man experience duality in its various forms of manifestation. It was the soul's mission in its many incarnations, to explore and express all aspects of its dual nature – both the good and the bad, and learn to balance them in harmony, thereby becoming one as God is one, in unity and a wholeness of completion; this would necessarily include the positive and negative attributes of the male and female polarities.

The masculine and feminine qualities so essential to the exploration and expression of our dual natures, can be experienced and developed to their full potential only if they are independent of their polar counterpart. Hence, it was necessary to separate the negative and positive qualities inherent in the wholeness of Adam/Eve. That was done by removing the negative portion of Adam, creating a woman that embodied qualities complementary to those of Adam. The separation was necessary because the unique characteristics of the male and the female entities could be explored and fully experienced only in separation, independent of the other.

It must be understood that the word "negative" is too often misunderstood to mean something opposite of good. It is not that. A negative is simply the opposite of a positive. These two are like the opposite poles of a magnetic field – one a positive polarity and one a negative polarity. Neither is better than the other, simply two poles of a magnetic field. Both are equally necessary, neither is good or bad.

There are four valuable steps to accomplish release when confronted by things of discomfort or harm. They are these: acknowledge whatever it is; accept it; be grateful for the learning experience; then release it for its value has been canceled out, and let it return to God where He will reuse the energy in new creations.

Adam and Eve expressed their polarity in their individual ways: in masculine or feminine qualities; in positive or negative expressions as creator or producer. It is these opposites that determine our identity. Over time, our ancestral soul mates lost awareness of their original unity and lived lives separate from the other in both time and space, unaware of the other's existence. Soul Mates have shared lifetimes many times, but often without awareness of who each other were. Mankind is now regaining the understanding of our true natures and when the time is right, we will be reunited with our soul mate in conscious awareness.

We are the heirs of Adam and Eve's legacy, the inheritors of their dual nature and the subsequent separation of our original unity. We have no recall of our primal wholeness, and only a cellular memory of leaving our garden of love and peace, which we did when we voluntarily assumed lives of duality. Since then we have enjoyed incarnations of difficulties, pain, and loss, but also ones of gain, peace, love and beauty. There persists in the back of our minds shadow memories, mysterious longings and feelings of something greater missing from the core of our being and beyond understanding. In a love we know nothing of, yet feel, we persist in what has been a fruitless search for our soul mate, yearning for a unity and a completeness of that love, which until recently we never imagined as real, and never understood that it is our destiny to once again be together. Only when we are, will we know the joy of completion and wholeness.

In like manner, we all have within us a longing for something we know not of. It is a longing to reunite with our creator, Father/Mother God. We too, underwent a separation of spirit bodies, rendering asunder the unity we originally had with God, leaving Him, going our own way, dependent on our own will and guidance. But in this way, seemingly a foolish and stupid thing to do, we separated ourselves from the power and wisdom of God, in what seems to be vain efforts doomed to mediocrity and failure. But only by doing this, by leaving Him and going our own way, were we, and are we able to develop ourselves to become one like Him, yet independent of Him – co-creators – Gods ourselves as Jesus tried to teach us. We are in truth prodigal children.

The Church has undertaken the role of creating a willful fabrication of the symbolical depiction of Adam and Eve, creating a religion based on untruths. Adam and Eve were merely symbols of the origin of humanity, convenient metaphors that explained and described the original forms of spirit to manifest on the earth. They were not the first and only humans on earth. There were four other races, making five in all. The metaphor illustrates the separation of Adam into male and female counterparts, or the transformation of spirit to flesh bodies of man and woman; and finally, the introduction of duality in the world and in their dual natures. The Church turned the symbolical eating of the apple of the Tree of Good and Evil – the tree of knowledge, into an act of original sin, casting over to our symbolic forbears a shame and guilt that has deadened our spirituality, and which we, as the inheritors of their legacy, have carried with us for all of our earthly lives. In their view, we are born in sin, live in sin, and die in sin, and unless we go out of our way to please God (which by extrapolation, means to please the Church) we will surely spend eternity in unceasing torture and unspeakable pain. (Would a God of love do that to his children?) We go through life encased in an aura of fear, which translates into guilt and shame. Guilt is the root cause of most of mankind's problems; sin is not, but guilt is! If it is not inherited guilt, then we create it for some reason, if only for self-punishment for a supposed violation of what we have conjured to believe is wrong or sinful.

The apple represents the symbolic infusion of a dual expression of positive and negatives in Adam and Eve, and is known in Christianity as *the fall*, which the Catholic Church declared was original sin. Their erroneous interpretation of the Biblical rendition of an event that established inherited sin in our lives of duality, resulted in man's separation from his oneness with God, forgetting our divinity. It de-spiritualized man and enslaved him to the Church's self-serving version of truth. It was accomplished through their imposition of fear and guilt. It created a separation from God that has persisted close to 2000 years. Their deceits and misrepresentations of God's truth are now being recognized and shown for what they are. The Church is being confronted with an outpouring of truth exposing their manipulations and misinterpretation of God's truth.

The world is being cleansed and scoured by a relentless tidal wave of truth pushing aside all obstacles and resistance to its reformation.

*The fall* was not a thing of disaster of original sin as the Church has made it out to be. It was instead, an opportunity for spiritual growth that the Church misunderstood and misapplied! It was a planned creation of God's that separated us from our original oneness and unity with Him, and split us into the duality of our polar natures and expressions. It created a system of positives and negatives in the material world in which we live, and also established a dual nature within us. It formed an illusion of reality and permanency of our dual natures. It fashioned a temporary schism of illusion that only *seems* to be our natural condition and our supposed reality. It was not an event of judgment and punishment, but one of blessing for it enabled mankind to explore and experience life in all its positive and negative expressions while doing it without guilt or punishment. In this manner, we can work our way back to our Godhead.

Our spiritual ancestors were not responsible for the fall, nor for the separation from our original wholeness into separated bodies of dual natures. The entire concept of illusion was orchestrated by God. He knew that if we were to ever become unified with Him in love and co-creativity, it would be necessary to experience life in all its varied forms and expressions, to know and be all that He/She is. He/She is the Tree of Life, in which all good and evil are balanced in a unity of wholeness and Love. One must understand that God is neither one nor the other, neither good nor evil; He is the gestalt, the completeness, the whole of all that is, the All expressed in Love. The only adequate description of God is that He is LOVE. Love is the totality, the completeness of *All That Is.* He knows all things, He is all things, and in this He is whole and complete. He is love.

13

# SOUL, SPIRIT GUIDES, AND LITTLE PEOPLE

In Webster's dictionary spirit is defined *as the vital principle or animating force within living beings: the incorporeal consciousness; the soul; a supernatural being; an angel or demon; a fairy or sprite.* It's obvious from this that spirit is pretty active, finding expression in just about everything and anything. And that is true, for spirit is in and of everything. Yet the definition doesn't encompass all of creation.

Spirit is the substance of God, the animating force, the creative energy that is individuated in various levels of spiritual expression, including the soul. Spirit is not limited in expression only to living entities. It is the life-blood or substance of all things – man, rock, earth, air, love and fear. It is the energy of the atom, the energy of love and of every form of creation: human, animal, and material; and also of the insubstantial elements of air, fire, heat and cold. Every desire and thought is individuated energy, for everything is of the nature of God, and comes from Him in individualized forms of intelligence. God is the Creator, the animator, the preserver of life and all the substantial and insubstantial forms of existence. Everything that is, is of His substance. As He created mind, even our mental activities are spiritual – whether good or bad, it all depends on what the experiencer wishes to experience.

To understand spirit, it must be realized that although spirit and soul are interdependent, they are not one and the same. Spirit is the essence of God in perpetual motion, the extension of God in all things, material and spiritual, organic and inorganic. It is without form existing in all things. Spirit is the life force of

91

soul; soul is the expression of the individuated spirit – the receptacle and manifestation of God's presence.

How spirit expresses itself in man depends on several things. One is the collaboration of spirit and mind in mutual dependency and cooperation. Its effect depends on the willingness of the individual to let divine guidance work in or through him. Another, is that spirit works best in a trusting environment, free of fear and doubt. Negative thoughts and emotions only set up a wall inhibiting, even prohibiting spirit from doing its part. At times, spirit will attempt to instill new information, and inspire new understandings within the mind and emotions. But because we have freewill, spirit is limited in what it can do, for it needs our approval. Its success depends on the intent and willingness of the recipient to cooperate, and sometimes in order to be cooperative, it is necessary to step aside and let spirit have its way.

Man has the wisdom of God within him, but because of misuse and disuse it has atrophied. Yet it is still available and only needs a little rust solvent and a restructuring and polishing of old attitudes, opinions and beliefs to get it going again. In the meantime, when Spirit is trying to give us what we have requested or needed, we should refrain from putting conditions on how it is to be done. We usually want it done our way, in our time, with little or no interference with our life or schedule. We don't want to wait until next week when we impatiently want it now. When impatience gets in the way of spirit, it only further delays the resolution of a problem or the granting of a gift. When we, on the soul level have asked for it, we must step back and let spirit answer our request. Often spirit has to work within the restraints of time and the space of a second person or persons, and it is not always for their best, or ours, to rush the granting of a request or need.

It is to be realized that we can do nothing to anyone, whether to friend or enemy; unless it is with the approval of the persons involved. And neither can spirit or God, because that is

God's law of non-interference with anyone's free will unless approval is obtained first. That approval is sought and given on the spirit plane, soul to soul. If more than one person is involved, then their approval is required also. Anything else would interfere with free will, our God given right to be masters of our lives. It is His law that cannot be broached or interfered with. It can be seen in this, that since nothing can happen to a person without that person's approval, there can be no accidents or events, or as it is said in legalese, "Acts of God" that can be considered as unfair or unjust, or even undeserved. So there is no injustice in anything, since everything is for a purpose, and is condoned and approved by all involved prior to the action or infusion of anything.

## SOUL

We are accustomed to believe that our soul is the be all and end all of our spiritual existence. From the perspective of our third dimensionality, soul is all there is. We think of ourselves as a body that has a soul, but we have it wrong. It is the opposite. Soul in a sense has a body. Far greater and far grander than a finite physical body, soul enfolds our body within its spiritual essence. Before birth, soul programs new life experiences for its incarnation in a physical form, and operates through the normal channels of male and female entities to conceive it. The female is impregnated in the usual way, and goes through the process of gestation, development and birth.

In a crude analogy, our body is to the soul, what our car is to us. The car is our means of transportation, carrying us from one place to another and from one experience to another. When it is past its prime, having satisfied its purpose and a new vehicle is needed, the old one is exchanged for a new one. In a similar manner, soul uses a physical body as its vehicle for life experiences, occupies it for a time, and when the body is no longer able to provide the experiences needed, the soul leaves it, programs a new one and reincarnates in another body.

Just as our body is finite, so too is soul. John and Susie may live a few years, or as long as a hundred years, but their physical bodies will eventually wear out and die. Soul lives much longer – we can say tens of thousands of years, even millions of years. But it too has an end. But spirit, which is the primal essence of God, the individuated essence of power, intelligence and love, is our reality and finds expression in our soul body. The spirit is to our soul body what our soul is to our flesh body. The body dies; the soul lives on and eventually dies also, but the spirit body, which is our true essence, lives forever. There is no ending to life, but there are constant new beginnings, new creations and new experiences to explore and savor. All that we have experienced as flesh and as soul, lives on in the spirit body – all that we are or have been remains a viable part of our ultimate reality as spirit. Nothing is lost or left behind except as we will it; there is only accumulation or gain, in other words growth, never ceasing, never ending, always an individuated heart cell of God.

Our reality is infinite love and creativity, with the ability to experience that in all its possibilities. To become one with God, which is to reunite with Him equally in all His greatness, we must be all that He is, which is the composite, the gestalt, of all things. We as intelligent spirit, a creative heart cell of God, need to immerse ourselves in every aspect of His creation.

The heart-cell of God is spirit; it is infinite and experiences life in many forms, in many levels of spirituality, one of which is soul. What we are at this moment, including all that we were in the past, and what we are yet to be, is all that God is! Yet we are not that, because we are not yet equal in development and in *expression*, and that's what we're doing here in a physical body, to learn to express our divinity. We are learning to *Be*. In this material world of duality spirit uses soul for its vehicle of experience and expression, using it to gain the experiences it needs for its spiritual growth.

In every transfer of intelligent energy there is never loss. All that soul has acquired in its many experiences in untold manifestations throughout time, remains and accumulates. There is only and always, gain. We are equal to God in creativity and love, but we have yet to learn to use it in harmony and unity with God. We live in the world so that we may learn to live as God.

## SPIRIT GUIDES

In the simplest terms, spirit guides can be said to be a part of God and a part of us. There is an infinite number of them, all helping mankind through all our trials and opportunities. They usually number two or three for each of us, although there may at different times be more or less. Each of us has a family of guides who have been with us throughout our many lives; some of whom we have walked with, lived with, loved or fought with in other times and other lives, and even in our present life – a deceased parent for example. But beneath our fractious duality, we all have one thing in common; that is unconditional love. Everyone has one master guide that is with them throughout their earthly life. The others are interchangeable, coming and going in accordance with our momentary needs. Each of them have certain abilities and strengths that are more appropriate or useful than a different guide for a particular person, or who are more in accord with that person's needs at a particular time. When that occurs, the one that is the most able to give the help or guidance that is needed, will take its place as one of our inner-circle guides. These guides are usually thought of as angels, sometimes guardian angels, or spirit guides. They all have a purpose, which is to help us whenever or in whatever way our needs may require, and they are always with us: whether in the midst of war; when we are lost and lonely; in poverty or need, or in our joys and sorrows. Even if we put ourselves in a virtual hell of our own creation, our guides are still with us. They will remain with us throughout our terrible ordeal in the darkness of the nether regions until we release our self-imposed condition and reenter the realms of life, light and love. We are never alone.

They help us in many ways. They instruct us through dreams, visions, feelings, meditations, synchronicities, and in a myriad of other ways. Sometimes their help is just an infusion of energy and upliftment of spirit and hope when needed. As they are cells of God also, they have access to God's wisdom and guidance as we do. But being in the spirit body, it is easier for them to access the higher knowledge than it is for us, because they don't have to cut their way through a jungle of mental confusion, opinion and conditioning to reach it.

They are spirit as we are spirit, but they are not encumbered with a physical body. They have lived before in material lives of duality just as we are currently living lives of our dual natures. They have lived as we now live with the same types of things of experience: loves and fears, pain, gains and loss, betrayal and abandonment. They have had personal weaknesses and problems to overcome also: selfishness, greed, impatience, cruelty, and they like us, have had to learn to embrace life in all of its manifestations of duality and live lives of joy and peace.

In a quotation from Lee Carol, he states: *"The actual guides are just like you, they exist on both sides of the veil. You're a group and so are they. They're part of your spiritual makeup, but their energy can change daily, if that's how often you change your vibration. Think of them as a helper energy group that is as much you as your higher self is you. The real you is angelic. It's interdimensional and infinite; it's a piece of God.*

## THE LITTLE PEOPLE

Spirit manifests in some forms of life that with a few exceptions we know nothing of. Our boundaries of understanding and knowledge are circumscribed by a narrow band of awareness, limited to flora and fauna – the varied forms of plant life, and all the variations of animal life ranging from the one-celled amoeba to man. All these are known as viable, recognizable entities, even though we may have to use a microscope to see the smallest of them. They are composed of physical matter, the substance of the earth from which they spring. Some are material; but there are others that are not material as we know materiality.

There are many intelligent life forms we can't see, but for which we have names. There are drawings and paintings of them, some claim to have photographs of them. Their material forms are invisible except by a few who have developed their extrasensory perceptions, and are able to see other dimensions of reality. These are the "little people", some are the fairies, others are sprites, trolls, elementals, and leprechauns, and there are many others of which we don't know. They are all a necessary part of nature, located throughout the world. Some are able to materialize their bodies so people can see them, some cannot, and some others have no wish to. But those who do, are careful to reveal themselves only to those they can trust, and who will accept them in love as spiritual equals. They are intelligent and creative and serve a vital role in the maintenance and health of the world about us.

# 14

# TWO TREES IN THE GARDEN

And the lord God said, *Behold, the man is become as one of us, to know good and evil.*

When Adam, urged by Eve, ate of the apple in the Garden of Eden, it started a chain of events that has never abated. The significance of that bite, embraced by the Catholic Church as The Fall, has been a thorn in our side ever since. The Church built a system of theology and dogma around an event that never occurred. From their false reasoning, a doctrine of Original Sin was developed by which all descendants of Adam and Eve – including you and me, are held equally accountable as though we were there and took a bite or two ourselves.

According to this concept, the mere existence of our genealogical roots condemns us to hell unless we achieve forgiveness, which we can't do on our own according to Church doctrine, because God doesn't hear sinners. They teach that since we were born in sin, we are therefore unworthy of going directly to God for absolution of something we had nothing to do with in the first place. The Church claims that God hears only the voices of the anointed, which are those selected by the Church to act as intermediaries for us when we need to communicate with God. In this light, the congregants of the Church cannot pray directly to God because of inherited sins. They cannot petition God for anything on their own, whether help in their illnesses, assistance in their financial plights, requests for love, or anything that is a natural part and parcel of life.

This is a reason why the saints of the Church play so important a role in the parishioner's lives, for each saint when appealed to for specific purposes, give the help that they are most qualified to give – some of healing, some of protection, some of travel, and there are others. They are a kind of super-intermediary for a petitioner.

Even at death, one is not able to pray directly to God to ask for forgiveness of sins. That is why one must go to confession and receive absolution regularly. If a person at the edge of death has not had a chance for a last minute confession of sins, a priest can provide unction – a last minute absolution that the dying person may not even be aware of receiving. Yet they are saved. But if a priest is not available, then it is possible that a person may not be saved – that is why it is so important to always receive absolution in frequent confessions to a priest. It's a further use of fear to bind one's dependence on the Church. If this were carried to its extreme, the only way a person could be certain of salvation would be to be in non-stop confession and constant absolution. Believers therefore are beholden to the Church for their salvation, and there is nothing that can be done except to obey their dictates.

Such is the position of the Church that was developed not by Jesus but by man in the years following his mission. It is a position that the Church still maintains as an influencing and controlling factor over its members.

After the Church established their erroneous doctrine of original sin, subsequent dogma and doctrines with their myriad rules and regulations, developed over time to be an all inclusive and enveloping system of faith and obedience. Original Sin is a doctrine based not on truth but on fallacious reasoning – perhaps well intentioned, but misleading and destructive nevertheless. As a result, the effects of it effectively destroyed man's direct connection to God. He was removed from the hearts and minds of man and placed in cubicles of stained glass windows, surrounded by frozen icons of marble, and confession booths.

In 2 Corinthians 6:16 it is stated: "And whatever agreement hath the temple of God with idols? For ye are the temple of the living God; as God hath said, I WILL DWELL IN THEM, AND WALK IN THEM, AND I WILL BE THEIR GOD, AND THEY SHALL BE MY PEOPLE." In simple terms, God is not the church of man; God is the church in man, and He can be reached and communed with as easily as one can commune with one's own feelings and thoughts. Intermediaries are not needed – never were and never will be. The Catholic Church has impinged on the role of God in our lives, assuming a role of judge, jury and executioner – establishing itself as a substitute god, but one that is despiritualized, and whose effects are materialized.

Altogether, the Church has created a very large package with a bomb in it and the fuse is lit. The fuse is an intertwining cord braided with all the lies and misconceptions and harm done to its millions of innocent members over the centuries who only wanted truth, and assurance of God's presence in their lives. The time is coming when all the packaged deceits will explode in a burst of truth and freedom, bringing with it a cleansing and purification of the Church that Jesus intended to establish in our minds and hearts.

But who is responsible for the despiritualized Church? It would seem a bit unjust of God if He were to hold all mankind equally responsible for it, since we were not yet born and not there to participate in it. It began with a curse imposed on us by men of the Church, who holds us equally responsible for the Mother of All Sins: the Original Sin, which occurred at what they erroneous call *The Fall*. If it were true, it would certainly negate free will, wouldn't it? And neither does it say much for unconditional love of which God is the cornerstone.

One must wonder how and by whom it was all put together, wrapped and tied with a nice pink bow for our approval and consumption. Upon reflection, it is not hard to see that the Church of men is responsible. And one must be aware of God's promise that He is not mocked, for what one sows, that he shall also reap.

Our basic concern at this point of discussion is with the Tree of Good and Evil and what it means to us. In the Garden of Eden there were two trees. One was the Tree of Life, and the other was the Tree of Good and Evil. Adam and Eve ate from the Tree of Good and Evil and accepted into their beings the dual nature the tree symbolized. After being confronted by God, they were banished from the Garden. They and their offspring, and that includes us, were condemned to lives of toil, pain and suffering. Then He posted cherubim and a flaming sword to guard the way to the second tree: the Tree of Life. But there was a reason for it, beyond that of mere punishment.

To ensure that the soul's dual nature would be balanced before the full experience of life could be achieved, it was necessary to be certain that all polarities of human thought and desire would first be balanced and unified. It was essential that this was done, because without the harmonizing of our dual nature, we could never become co-creators and one with God, which is the whole purpose of life.

The doctrine of Original Sin is a misconception of the meaning of that tree, and it shows a lack of understanding of the needed balance provided in its symbolic essence because it stresses evil to the exclusion of good. The tree is a composite of both good and evil – the duality of negative and positive quantities, so to concern ourselves with only the negative aspect of the tree is to minimize and negate the tree's value to a meaningful understanding of life, of ourselves, and of our relationship with God.

The Tree of Good and Evil is a symbol of balance and harmony for it contains the complementary qualities of our positive and negative makeup. These are comprised of competing, yet supportive opposites found in nature and man. Learning to balance these opposites is what life is about – necessary for the complete harmony of our dual nature and full expression of our innate spirituality. These opposites are so much a part of our daily lives we are often unaware of their dual nature and how they impinge on our peace. A cursory look will reveal some of the more common ones such as love and fear, honesty and dishonesty, sharing and selfishness, light and dark, and passivity and aggression – and of course good and bad.

Every quality or factor in life needs its complement in order to keep from developing to its extreme. For some examples:

if love is unrestrained it can become conditional, demanding responses from others not in their best interests, and it can become stifling, preventing others from being themselves as they choose to be. Zeal can become fanatical, unbalancing the individual by focusing his interests and potentials on one narrow goal to the detriment and productivity of the whole.

Another set of balancing opposites is that of light and dark. If there were light without darkness it would interfere with the natural cycles of nature and man – the cycle of productivity and regeneration. Darkness without light would be equally destructive for there could be no life and no growth in either nature or man. Additionally, there are the opposites of male and female, the generators and the producers. All of life is predicated in all their forms in flora and fauna. Without both there would be no life in a world of polarities such as ours.

In the realm of duality, one of the most misunderstood and misused of opposites is the concept of good intention. It appears in people who do for others what *they* believe is best for the others – interfering with another's life and their free will to be themselves, without meddling by someone else. The claim of good intentions will often be erroneously used to justify evil actions. Historically, the claim of good intentions was used to justify perhaps the most heinous and cruel example of evil in the history of the world. It was the inquisition, promoted and conducted by the Catholic Church. It was not good intentions alone that were responsible for the unspeakable cruelty, but equally and just as important, it was lust for power and greed. It was a tribunal formerly held in the Catholic Church during the Middle and Dark Ages to suppress heresy. What is heresy? Nothing but disagreement with or disobedience to the rules and doctrines of the Church – not to God, but to the Church that had decided by itself what God had intended. In order to maintain absolute obedience and loyalty to the Church, people were forced to confess to heresy and other conjured sins whether they were guilty or not. There were few restrictions on what means were used to break the will of people accused, anything to get them to confess their sins of heresy before they died. The inquisitors used the rack that could stretch a human body until it was literally pulled apart; they burned people alive; they encased people in coffins (the Iron Maiden) with spikes protruding from the interior wall that would pierce the live victim's body when it was closed tightly. There were times when without provocation, it was used solely for murder. If the victim was a Jew, he or she would be locked into an oven and baked alive. Often innocent people would confess and still die from the torture. The Church falsely justified their use of torture by claiming that their actions were used to save a heretic's soul from hell.

The Church did these things, supposedly out of love and for the benefit of the accused. All with good intentions and done under the auspices of God for the purpose of saving souls. But that is not truth. It is inconceivable that God would encourage, even approve such horrendous evil. Was the Church at that time, a church of God? Is it still a Church of God? The real motive at the time was power and control, nothing else, and the Church is still exercising tight control of its members. It is unwilling to let people exercise their God-given right of free will and expression to choose for themselves without censure and fear of punishment.

In the realm of evil, it is hardly necessary to outline the results of evil if left alone without a balance of good. We have seen the results of evil unchecked; it is evident in the cruel and wanton sadism of dictators who have concern only for themselves. Some examples that come to mind are Hitler, Stalin, Pol Pot, Idi Amin, Saddam Hussein and his sons. On down the list are the minor sadists: serial killers and those who torture and kill just for the pleasure of it. It is easy to see in these examples why there must be a balance between all things. Aristotle said it well a few thousand years ago: "Everything in moderation, nothing to excess."

This thing of opposites is the duality that we, in this three dimensional world, live in. All of life is founded and maintained in this duality. It is in us, and of us, and without it we would not and could not be us. It is our dual nature. It is that simple. And this is where the Tree of Good and Evil exemplifies this duality. It is the symbol of our innate duality – the duel nature of opposites.

Why did God create our world and us in conditions of opposites? The answer lies in the understanding of why God created man in the first place. He wanted to know Himself, and He wanted companionship of souls of equality with Him. We choose friends and companions that offer something we would not have without them, such as friendship, laughter, respect, fun, and the enjoyment and enrichment of each other's company. God enjoys these things too. And contrary to what some churches teach, God has a sense of humor and He loves to laugh. Didn't He create all things? Then He created laughter also. Could He give us something He doesn't possess? Impossible. If He didn't have what He wanted to give, He would have nothing to share. The Puritans are an example of misunderstanding God's intention for us, and encasing us in an inescapable straightjacket of joylessness. What a sad group of people they must have been, going through life with no joy in their hearts, possessed with fear of doing anything that might be enjoyable and pleasurable.

Why would God even consider giving us the things of joy and laughter and beauty and friendship if He didn't know their value and how important they are to one's health and enjoyment of life? As it is said, "Laughter is good for the soul." It's being realized by science that laughter and a sense of humor are essential to one's health and well-being.

To be the companion that God would like us to be, it is necessary for us to experience all facets of our dual nature. We were created in balance and harmony, but when we chose to become co-creators with God (it *was* our choice), we had to experience life in an unbalanced state, tasting the fruits of each condition, each experience, exploring the dark side of our natures as well as glorifying our spirituality. In our many lifetimes, we have experienced life in its most degrading and unloving and dreadful qualities, but we have also experienced the sublime joy of love, compassion, and oneness with God. It is our destiny to regain the balance we deliberately set aside for the greater attainment of creativity and ultimate oneness with our God of love and light. In time we will balance the negative and positive qualities of our dual nature and unify them becoming a unified whole as God is whole and complete.

When we symbolically ate of the apple of the Tree of Good and Evil we made the decision to separate ourselves temporarily from any awareness of our divinity. It was then that we embraced the dual qualities the apple represented. We lost our innocence and became unbalanced knowing the opposites of all things. From that time to now, we have dedicated our lives to experience life in all its possibilities, exploring both sides of our dual nature and one by one bringing these opposite polarities back into a unity of balance. But before that can be understood, the cobwebs of misunderstanding and faulty reasoning will have to be removed from our dusty minds, and replaced with minds open to alternate possibilities, to concepts never before considered.

God planned and established a system of birth and rebirth so that our souls could experience life to its fullest. This has given us the opportunity to explore and develop the positive and negative characteristics of God that we His children, were created with. In time, we will be balanced in all things, and become one with Him in love and creativity. This cannot be done while reclining on a fluffy cloud with a guitar, and no opportunity to prove ourselves spiritually. Only through trials and errors, tests and accomplishments, through tears of pain and tears of joy will we ever achieve that destined result. We must use the opportunities God has provided, to explore anything and everything. We need occasions to experience honesty and dishonesty; trust and unbelief, constancy and inconstancy, compassion and cruelty, reliability and fickleness – all things need to be explored. Only in freedom with adventures outside the realm of safety and conformity will we ever develop ourselves in balance, spiritually and materially. We need to achieve balance and become one once again with Him. This is why we live in materiality with physical bodies as vehicles for soul, enabling us to experience life in all its myriad possibilities. And this is why one must never judge another, for we don't know why he or she is as they are. Only God knows that, and He does not interfere with their choice, nor does He judge them. But He does applaud them when they show courage to try new things that society might consider harmful or even evil, because in the experience, they can grow in spiritual understanding and balance.

This growth in our ultimate oneness with God can't be done in a single lifetime. There's just too much to be experienced and developed. It's not that we have to become perfect – even God is not perfect. Jesus was not perfect; neither was Buddha, nor Zoroaster, nor Moses, nor Mohammed, nor Mani ... and certainly not us! Nevertheless, we must continue to work at developing the desirable traits of Godliness, and this is done in successive lives by exploring life in its fullness, experiencing everything, leaving nothing untouched.

The Fall, was not the disaster that religion trumpets; it represents a blessing – the greatest blessing God could give us, for it provides the opportunities for us to realize our true sonship and daughtership with Mother/Father God. It was not original sin as the Church says it was. It was not punishment – it was quite the opposite. It was a gift from God to us – the greatest gift possible, for it set the stage for us to learn what and who we really are, and ultimately what our destiny is, which is to reunite with God. Man, contrary to religious teachings, is not inherently evil. The Church is wrong! We are children of God! How then could we be evil? Is God evil? Does He create evil? How then could we be evil since he created us in his image, as like-kind?

We should be grateful for His gift of the tree of duality, for it gives us the opportunity to experience the full range of our potential being – spiritually, mentally, emotionally, and physically – to experience all the situations and conditions of life. Without it we would never be able to become one with God, for He is the composite of all things, positive and negative, and we must be too. He/She is a wholeness, the gestalt of all in one. That is our purpose, our destiny – to become whole and complete in God. But we can't experience that which is not already existent in God. We can only reflect His reality. We can only be what He is, and give only what we have.

There is no devil or Satan; they are the personifications of evil that exist in our own being, self-created and self-maintained. Evil is not created by an outsider, or outside force – a nebulous something unseen. Evil is nurtured and expressed in our own minds through desire and thought: anger, hate, selfishness, greed, power, cruelty, and the many other aspects of negativity. But it is to be remembered, that the opposite of evil is good, and it also resides in us through our desires, thoughts and actions.

The Fall is symptomatic of our condition of duality – a dualism that governs everything we are, say and do. It represents a time when soul came into the consciousness and experiences of physical life – the inborn impetus that God purposely established for our total development in all phases of being, physically, mentally, emotionally, and spiritually. Far from being an event that was sinful and wrongly deplored and maligned, it was a symbolic happening that facilitated our move to reunite with God – the balancing of our duality in a wholeness, a completeness in the unity of God. God is already a unity of opposites, balanced in harmony and love, and we too in our time of many lives will achieve this unity. It is our destiny because God wills it to be. We cannot prevent it, no more than we can prevent the dawn from heralding a new day, or the moon from lighting our way in darkness. We can only delay its inevitability.

# 15

# KARMA –

# WHAT YOU SOW,

# YOU SHALL ALSO REAP

As we pursue the daily rites of living, we encounter things and situations not of our choosing, things that seem to lack the imprint of justice and fairness. How is it determined what justice is? How do we decide what is fair? How is it resolved who gets what in life: that this one gets health and that one gets sickness, that this one gets luxury and that one reaps ill harvests? Is chance the deciding factor – the mere flip of a coin, or is it perhaps God, careless and uncaring? Where is the justice in life, a fairness that of necessity requires an intelligent and compassionate Source for its impartial administration?

We ever wonder why unfavorable things happen to virtuous people, and favorable things to immoral people. Why do some gain and others lose in situations and conditions that seem to be not of their making – the innocent child for example who dies of leukemia, or the living saint who struggles in poverty and ill health. Or how about the drug pusher who destroys the lives of others through greed, yet lives in luxury and good health untouched by laws or justice?

On the surface of things, there is often an appearance of injustice, and with the cynical an attitude of, Who cares? But such appearances can be misleading and wrong because there is justice in all things, even in "injustice," for nothing happens by accident or chance. Behind everything there is purpose – a reason for the season it has been said. In our inability to understand the what and why of things, we seek out our spiritual shepherds for guidance. But they, who mostly don't know either, attempt to explain the "unexplainable" by resorting to weak and ineffectual excuses for their ignorance, such as: *God works in mysterious ways his miracles to perform*; or perhaps in desperation, *Ours is not to reason why; don't ask, just do or die.* By default, we are compelled to blindly accept their inadequate explanations in our faith of their supposed wisdom, or in frustration of their inability to explain the why of a thing. But still we question and may in time come to resent what appears to be unjust, and then begin to see injustice everywhere. Eventually that can lead to cynicism and even rejection of God, blaming Him for our misfortunes.

Would we do that? Why? Because of ignorance and vanity. We have to blame something or somebody – certainly not ourselves! So if it's not the fault of those afflicted, and if it's not the fault of others, and if it's not us, then who else is there to blame but God? So then it must be God's fault – right? Wrong.

We may believe that we have no right to know Truth, and even if we do, there is no access to it. In spite of appearances, we can know the Truth, and we have the right to it because God wants us to know! Doesn't He say that the Truth shall set us free? Yes, He does, and He also provides a way to get it.

There is an explanation behind everything. The understanding of the root causes of events and conditions, the good and the bad, lies in the Biblical statement: *What you sow, that you shall also reap.* Edgar Cayce explained this concept in a few words, as *"Self meeting self."* In the eastern religions it is called *karma.* The things we meet are the fruition of seeds that create the conditions and incidents in one's life, seeds that were planted at an earlier time. What a seed represents may not be recalled at the time of coming face to face with its fruit. But in patience, the justice of it, if accepted, even if not understood, can bring peace. The understanding of this conundrum lies within us. Just because we may not realize that we reap what we sow, or understand what it means, the responsibility for planting seeds, whether of unrest or peace, regression or progression, the resultant fruit is still ours because we spawned them.

There are an infinite variety of seeds, some are of intemperance, anger, dishonesty, and gossip; and conversely, there are seeds of compassion and kindness, of sharing what we have no matter how little, by giving a warm smile to a stranger, or a word of encouragement to one in need. In these things we lay the foundation of what we are building for ourselves. These are seeds that after planting will in their time sprout, and in their maturity we will reap their fruit. It's that simple. What we sow, we will reap. This is our karma, whether good or bad. Contemporary slang puts it this way: what goes around comes around. When this is understood, the unexplainable can be explained. It removes injustice from our vocabulary. It is only those who don't understand this truth that see injustice where there is none, capriciousness where there is order and purpose.

If karma is to be fully understood, it is necessary to understand that we live more than once. This is the rebirth of soul in a physical body and is called reincarnation; it is the handmaid of karma. Its purpose is simple: among other things, we are reborn to meet the things we have sown, to pick the fruit of our labors, and whether the fruit is sour or sweet, it's what we planted. This explains why we sometimes meet, or experience things that we can't trace to a cause. It may be because the cause, or seed was planted in a time forgotten, in an earlier life perhaps, and all conscious memory of it is temporarily blacked out during a current life. Nevertheless, they are our plantings, and they present opportunities for change and growth.

As we go through life, we encounter situations and conditions, some of which are positive and some are negative. This can, for example, include relationships with people. Encounters with others are reunions in a sense and not at all accidental, but spawned by what they and we previously set into motion – seeds that have since sprouted and matured. Indeed, there are no such things as accidents. Such meetings or

111

encounters are the results of seeds planted in an earlier time, often in another life, which then mature and are ready for harvest. They give us the opportunity to share again a long-lived relationship, perhaps one of love, or maybe its opposite of hate, jealousy or envy. But being one that gives us the chance to make amends if needed and to change a negative relationship into one of respect and amity.

Because we don't realize that we create our encounters with life experiences, we attribute their cause to a variety of things outside of ourselves, some good and some bad, such as luck, actions of others, retribution for sins, jinx, forces of nature, justice, injustice, accidents, even the anger or love of God. But *we* are responsible for everything that happens to us – the good and the bad. That's difficult to accept because we lack understanding. It's much easier to blame something or someone else for our misfortunes rather than looking within and accepting responsibility for what is affecting us. But that's where Truth is lying in wait, and where freedom beckons. The reason we don't understand is that we look at life through the blurred vision of vanity and in myopic perspectives of truth. We don't see ourselves as God sees us in both our faults and in our grandeur, and that should ever be our goal. When we remove our blinders and see life and ourselves in truth, we can gain peace in the understanding that there is justice in all things, that God is in charge and is doing His job quite well, thank you. He is loving and merciful, generous and kind, wanting only good for us, and does everything He can to help us get it.

We erroneously believe that the life we're living is all there is, and there ain't no more. That's wrong, but before understanding can be achieved, it must first be asked, "What is life? What is its purpose? Why do I have the life I have? Why must I live like this? Why can't I have what Joe and Jane Jaberwocky have? Or maybe, why do I have such good fortune and wonderful friends and others don't?" There are answers to all this and they are available. In the search for them, it will be found that knowledge and wisdom are handmaidens, and when they are attained, understanding follows. In Proverbs it is stated, *"Wisdom is the principal thing; therefore get wisdom; and with all thy getting, get understanding."* The answers to all things lie within us and are available to those who earnestly seek truth. If you go to God for help, He will show the way and give all that is needed and more. He is not stingy.

When our spiritual leaders, the pastors, teachers, ministers, and priests don't understand the in-depth meaning of their own biblical readings of "What you sow, that you shall also reap," or who don't want to acknowledge the full ramification of what it means, they struggle to escape responsibility for their ignorance or deviousness by tossing it into the trash bin of the "unexplainable." They won't or can't say why they don't know, or even that it is possible to know; they simply say *it's not for us to know*. But they're wrong; we can know. God wants us to know! He wants to give all truth to us, and only refrains from giving certain things when He knows we are not ready to understand and use it wisely for the benefit of all concerned. The wisdom of God can be ours when we have prepared ourselves to receive it and use it wisely. His knowledge is so vast that when we do attain even a minuscule portion of it, we will realize that we are intellectual pygmies. It is a knowledge so encompassing, so broad and detailed, and so comprehensive, that it's beyond the scope of science or man to even imagine its magnitude. But the first step on our path to truth is to remove the mistaught and misconceived teachings and conditionings of well meaning but ignorant mentors that go back many lifetimes. That takes time and more than one additional life to do it in.

There's really nothing illogical about reincarnation and karma. It is man that refutes the logic and reasonableness of it. God defines it; man denies it, and to live more than one life is all in His perfect plan, for He knows that mankind is not able to achieve oneness with Him in a single lifetime. The goal is not unreachable but highly difficult and not easily attained, yet it can be and will be accomplished by all, because it is supremely simple: one has only to be Love, unconditional, all encompassing Love.

All religions are of God. Each one contains only a part of His truth and this includes traditional Christian religions. No one religion has it all; none of them have none; and all of them have some. Much of the world believes in reincarnation, and there are many hundreds of priests, bishops, ministers, and teachers in Christian churches, both protestant and Catholic that accept reincarnation as truth as well, and the number is growing. The Essenes, who were Jesus' mentors, believed and taught the concept, and his remarks show that he did also. It is important to know that the Christian Bible *does not* deny reincarnation. Not a single passage can be found that denies it, only the misled and the ignorant do that. For those who really want truth it's available for all to understand and claim.

The Bible was inspired by God, but not written by Him, nor by Jesus or any other one person, but rather by many over the years. Various writings regarding Jesus' ministry such as the letters of St. Paul, and some of the Disciples and others, were collected and compiled over the course of the first several hundred years A.D., into a single volume that came to be called the New Testament. In the many years following, it was edited, revised and rewritten in which much of the original teachings were misinterpreted, subverted and bastardized. There is much inspired writing in the Bible, but one should be cautious and read it with discernment. It is not a book of absolute truth; no book is when it is written by the hands of man, who then are prone to revise it and rewrite it.

When we hear a sound from outside our body, there is no doubt that we heard something and can usually identify it as to its source. But when the sound comes from within, we are often unaware of it, or if we are, it is easily misunderstood or mistranslated. It has various names: subconscious, intuition, feeling and inspiration. What one hears with the inner ear is a still small voice with a sound that is not a sound. It is a sound so soft as to be almost indistinguishable from normal mental activity, having less substance that thought, as though it has passed through a filter with all distracting sounds and images removed, yet leaving a coherent sense of feeling and knowing. When it comes through clearly, it is unmistakable. But at other times, the filter can get clogged and permit only faulty transmissions that are easily misinterpreted by man-mind, sometimes coming out as something unintended. It can easily happen this way when one receives from within.

The writers of the Bible and subsequent translators, those who were inspired, underwent the same process and were equally susceptible to misinterpretation and misunderstanding. Then there were the others who were not inspired, but who calculatingly altered passages or removed them for personal gain, usually power. The example most destructive of this to the spirituality of man was the intentional removal from the Bible of all references to reincarnation.

In 553 AD, the Byzantine Emperor Justinian, at the urging of his wife and advisor Theodora, convened the 2nd Council of Constantinople. He issued a decree that required the assembled bishops of the Church to remove anything pertaining to reincarnation from the Bible. The council obeyed his edict and did a pretty good job of it, but they missed a few passages: refer to John 9:1-3, Mathew 17:10-13, and John 3:3-7. Enough was left to provide significant confirmation of the proof of reincarnation. This is an obvious indication that if man doesn't like what he finds in the Bible, it can be changed or removed. It has occurred many times over the centuries.

There are many men and women of religion, shepherds in almost every denomination and belief system that accept the inherent truth of physical rebirth. But there are a greater number of false prophets in black cloaks and white collars, and many in scarlet cummerbunds who deny it and lead their flocks into error. And there are too many sheep who blindly follow their misguided shepherds down the thorned paths of doctrine into swamps of errant theology, simply because they are unwilling or unable to reason for themselves. But after a lifetime of indoctrination and conditioning, it is understandable. It takes a determined will and great courage to pursue truth on one's own without the false security of a leader to direct one's thinking and actions at every step. But it must be done if one is to be liberated.

The greatest disservice of the church to the growth of spirituality in man, is not so much that it teaches error and compromise, but that its members become dependent on a material construct – the church, for their salvation. They are comfortable to have someone else tell them what to believe and how to express their belief in their lives. It doesn't enter their heads that what they are taught may not be entirely true, and that truth is to be found outside the boundaries of church doctrine, in of all places, their own hearts and minds. They have no reason to think that what they believe might not be truth. They are complacent in their belief and remain stuck in it, having no desire to think for themselves or to look elsewhere for the truth that will set them free.

We have been conditioned since infancy to believe without questioning the advice and teachings of our elders. But how do we know that they know the truth of what they're saying? It would pay us to consider that they in their turn were also conditioned by their elders to believe without questioning. And their elders....? Redundant in our religious history, we see where someone came to believe something, and with conviction convinced others to believe it also. But where did their opinions or knowledge come from? Did it come from their higher mind... from spirit... from God? Did it come from pure intent, or from hunger of prestige or power? If from within, or from spirit, was what they heard or given, accurately transcribed or translated? So, is what they have claimed to be truth, reliable and trustworthy? The point that is being made here is that it is necessary to consider these things without having your conditioned responses activated to automatically reject what could be a major turning point in your spiritual evolution. Much of what we have been taught is at the best misunderstood and faulty transmissions from within or from spirit, and at the worst, outright lies and manipulations of truth by those we should be able to trust with our spiritual development.

We were created sons and daughters of God. Our purpose then is to become one with Him in knowledge, purpose, creativity and love. Words alone, whether written or oral, spoken or thought, do not have the power to make us one with God; and neither will the surrender to doctrine, or obedience to creeds and dogma.

If one is to achieve wisdom and understanding, it is essential that truth is pursued independently, free of coercion, on one's own initiative by going within to the Source of All and receiving from God the guidance needed. With an open mind and a little digging, using what God has given to everyone, all can know the truth about all things, including reincarnation, which is a most misunderstood and rejected of God's verities.

Until one understands that we live more than once, any possibility of achieving any meaningful degree of wisdom and understanding is impossible. Truth is available for all to find and claim. But keep in mind that truth is not handed to one on a silver platter like John the Baptist's head. If it were, it would be about as valuable. So keep your own and dig into it and find the gift of truth that is lying in wait for your unwrapping.

No longer is it not for us to know. It is in this New Age, our responsibility to know! It is now that with our new found freedom from fear of persecution and threats of damnation, our obligation to ourselves is to know. When one understands reincarnation and karma, sense is made of the nonsensical, understanding replaces confusion, the unexplainable can be explained, and peace and harmony can ensue. Understanding can lend credence to justice and fairness in all things, and tranquility to a mind in turmoil. The vast smorgasbord of God's knowledge and wisdom can then be spread out before us for the taking. And in this is God's promise: "The truth that shall set you free."

# 16

# REINCARNATION

The Church has made many alterations to the original teachings of Jesus. Among them, the most far reaching and damaging to man's spiritual understanding and growth, and to his relationship to God, was the purging of references to reincarnation from the bible. The result was to believe that we have only one life to live in a physical body. The removal made it possible for the Church to fundamentally alter the original teachings of Jesus, setting the stage to create doctrines and dogma to their liking, irrespective of truth. It opened the door to widespread abuse of truth, and unbridled power.

The lasting effect of their changes severely damaged and distressed the intent of the early Church of Jesus because it created in the followers an unquestioning obedience and dependency on the Church. It was a dependency that was based on fear, and it effectively removed free will from God's mandated right of free choice and self-responsibility in his spiritual affairs, beliefs and expressions. It made it possible for the Church to defend the alterations and additions it had made to Jesus' teachings, and maintain control of its member's expressions of faith and worship. It created a situation that enslaved the people to the Church – their very salvation became dependent on abject obedience to the Church's wishes and demands. It altered the very foundations of the Church that Jesus established. The church of universal love and forgiveness became a Church of fear and judgment.

The removal of reincarnation from the Bible was done under the orders of Emperor Justinian in 543 AD, at a time prior to the Church's ascendancy to uncontested ecclesiastical and temporal power. Fortunately, they missed a few passages, enough to give credence to the claim in later years that reincarnation is fact. Regretfully, when the Church later gained supremacy over its own affairs, the topic became one of denial, although unofficial, and it has become an accepted part of their unwritten dogma ever since. Following the Protestant Reformation promulgated by Martin Luther, this virus lived on in the protestant churches and the offshoot sects as well. It remains in good health today as it is denied by most of the theologians and clergy of the Christian churches. There are however, people of clergy and laity alike of most, if not all, the various sects who firmly believe that reincarnation is fact, although it seems to never be preached about during Sunday sermons. Rather than being acknowledged, it is conveniently overlooked, if not denied.

The Church did not and could not have restored the concept of reincarnation as part of their official doctrinal system of belief even if they had wanted to. If they had restored it and accepted it as truth, it would negate their claims of original sin and all the various canons and doctrines that were spawned from it: punishment, hell, damnation, confession, penance, absolution, and priestly intermediacy, all of which were needed to instill fear for the retention of power.

The survival of these nefarious doctrines depended on the claim that mankind has but one life. In this view, this life is all there is, and man has to make it or break it in the span of a few years – there are no second chances. All of their doctrines rested on this and enforced their claim that salvation depended on absolute obedience to Church dogma. The Church was caught in a trap. They could not restore the concept to the Bible as a basic truth, for if they did, what they had labored on for over many centuries, would be destroyed. They had successfully altered Jesus' teachings to convince the people that there was only one life, and only through the church could they be saved. To restore the concept of reincarnation to the level of truth, it would cost the Church credibility and damage the authority of the clergy with a consequent loss of power and prestige, which were the reasons why they made the alterations in the first place. That, they would not countenance.

If people were to understand that they had a second, a third, a fourth, and even multiple lifetimes for repeated opportunities to correct errors of thought and conduct, then a priestly hierarchy and all the rest of the contrived dogma of the Church would be superfluous and unnecessary for one's salvation. It would shine a glaring light of truth on all the misinformation and lies the people had been conditioned to accept as sacrosanct. The people would have the freedom to be what they were created to be: self-responsible and self-directing of their lives and spiritual growth. The responsibility of one's personal relationship with God would then be the individual's. The priests, pastors and ministers of the varied churches would be what they should be – humble torchbearers to show the way as Jesus did. They would be teachers of truth, guides and lovers of freedom and God's word – true representatives of God. There would be no sin punishable by priestly condemnation, or above all by God, and there would be no hell and no forgiveness because there would be nothing to forgive and nothing to punish. There would be no guilt and no fear. Love would predominate and fear would be negated and lose its dominating and coercive influence of man's thoughts and actions. Love would replace fear.

God emphatically states that He wills that no man shall perish. That statement is not just a nice platitude. They are words of power and truth in that there is *no one* that will ever be condemned to hell, not by God anyway, regardless of belief or conduct, or of what someone may have done to themselves or to others. *There is no hell, except in one's imagination!* And God's forgiveness is guaranteed because there is nothing to forgive. But it must be remembered that God says: *What you sow, that you shall also reap.* That is fact for it is the warp and woof of our tapestry of life. It will be reaped, if not in the present life, it will be in a subsequent life. It must be understood that the reaping of what we have planted is not for punishment; it is only for an opportunity to learn from our mistakes. And it is also possible that if we should learn and correct our errors of thinking or action before meeting our karma, it may not be necessary to meet it at all. God's grace would be sufficient.

Although there is nothing to be forgiven, there still remains the possibility of a hellish experience, real in its effect but not real in fact. Instead, it would be an illusion of a seemingly never-ending nightmare of a person who has inflicted it upon himself through misunderstanding of what is accepted as true. It is temporary, not permanent – no more than a nightmare is. One who wills himself or herself into an illusion of hell stays locked in the illusion only as long as they continue to believe its reality and resign themselves to a fate that is not preordained or inevitable. The time will eventually come when it is realized that their experience in their hell, which has been accepted as real, is not real and is not necessary. At that point the individual will begin to seek a way out of his torment. The simple recognition that hell is only illusion will be the key to freedom. That may take years, maybe thousands of years of our time, before questioning begins and realization sets in and hope arises that the condition is not an unchangeable judgment of a vengeful God. Or again, his release could happen rapidly. It depends on how strongly attached a person is to the condition he or she created, and how deeply embedded they are in their conditions, such as unbridled hatred. Hate for example, can be so intense that it can wrap itself around the hater like an unbreakable chain holding him in agonizing captivity for what can seem like eternity. The only release will come when what is being experienced is no longer bearable and hope arises that there may be something else, something that can free him – maybe a spark of love, or maybe even God.

All during his imprisonment he is under constant care and guidance of angels assigned to watch over him, whispering words of truth, of hope and understanding. Eventually their words will take hold and a spark of illumination will be birthed, followed in time by the realization of God's never-ending love and non-judgment. When that is accepted and he follows that beacon of light, he will be freed of his nightmare.

Reincarnation is not a fable, and it is not wishful thinking of people looking for an easy way out, trying to evade what they fear may be in store for them. It is not escapism; it is liberation. It may be said that it is the truth that sets one free.

It's hard to envision and impossible to believe that God inflicts pain and punishment on His own children, regardless of what is commonly believed and taught by God's supposed spokespeople in our churches. He is not vengeful. He does not, and cannot punish because he is Love. Neither does He judge. We do that, and wrongly so. Just as we should never judge another, neither should we judge ourselves in a condemning manner. However it is necessary to see our errors for what they are, but not for punishment, for that only leads to depression and defeat.

God gave us free will for the purpose of learning to use it in a Godly and creative manner. If he punished us for our errors, and one can be certain that there would be many, would He then punish us for trying? Would we do that to our children after we have encouraged them to choose and give them the freedom to try and fail? Would we tell them that if they fail, they would be severely punished? How could they learn to be responsible and creative individuals if they were punished every time they erred? It wouldn't take too many times before they either quit trying, or rebel. We wouldn't do that to our children, and neither would God do it to His. It is inconceivable that He would or could, and difficult to believe that God who is love is thought by some to be capable of such things.

How else could we as soul, our real self, ever learn to walk on our own and make our will one with God's will if we must constantly hold His hand, afraid to walk on our own, never having the opportunity to exercise our freedom to choose according to our desires? He doesn't want sycophants hanging around aping everything He does, doing only what He wants. He wants us to develop our individuality and be co-creators with

Him. But that is impossible without exercising our free will, and that requires choice with the possibility of error. To develop our will to eventually be one with God's will, simply cannot be done in a single lifetime. There must be opportunities to try again and again if necessary to increase our greatness and transform our weaknesses into strengths, and our fears into love, and our love into oneness with All That Is.

Let's say we live a life without concern for the welfare of others, maybe trample on their rights of individuality, and imprison them in circumstances of financial or emotional conditions from which they can't escape. We hold the key to their liberty but won't use it. Instead of freeing them, we keep them tied to us for our selfish advantages. After a life of this, we die. In the afterlife, we are shown the akashic records (the Book of Life) of what we did in that life and are helped to see where we went wrong, and what must be done to correct the mistaken values we thought were so important and necessary for our physical and emotional survival. That would necessarily require that we are reborn and reenter physical life and apply what we learned in the time of in-between life.

Before our rebirth, a life pattern or outline is formed for us to follow, enabling us to meet circumstances, conditions, people – whatever is necessary for our re-learning opportunities. We are reborn – reincarnated – and begin life anew in a different body, with a different family, and in different circumstances and try again. Upon our death, we again evaluate our experiences to see what we did right, and where we may have gone wrong, then incarnate again and continue our spiritual growth. Obviously, this process requires more that one life to accomplish our soul's purpose to become one with God as a co-creator.

We are already one with Him, just as Jesus was. The difference is that we have not yet realized our potential and our understanding and application of this truth. Peter walked on water and succeeded until he lost faith in himself. Jesus said we could do even greater things that what he had demonstrated, meaning that we have potential equal or greater than what we know of him and his abilities. Tragically, the Church has denied that truth by substituting in its place the belief that we are incapable of walking alone, and that we must rely on the Church for our guidance and salvation. Ignorance is the locked door to our prison of fear and defeatism; understanding is the key to freedom.

Religion emphasizes salvation; in fact its entire theology is based on it. All its dogma, rituals, rules and regulations, do's and don'ts are derived from the concept of sin and salvation and are used to buttress its foundation of error. The term salvation is misleading because there is nothing to be saved from except from our fears and misunderstandings – there is no hell and there is no punishment. Salvation therefore is a no-brainer and meaningless. We are saved before we are born; we are destined from the moment of our creation to reunite with God, to be one in love and creativity, and there is nothing that can stop our inexorable march to that goal. There is only that which can delay but never stop our progress. It is not God's will that any should perish; it is His will that all His children – we, his prodigal sons and daughters, shall, after trying our wings and fall, get up and climb back up the tree of knowledge and experience and try again – then again and again if necessary until having gained in understanding and love, we learn to fly and return home. That is our inescapable destiny – the only fate we will ever meet.

In our journey of many lives, many times, of many names and many failures and successes, we may get corns and bunions and blisters on our feet, we may take wrong turns, we may meet many detours, and all kinds of delays and obstructions. And after a time, we will need to exchange our tired and worn-out vehicle, our physical body, for a new one; but before our next birth, we will stop for a needed rest in paradise. We will patch up our sores and pains, our discouragements and lost hopes, we will restore our strength, and then with renewed will and renewed purpose, we will get up and continue on our journey of soul. That is our destiny. It will not be denied, it can only be delayed. We will arrive home from our many journeys to be greeted by the welcoming arms of our Mother/Father God.

# 17

# IT'S IN THE BIBLE

There are people numbering in the thousands of millions in both eastern and western religions who believe in reincarnation. But the question that remains especially pertinent for western peoples is, is it truth or just foolish nonsense perpetuated by the errant thinking of the gullible? There are more than enough detractors who believe it is just that, yet there are also a great number of others of all stripes and hues, men and women of probity of all religions and faiths who believe it is true, including Christian ministers, priests and theologians of both Catholic and Protestant persuasions. In spite of the denials of prevailing theology, there are Biblical references to the teachings of Jesus in which it is presented that there is more than one life for every person.

Countless arguments can be made to substantiate the truth of reincarnation. There are people in varied nations and different cultures whose verified memories of lives in other times and places support the truth of reincarnation. See "Many Mansions" by Gina Cerminara, and "Twenty Cases Suggestive of Reincarnation" by Ian Stevenson, for two books of enlightened support of the topic; and then there is simple logic.

The belief in reincarnation is not against the teachings of the Christ. Support for this can be found in much of his teachings wherein they were explained in the concept of rebirth, or reincarnation. Jesus referred to rebirth not only in regard to our final resurrection from the material body to the spiritual body at the time of our death; but most importantly to this topic, to repeated incarnations in physical bodies in the material realm. Yet some will ask: if reincarnation is true, why isn't it in the Bible, or why didn't Jesus talk about it? The answer in both cases is: it is, and he did. For example, there are statements made by Jesus that are corroborative evidence of his belief in it. In John 9: 1-3, for example, the disciples when walking with Jesus encounter a blind man by the side of the road and ask: *"Master, who did sin, this man or his parents, that he was born blind?"* Jesus answered, *"Neither hath this man sinned, nor his parents, but that the works of God should be made manifest in him, "* and he then proceeded to restore the man's sight.

The question makes it obvious that the disciples understood reincarnation as a fact, and in Jesus' answer that he did also. This poses an interesting question for those who don't believe in the concept. How could the blind man have sinned before he was born? If Jesus' answer is to make sense, it must be that the man had to have lived a life prior to that one. This point cannot be easily dismissed or tossed aside as though it is unworthy of consideration. After all you may reason, the church denies the physical rebirth of soul, and it claims that man lives but once, so who am I to question? But which church denies that, or do they all? In truth, there are some who do and some who don't. So which church? Yours? Mine? Whose?

Consider also, that above all else a church is composed of individuals, all sons and daughters of God, and many if not most, have a gnawing feeling that what they've been told is not the full Truth. With a growing certainty that there is more, their faith erodes because truth is being hidden from them. In spite of the power of authority, of rules and regulations, dictums, tenets, doctrines, creeds, and threats, members are still individuals and they will at some point in their soul life, seek the Truth. It is their destiny and unavoidable. When the spark of free will yearns to express soul's desires and urges them on, knowledge can and will be attained and the truth will out, even if it takes another 2000 years, or another twenty lives.

On another occasion, the disciples asked Jesus if he was the prophet Elias reborn, and Jesus said that it was John the

Baptist who was reborn. In Mathew 17: 10-13 it is written:

*Vs. 10     And his disciples asked him, saying, Why then say the scribes that Elias must first come?*

*Vs. 11     And Jesus answered and said unto them, Elias truly shall first come,  and restore all things.*

Vs.12     But I say unto you, that Elias is come already, and they knew him not, but have done unto him whatsoever they listed. Likewise shall also the Son of Man suffer of them.

*Vs. 13     Then the disciples understood that he spake unto them of John the Baptist*

Additional support can be found later in the Bible when Paul says that if one man, referring to Jesus, was resurrected, all were. And again at another time, Jesus made the statement: *Before Abraham was, I am.* Consider also that Jesus was raised in an Essene community where it was accepted as fact that man lives more than one life, so it is logical to assume that Jesus was taught the facts of it and in turn, taught it also.

For further consideration, the biblical statement, *to be born again,* is misinterpreted by religion to mean to be born of the *spirit.* In this they are only partially correct, for when one examines the statement of Jesus in John 3: 3-7, it is found to include being born of water as well as spirit.

*Vs. 3     Verily, verily, I say unto thee, except a man be born again, he cannot see the kingdom of God.*

*Vs. 4     Nicodemus saith unto him, How can a man be born when he is old?  Can  he  enter the second time into his mother's womb and be born?*

*Vs. 5     Jesus answered, Verily, verily, I say unto thee, Except a man be born of water and of the Spirit, he cannot enter into the kingdom of God.*

Vs. 6     That which is born of the flesh is flesh; and that which is born of the spirit is spirit.

Vs. 7     Marvel not that I said unto thee, ye must be born again.

Notice that Jesus clearly considered water as separate from spirit by saying, *that which is born of flesh is flesh; and that which is born of the spirit is spirit.* These are two separate things. Water is not spirit, it is a material substance and it exists in a material world; metaphorically it is flesh. A fetus lives in a fluid environment, the amniotic fluid, before it is born. This is commonly referred to as water. To be born of water is an obvious reference to the fluid. Without it, gestation would be impossible, and birth could never occur. Jesus is saying in effect that man is born both in the spirit and in the flesh. This supports his belief in reincarnation as fact. But the church theologians, in order to support their position that man lives but once, twisted this straightforward statement into a misleading falsity by claiming that to be born again refers to the birth of spirit only. Such a position is specious and not true.

In spite of the fact that reincarnation was an accepted belief by many, and rejected by many in the days of Jesus, it is most interesting that there is nothing in the Bible that refutes the belief – there is not a word against it, indeed as it has been shown, there is support *for* it. Those who do reject it have accepted a theology that is not substantiated by biblical writings. Reincarnation, or the opportunity of living more than one life, is all part of God's perfect plan for our spiritual development. The rejection of the concept was conjured by man-mind, not by God – quite the opposite. It was an accepted part of the early Church's belief systems until at the 2nd Council of Constantinople, 553 years after Jesus' resurrection, the church removed it from the Bible.

While the flesh body is finite, the soul body is infinite and never ceases to be. When we recognize that our true self is an indestructible cell of God, and that our flesh body's destiny is only decay and rot, followed by a recycling of its energy, it is reasonable to assume that life continues with the virtual certainty of rebirth in another human form. For soul to have the opportunity of further experiences in material duality, succeeding lives are essential if spirit is to grow in truth. It is reasonable to understand why God provides the opportunity to be born again in the flesh.

The reason for rebirth is simple: we live in the flesh so that we may learn to live in God in oneness and co-creativity. A high level of spiritual attunement is required to achieve oneness with Him, and repeated lives in physical form, give us that opportunity. It enables us to correct past mistakes, enhance desirable qualities, acquire truth, cast off any chains of doubt and disbelief embedded in materiality, all so that we may recognize and nurture our real self, our divine cell of God – our true self, which is Soul, and become one with Him in love and creativity which cannot be done in the span of a single life.

Unfortunately reincarnation is so misunderstood, it has been derided and ridiculed to the point of disdainful rejection. It is a topic often misunderstood with some believing as the Hindus do, that as a rule rebirth means reincarnating in animal form. Their understanding is better called transmigration – the rebirth of soul from man to animal, rather than reincarnation. In non-Hindu belief, it is accepted that soul reincarnates in human form, not in animal form.

The primary reason for the widespread rejection of physical rebirth is its historic denial by the Church, a denial based not on doctrine, nor on fact or reason but on fiction, on a created need to defend false doctrines and tenets. So in this view we have only one chance to make it… or down we go.

All religions worldwide are of the One God. Each one however, contains only a part of His truth and this includes the Christian religion. No religion has it all; none of them have none; all of them have some. Much of the world believes in reincarnation, and there are many hundreds of priests, bishops, ministers, and teachers in Christian churches, both Protestant and Catholic that accept reincarnation as truth as well, and the number is growing. The Essenes who raised Jesus, believed and taught the concept, and his remarks show that he did also. And again, it is important to realize that the Christian Bible does not deny reincarnation. Not a single passage can be found that denies it, only the misled and ignorant do. For those who really want truth, it's available for all to understand.

## 18

# THE TIDES OF LIFE

In spite of the Christian Religion's repudiation of repeated births, or reincarnation, God does give us extra chances. He wants us to realize our Godly potential and that can not be attained in a single life. It could take thousands of mistakes requiring thousands of corrections, and hundreds of lifetimes to do it in.

In each life we have objectives: goals to reach, special undertakings that may be the overcoming of a particular weakness such as egotism or wrong attitudes, and perhaps selfishness or greed. Conversely, it could be the development of special gifts, increased knowledge and understanding, and other things of a Godly nature. In the different lives we will have varied projects of self-improvement materially and spiritually to undertake. We may advance spiritually in one or more qualities of soul in a single trip, but we can also regress in one or more of them, and then need to work on it again in another life. So it behooves us to be on guard.

It is not required that we reincarnate. It's our choice. It is also possible that a rebirth is no longer necessary or desirable from the standpoint of spiritual growth because when we attain the supreme achievement of universal and unconditional Love, there is nothing more to acquire since Love is all there is. God is Love and Love is God. When we are truly Love, having achieved the very reason for our being, we can then say that we are one with God. Then there will be no further purpose in coming back for another go at life, for we have attained what we came here for.

There is no end to God's patience in helping us realize our potential. He gives us unlimited opportunities to be reborn as many times as we desire or need, enabling us to find the truth and align ourselves with His will. As in all things, the choice is ours.

For some it may be hundreds or more of rebirths, and for others, fewer. But in all things, we have the choice to proceed rapidly or slowly. Our progression is up to us – even whether we choose to reincarnate or not. Frater Achad says, *"It is not a decree of God that man should so pass from rebirth to rebirth. He or she who lives in ignorance of that fact is the one who experiences such."* He also says, *"We have frequently stated that God is birthless, ageless, deathless. Man, the image of God, is birthless, ageless and deathless. Rebirth is not mandatory by any established law of God. Rebirth is man's choice."* In other words, we have free will to choose our destiny. Reaching our goal doesn't have to take forever. It can be done in a single lifetime when one becomes Love.

Reincarnation and karma explain the unexplainable, but this too often emphasizes only negative karma – the things experienced in thought or action that are considered unhealthful, immoral, antisocial or destructive. But this is only one side of the coin. The obverse is positive karma – the thoughts and actions that are good for others and oneself, those that are in harmony with God's will – for example talents and abilities and expressions of love and compassion.

Our belief systems of values, morals and mores are inevitably the result of conditioning. Our spiritual mentors – our pastors, priests, teachers and parents have been conditioned in their youth to believe certain things in certain ways, and retain their faulty understandings long after they should have progressed into greater maturity with deeper insights and wisdom. In a very real sense they are brainwashed and conditioned to accept faulty opinions and beliefs as inviolate truth and incontrovertible law. They are representative of all of us; no different except by degree. Paul states in 1 Corinthians 13: 9-13: *For we know in part. But when that which is perfect is come, then that which is in part shall be done away. When I was a child, I spake as a child, I thought as a child: but when I became a man, I put away childish things. For now we see through a glass, darkly; but then face-to-*

*face: now I know in part; but then shall I know even as also I am known.*

Over the centuries the Bible has been rewritten and reinterpreted many times, and all but a few references to reincarnation have been removed, and it appears that they were left in not by intent, but by oversight. For our benefit some passages escaped the ravages of Ockham's razor and are still there for our education and understanding.

Jesus called attention to the Temple of God within, which is the church that is based on truth as exemplified in his life and teachings. But in the following centuries it devolved, losing its distinction as a church of spirit and truth, becoming instead a church of stone and distortion. In the centuries following Jesus' death, his teachings were subverted and his church of truth and freedom degenerated into the moral ambiguity of *churchianity.*

In the prevailing attitudes that are based on false impressions and inadequate understandings of things deeply embedded in conditioned beliefs and attitudes, we often live in fear of punishment, even eternal hell should we transgress any of them. That is so sad, because God is anything but vengeful. He is LOVE, not hate or revenge. When there is punishment, it is we who punish ourselves, and that is ridiculous because punishment is never necessary. Recognition of an error is, but it's for correction, not for punishment.

It should be encouraging for people to know that their next life will not necessarily be a continuation of the same trials, mistakes, lack of success, poverty, ill health, or other debilitations of the flesh and emotions. A rebirth is a new beginning, physically, mentally, emotionally and spiritually; it's a doing away with the old and a birth of the new. However, there will be certain things such as innate gifts and abilities, or traits of character that are not lost, for *nothing* is ever lost. They remain a part of the real self – soul, and are an influencing factor in a new life.

One or more inherited traits from a previous life could form the foundation of increased maturity and perfection in a new incarnation. Attitudes, proclivities, values will remain viable and help form the framework of the new person. They integrate with one's life, influencing the development of character and personality. Things of likes and dislikes, certain attitudes and attachments such as a respect or disrespect for authority, perhaps an inner longing for desert climates or mountain landscapes, certain fears, predilections for certain tastes such as blondes over brunettes, or vanilla over chocolate ice cream, or a preference for certain types of music are a few of these invisible, intangible aspects of one's soul carried over from a past life. They help to make us the person we are, shaping our personality and character.

The mission in one's life is established before birth. It is determined by desire or the need of soul to experience certain things that will advance one's material or spiritual growth. It can be something such as developing patience and tolerance, or maybe compassion, self-control and discipline. Or it may be to be born in great wealth or luxury for the purpose of learning the proper value and respect for money, or maybe as a test to see if it can be used unselfishly and for the benefit of others as well as oneself. It could be to develop a musical gift to a higher level of perfection, or to explore an acquired interest during a past life. But in any event, a new life is a new beginning with a new physical body, a new mentality, new opportunities, and a renewing and regeneration of spiritual values.

There are men and women of religion, shepherds in almost every denomination and belief system throughout the world that accept the inherent truth of physical rebirth. In the Christian religion there are those who believe its truth also, but there are a greater number of detractors in black cloaks and white collars who deny it and lead their flocks into error. And there are too many sheep who follow their misinformed shepherds without questioning, simply because they are unable or unwilling to reason for themselves. But after a lifetime of indoctrination and conditioning, it is understandable. It takes a determined will and great courage to pursue truth on one's own initiative, going against a lifetime of feared authority. But it must be done if one is to be liberated from the shackles of indoctrination and fear. The greatest disservice of the church to the growth of spirituality in man is not so much that it teaches error and compromise, but that its members become conditioned and dependent on a system of belief that is destructive to their spiritual growth. They are comfortable to have someone else tell them what to believe and how to express their belief in their lives. They don't consider that what they are taught may not be entirely true, or that the Source of truth is to be found not in the Church, but of all places within their own hearts and minds! They have no reason to think that what they have been taught can be wrong. Nor do they have a reason to believe in their own ideas of what they think truth can be. They are complacent in their beliefs and remain stuck to them, having no desire or inclination to look elsewhere.

Frater Achad states it eloquently:

*The treadmill of life is endless until man finds Truth and it shall never be found in that which man has learned to call churchianity. It can only be found in the higher precepts and principles of Christianity.*

*What is Christianity? It is void of form. It never becomes a fable. It does not give its appearance as a phantom. Christianity is living the Christ principle, the wise man in the manger of consciousness in action and it meets you through every house of the Zodiac and through every experience.*

*Do not be deceived. Ritual, form, confession of faith, does not make you a child of God. You are God's child from the beginning of time and it shall ever be thus.*

We are born as Sons and Daughters of God. Words alone, whether written or oral, spoken or thought do not have the power to *make* us one with God, and neither will the surrender to doctrine or obedience to creeds and dogma. It is the wisdom of our soul, and the love in our hearts that make us so.

If one is to achieve wisdom and understanding, it is essential that truth is pursued independently on one's own initiative by going to the Source within and receiving from God the guidance needed. With an open mind and a little digging, using what God has given to everyone, all can know the truth about all things, including reincarnation, which is a most misunderstood and rejected of verities. Until one realizes that we live more than once, any possibility of achieving the highest degree of wisdom and understanding is impossible.

No longer is it not for us to know; it has always been our right to know, and now at this point in our spiritual evolution, it is our obligation to know, free from interference and restrictions. When one understands reincarnation and karma, sense is made of the nonsensical, understanding replaces confusion, the unexplainable can be explained, and peace and harmony can ensue. Understanding can lend credence to justice and fairness in all things, and tranquility to a mind in turmoil. The vast smorgasbord of God's knowledge and wisdom can then be spread out before us for the choosing. The centerpiece of His table will be His promise: "The truth that shall set you free."

# 19

# *OF LIFE AND DEATH*

Death is personified as a black cloaked horror whose hooded face we never see. Its countenance evidently is too horrible to be looked upon. It is aptly depicted because it represents the reaping of life and our inescapable future. We fear death because the unknown is always feared, and when it becomes so personal and so inescapable that there is no chance of escaping what fate has in store for us, we cringe and set it aside, out of our minds and thoughts.

Death does not discriminate. It comes to everyone, some sooner, some later, some fight it and some welcome it, but there are few who don't fear it. But there is really nothing to fear. Death is feared because it is not understood. Fear is engendered by ignorance, whereas with knowledge there is understanding and freedom. With an enlightened perception of death, the logic, the rightness and even the wonder and mystery of it will be understood and appreciated. When it is identified with what it really is, it can be welcomed. For with knowledge, it will be seen that there is no end to life as it is usually thought. In spite of doubt and false impressions, life is perpetual and never ending. Death can be thought of simply as transference of awareness, with an unnoticeable switch in consciousness from the illusion of materiality to the full expansion of freedom and unlimited knowledge of all that we are as soul and spirit-mind. It is nothing more than a change of vehicles, which is what our body is for the soul. When one wears out, it is respectfully exchanged for a new one.

The basis of our fear of death is that we identify our reality with a flesh body. We are that but only in part. Our reality is intelligent spirit without form or material substance expressed as soul. Death is only a point in non-time when soul leaves the physical body and returns to its true state of spirit to continue its spiritual growth in other realms. There are different realms of life, most of which are expressed in spirit form. One realm is the astral plane, others have different names – all of them are often lumped together under one term: heaven.

Death is feared because we have been conditioned to believe that there is only one life. We are taught that if we live right, obey all the rules and regulations of whatever church we belong to, if we attend church every Sunday, pay our tithes, don't swear, obey all the ten commandments, and all the other items on the long list of spiritual conduct, we will be saved and receive eternal life in heaven. There are those who do all the right things, just the way they were taught in Sunday school and sermons, and by all that, they have it made. Yet deep inside, they fear that they don't qualify because they have done things, maybe unknown to others, that in their minds were sinful. And so they fear death, not knowing what to expect.

The chief requirement of Christianity's concept of salvation is that we must accept Jesus in our hearts. So we try, some earnestly and some too earnestly, becoming religious zealots. Some half-heartedly paying only lip service, and some don't even try, believing they don't have a chance anyway because twenty-three years ago, they shoplifted, or got drunk and hurt someone, or something terribly sinful like that. But they're wrong. Some, of course, may have done something really horrendous such as murder, and then they *know* that they're going to hell, but they're wrong too. They will not go to hell for two reasons: first, there is no hell; second, their beliefs are based on illusions without substance, self-created and nurtured with every little or big error they make. If they believe it strongly enough, hell will manifest for them, but it will be a virtual hell, real in its effect, but not real in God's reality. Therefore, it can be undone, or uncreated.

The understanding of death will come when we realize that we are more than a body of flesh composed of energy that has only a momentary flicker of substance that lasts a few years, then disintegrates and returns to its primordial state of dust. There it remains in chaos intermingling with the creative energy of the universe until used by God in another creation. Nothing ever dies; nothing is ever lost – including energy. The old energized form of flesh is gone, but the energy itself – God's life spirit, continues without end. *"Then shall the dust return to the earth as it was: and the spirit shall return unto God who gave it."* *Ecclesiastes 12: 7*

Soul, which is a heart-cell of God, is the animating force of flesh, and continues to live apart from a human body after its demise; how could it not since it is a part of God? It lives in a form that is not flesh, but individuated spirit – a spiritual body. As such it has life eternal, without end. As soul we will continue to experience life, living in a multitude of forms, some of spirit, some of flesh, and continue to grow in perfection and wisdom. It may be said that physical life as we know it, is a temporary spiritual aberration – a needed experience for the souls growth to perfection, but it is not the reality of life. It is but a virtual reality, an illusion created by soul. It is a mirage, a dream, which is to be experienced, savored, and used by soul to obtain greater perfection, knowledge and understanding. But it can be experienced only in the illusion of reality, in which what we experience is as real to our concept of truth as the rain is to a thirsty land.

So what do we have to fear? Death? Or is it the virtual reality of *life* that we fear, because we don't understand life. In the midst of a nightmare, are you in fear of awakening? No, you would welcome it to escape the horror of the illusion. We have less fear of what is known, than of what is imagined, because fear is the false reality of mistaken ideas, concepts and false projections. Fear, worry, and anxieties are born in the unknown and in our misunderstandings of life and death. When these are accepted into our thoughts and activities, they become tyrants, destroying peace, even hope, if not controlled.

Fear is love's opposite; it's a destroyer, killing all that is good and sacred if left unchecked. Love is the counterpart of fear. When one lives in love, fear doesn't have a chance. People who are afraid of death, are often afraid of life as well, because they don't understand either. Those who do understand life and death have no fear of either because they realize that death is only an extension of life and the precursor to another life. In other words, death is not an ending, but a beginning. Thomas Mann says, *"The only religious way to think of death is as part and parcel of life."*

What man may think is true has no bearing and no effect on what the reality of that thing is, except when it is misapplied through ignorance and misunderstandings. Truth itself cannot be affected, because truth stands alone and is inviolable. The beliefs of mankind and their negative effects on our lives are governed and restricted not by truth, but by truth misconstrued. When truth is understood and accepted, it does not restrict, it frees. Truth is often uncomfortable, yet it is the liberator that frees mind of doubt and fear.

There is nothing to fear following death. There is no hell, no punishment, and no distress except what the individual has created for himself through shame and guilt. God does not judge us, we do. If there is to be judgment, it is we who do it, and that's stupid because it's not necessary and not needed. What we will do, is evaluate our life and determine how it has affected our overall soul growth. Any pain we experience is self-inflicted. And in this too, God does not do it to us, we do. It is against His nature to inflict pain; it's simply not in Him, for He is love. He assuages, not distresses. He does not judge, but forgives. The judgment at the end of our lives comes not from God, but from an *evaluation* of us by us. It is for the purpose of seeing where we may have gone wrong, and helping us to see what we may need to do to correct it in our next go-around. There is no pain involved except perhaps regret and the resolve to do it differently next time.

In order to give something to someone, it must first be possessed. To give love, one must be love. If one is love, there is no room for hate, or any negative emotion. There can be one or the other but not both. As one matures in intelligence and spirit, with increased understanding it will be understood that as God is love, He can only give love. So one can expect only love from Him – not anger, not pain, not judgment and certainly, not eternal separation in a place of flame and pain. Only love. Edgar Cayce says, *"The fear of God just waiting to catch you or punish you, appeals to the child mind. Do not fear God, but love God. Do not fear death, but conscience."*

So if this is true, which it is, then what is there to fear when the physical vehicle wears out and it's time to get a new one? Just enjoy a well earned between-life vacation, and when rested, resume what you are destined to do and be – a soul to select what it chooses to experience as a replanted seed. It chooses to be reborn if it desires with a new body with no miles on it, paid for in full with the love of God and its new mother's travail. And with your first breath, take your first step on your next journey of soul. It's really that simple.

Life is a process of experimentation and adjustment. It is a series of journeys of indeterminate length and purpose. Each journey represents an opportunity for change and advancement – greater understanding, the development of desired traits, the elimination of undesirable ones, the meetings with others of whom we have a karmic relationship – some of good, some of bad, but all of which can be strengthened or corrected – whatever is needed for soul's growth. Life is to be savored and enjoyed – even the experiences we'd rather not have because in them there is good and potential growth. Robert Browning eloquently reveals his love of life: *"How good is man's life, the mere living! How fit to employ all the heart and the soul and the sense forever in joy!"*

People identify themselves with their flesh body, which is tragic, for that is the source of their fear. They see at death, a body that was once a vital, functioning human vehicle for soul, but now only decay and rotting flesh. They don't see the freed spirit that once inhabited the body, but has since escaped its prison of flesh and gone on to experience true liberation like a butterfly in the freedom that comes only with release from a cumbersome cocoon bonded to the earth – the freedom to enjoy the peace, laughter, creativity, and love that comes with the transformation.

There is a purpose in life for every soul that enters a physical body – a mission to perform for its spiritual growth. The purpose, or mission could be one that will shake the world. But it's more likely to be one of simply living life in as Godly a manner as possible, gaining and giving love, joy, peace, and compassion in service to God and others in selflessness and good will. This mission may require a life span of 120 years or longer, or only a few days or even hours. The mission may not be only for the soul's adventures in material expression, but also for the opportunity for someone else to learn and grow spiritually in the trials that may be offered to it. An example would be the parents of a child that lives but a few days or a few years. Death is not capricious, visiting its so-called victims haphazardly; death is part of an organized pattern of a soul's brief sojourn in materiality, unfolding in accordance with the pattern established before birth by soul with the approval of spirit.

There is a purpose and a time for every life and death, and for every experience. There are no accidents. Every life has a purpose with things to do and things to be, and things to be recalled and experienced. When that has been fulfilled, one graduates and goes on to a higher level of awareness and development. The death of someone is not to be mourned, but *celebrated* for his or her graduation from a life of materiality to a new life of unsurpassed freedom and joy. Mourning is for the survivors, not for the deceased.

Death is not an ending, but a beginning. It is a rebirth into new and glorious experiences that expand on what we have already experienced in material life. A going beyond the known to new experiences and opportunities to correct past errors of thought and activities, and in the re-creation, constructing a new being. Death is not to be feared – not at all. *"O death where is thy sting? O grave, where is thy victory?"* 1 Corinthians 15:55

Death should be welcomed, not feared, but not necessarily encouraged either, for to do that it could create the possibility of leaving life before we are ready, before we have finished our purpose for that lifetime. Soul has a reason for experiencing material life, and everything that is part of it, and it determines its coming experience carefully before birth. But after its birth, its knowledge of its true self, its past lives, its reason for being born is veiled to the conscious mind. But the purpose, the reason for its current life is still viable and needs to be expressed. It would therefore be a waste of energy and of soul's time to seek death before the purpose of life has been fulfilled. However, as we have free will, we have the freedom to choose whether to live or die. But choose carefully, for if one leaves before their mission has been fulfilled, there may be a need to return to a human body and go through the whole thing again until its purpose has been fulfilled. Suicide is not an unpardonable sin – there is no such thing! That is a conjuration of man-mind, not God-mind and in this too, God does not judge. We choose to be reborn and we also have the right to choose when to leave life. God respects our choice and does not punish. We may still have to meet the things that precipitated suicide, and that will require experiencing the situation and conditions again in a succeeding life. So in that event nothing is escaped and nothing is gained.

It has been spoken here of life and death, with emphasis perhaps wrongfully stressed on death, for death is only the flip side of life. Life is the precursor to death and death is the prelude to life. Without the one, there cannot be the other. Death is but a rebirth into a new life with renewed talents, abilities, loves, opportunities and new chances to recreate those things of soul that need changing or developing, or even trying for the first time.

It is said that we begin to die with our first breath. So we have a conundrum: which comes first: the chicken or the egg – life or death? Life and death both precede and follow each other. They are not separate, but integral. They are both the parent and the child. One doesn't eliminate the other; rather they complement and support each other; each is necessary for their fulfillment. Death will always follow life; but one can rest easy knowing that life will always follow death. As there is no loss of consciousness and awareness at the point of transition, the prevalent concept of death as an end-all is erroneous because there is no cessation of mental activity. Thought goes on, awareness continues without interruption, and what soul has acquired in the way of knowledge and experience, remains forever as part of its total being.

We must realize that our reality is not the body we see in a mirror; our reality is that we are a God-cell of intelligent spirit – soul. Though we may not see our invisible selves, we are nevertheless real and experiential. We are creative reality. There is in the cycle of birth and death, a continuation of soul's evolution in spiritual growth and perfection.

Seattle, a Native American leader of Northwest Indians, stated: *"If we are to understand death, we must first understand life."* The transition of soul from a material body to a spiritual body cannot be understood separately one from the other for they are interdependent. So cheer for life; it is a glorious and beautiful opportunity to express soul's exuberance in becoming one with God. But greet death also with cheer; welcome it when the time comes for soul's transition, for it's the first step to a new life.

There is a time for the transition, a time to pass through the veil of death to a new and different life with a new body, a new mind, and new opportunities for exploring and expressing soul's innate abilities and needs. It matters not whether the life span is 100 years, one day, or one hour, for there is in the living, no matter how brief, a great deal accomplished. The passage of life should be celebrated, not mourned. Mourning should be for the assuaging of the survivors emotions, and that is good, but it has no value for the deceased. The essence of a deceased person does not remain in the dead and rotting corpse, held there by some unknown and desperate malevolent force not wanting to relinquish its hold. With the body's last breath, soul is freed and flies away – rising in spirit to a new level of freedom and a new life of joy, peace, and love. So why should a dead person be mourned? Why not celebrate the death as one would a graduation, because that is what it is. So have a memorial service, but for the living, not for the dead. For the departed, celebrate – drink a toast in salute to the deceased's graduation to a higher school, and to a new life of peace, joy, and love.

# 20

# DESTINY AND FATE

Fate is the inevitability of an event or condition beyond our control to affect or change. In its effect, it is death because it is immovable, static, unchangeable, and therefore without life; without change there is no life. Destiny is in the living – expressed in progression toward pre-determined goals or events. They are those that have been established and nurtured by the individual, and maintained as long as it serves the purpose of its creator.

Destiny is the result of choice and it is dependent on the will of the individual to keep, change or let go when it is no longer wanted or useful. It is an expression of free will, whereas fate is predetermined by an outside force. While fate is preordained and inevitable, destiny is selective and amendable; it is not inescapable. Destiny is subject to a person's will and it can be changed or altered as the person sees fit.

People commonly identify destiny with fate. When they do, it can create cynicism and defeatism when one believes that nothing can be done to change what seems to be unavoidable. It can involve surrendering to a supposed lot in life that deprives them of the freedom to direct their own lives. It can rob them of the ability to create the good things of their future, or remove what is not good. They can be locked into a *fait accompli* by their misunderstandings, unable to re-recreate a situation or condition that is untenable such as a life of poverty, illness, fear, depression, or lack of love.

Too often, people believe that they are living an inescapable reality, bonded to a fate beyond their ability to resolve or change. But they are wrong, for nothing is inevitable.

Everything can be changed. The problem is that chosen destinies are often confused with pre-determined fates. The terms need to be defined for a clear understanding that all things can be changed, and when that is understood, to decide whether a thing *should* be changed, or if it would be better to leave it alone. But in every case, the choice is ours to make.

One's destiny in life is not set in concrete, inescapable and forever fixed. This includes the meeting of karma, or the meeting of what has been sown. Events and circumstances are not fated in themselves. They are the results of choice and subject to change. Therefore nothing is untouchable. All but death can be altered, or eliminated. However, the manner of death and its timing can be determined by the person. It can be postponed; it can be hurried, feared or welcomed but it cannot be prevented. It all depends on attitude, desire and choice. But it cannot be prevented, thus it is fated.

Fate is believed by most to be those things that await a person at some point in their lives or upon their death that enfold uncompromising, inevitable events or situations. In this belief, fate is predestined by an unseen force, principle or power that predetermines events. It lies outside the pale of freedom and free choice. It is locked into the certainty of a thing happening, in the belief that there is nothing that can be done to effect it. In truth, there is no such thing as fate except for death, because all things are subject to change in accordance with the free will given to us by God. We create what we are and what we experience; but along with our power to create, we can also undo, or recreate, thereby changing our creations if and as we will. Nothing is immovable or unchangeable, including ourselves. Only *we* have the power to bind us to a condition or situation that is not for our best, and then only if we accept it and allow it to control us without any attempt to change.

In most minds, destiny is equated to fate, allowing it to slew toward inevitability, and its acceptance as unchangeable or unalterable. In this manner it can be said that Old Joe was destined to experience a loss of some sort with an implication of inescapability, which is just short of a certain fate. But Old Joe had the opportunity all along to change the course of the situation or condition and its result during its development, but he chose not to, which may have been deliberate, or simply failure to act. He may have been destined to encounter a certain thing, but not necessarily to experience it. The experience, or the effect of it, was not fated – it was permitted through choice, or usually, through inaction; yet even inaction is the result of choice.

Predestination is a different breed of cat. It is related to destiny and fate but with a twist. It is an extreme religious concept of life after-death, a dressed up word for fate and also lacking in self-determination. It is fatalistic in that it is conjured by a religious belief that effectively removes free will from our inventory of God's gifts. In its concept, God determines our fate for us, before we are even born – a rather ridiculous misunderstanding of merit or justice that completely negates God's unconditional Love. Pre-selection is an arbitrary decision without justice, like the throwing of dice or flipping a coin to see who wins and who loses. It compels and binds a person to a fate that is inescapable, which may be heaven, but it can also be hell. But in either case, it is not known until it's too late, and neither is it amenable by choice before or after death.

In such a scenario, its belief can have a devastating effect on one's life. A person can live the life of an angel in loving obedience and deference to God, and selfless service to others in unconditional love, but if that person is not on God's list of those He pre-selected for heaven, he will be consumed in the fires of hell as surely as the burning sun will consume a snowman. Such a concept of injustice could compel one to believe that God is not just, and that justice cannot be obtained no matter how deserving. It is easy to imagine how this could infect one's faith and trust in a loving, compassionate and caring God. Fear of the unknown would infiltrate one's life, hope could die and everything a person thinks, says and does would be affected. A life of fear and slavery to conditions not of one's choosing such as poverty, abandonment and illness could likely be accepted as an inevitable fate. Without hope, there would be nothing to live for. This is a good example of how a church, or a religious sect can infect truth with self-deception, deceiving people into accepting the most ungodly of things as truth, and all with good intentions.

We are born into physical life with a pre-determined outline of a format or a life-program that has been established by soul before birth, all done with the advice and guidance of our spirit guides and angels. Destiny is the meeting of that which is included in our original life program, destiny conceived not by uncontrolled events and inevitable fate, but of events and situations created and energized by us with the guidance of spirit for their desired effect on us. This format is of our creation and consists of the elemental events and conditions to be met through life experiences. It creates our DNA that determines our physical, mental and emotional characteristics for that lifetime – whether they are sickness or health, homeliness or beauty, genetic abnormalities or superlative gifts of genius – they are the things that develop and affect our physical and material existence.

Destiny is nurtured in freedom and expressed in opportunities resting easy on desire and choice. The purpose is to provide effective conditions and situations that will enable soul to experience those things that are determined effective for its spiritual growth. This includes our choices before birth of parents, conditions of health and wealth, vocations, successes and failures, loves, gains and losses. We can select situations of fear and destruction, or love and construction. And we can also select opportunities of developing talents and abilities, or maybe to correct relationships with souls we had difficulties with in previous lives. And it may be to enjoy the warmth of love and friendship with souls we have been close to in other lives.

We will meet in our life, a framework of pre-determined destinies with the details of opportunities and experiences left open, to be filled in as we live it. Our life will be a series of experiments and adjustments, of learning and growing while planting seeds for our future, then reaping their fruits, sweet or sour, as they mature. In our life-program we have free will to fulfill our chosen destinies according to the conditions of the moment – or changing them and creating new ones as we choose.

Although we have pre-selected the major events and conditions to be met, they are only the outlines of our lives to live. We are born with the opportunity and freedom to create and recreate the events of our lives as we choose, filling in the outline with the details of experiences we so choose. In this is our responsibility, and in this is our opportunity to be and express ourselves as we wish, therefore satisfying the desire of God for us to develop our individuality and become one with Him as co-creators.

The greatest hindrance to a successful resolution of one's destiny is the lack of understanding of our God-given powers of creativity. Most people don't realize that they are co-creators with God and have the ability and the power to create and re-create not only things, but also the subjective influences and essences of life as well, such as happiness, peace and future opportunities. It is not only our right but also our duty to fulfill our responsibilities as co-creators and determine what kind of life we want, and when and how we will experience it. If a person chooses something in life that may turn out to be a mistake or not in his best interest, it is always the result of choice. But as he chose it, so can he re-choose, undo or re-create it. In a nutshell, our life is what we make it. We are not compelled to accept anything. The choice is always ours; that is our God given right of free will.

# 21

# DESTINY AND FREE WILL

Life is predicated on free will. Without the right and the duty to choose in our lives of duality, there would be no reason for physical existence. The purpose of life is to become one with God, and as such to be co-creators with Him. We are given opportunities in life to develop our creativity, and this can be done only through the process of choosing expressions of free will. We are destined, but not fated to anything, for if fate existed, it would obviate free will.

Every person is born with a life-program to follow – a pre-determined framework consisting of the elemental events and conditions to be attained through the application of free will. We contracted before birth to undergo certain things, to meet certain conditions, to alter negative mind-sets, to develop new belief systems, or perhaps to improve performance in whatever area it is desired or needed – all for our greater spiritual growth. Although we have pre-selected the major events and conditions to be met, they are only the outline of our life to live. We are born with the glorious opportunity and freedom to create and recreate the events of our life as we choose, filling in the outline with the creations of our choice. In this is our responsibility, and in this is our opportunity to be and express ourselves as we wish, therefore satisfying the desire of God to develop our individuality and become one with Him as co-creators.

In our living, we can reach out, expand our interests and investigate other things as we wish. With this freedom to change the tides of our lives with its ebbs and flows of destiny and uncertainty, our life can be compared to a lucid dream during which the dreamer is aware that he or she is dreaming, and assumes control of it by altering the content or course of the dream, even changing its fundamental rationale or purpose. What we experience in life is tied to free choice in the application of our will. The creation of destinies, or their manifestations in our lives do not unfold in a script that cannot be revised or rewritten. They are not written in indelible ink nor anchored in cement. Everything in life is movable and changeable and is the result of willful creation and re-creation, and we are the shakers and the movers. Although our pre-established life program provides the opportunities to harvest what we plant, it is not inevitable that we must, for what we planted can be pulled up and something new can be rooted in its place.

A person is destined to meet certain things that are set in motion beforehand by oneself, whether before birth or during a current life. It is a meeting of that which is conceived, not by uncontrolled events and is inevitable, but by what is envisioned and energized for its desired effects by the person it's affecting. Destiny is conceived in freewill and expressed in opportunities of desire and choice.

People too often believe they are living an inescapable destiny or fate, locked into something beyond their ability to resolve or change. They are in error because they confuse the two. They need to define terms and determine what destiny is, what is predestined or fated, and what the results are of their own creations. They don't understand their God-given powers of free will or creativity. They don't realize that they are co-creators with God and have the power to create, uncreate and re-create not only things, but also the subjective essences as well, such as happiness, peace, and opportunities.

Fate is considered inevitable. But that is not true because nothing is inevitable except death, but even that not always – do you recall Elijah who was lifted up bodily into heaven without having to die first? Nothing can be inevitable for if it was otherwise, there could be no free choice. Without the ability to choose, it would be impossible for us to ever become one with God, which is the whole purpose for soul to take on the heavy weight of materiality. But since we have the ability to choose, we must also have the ability, and the right, to change anything in our life we find disagreeable or incompatible with our desires of free expression. In other words, there is no such thing as fate, only opportunity.

We are not locked into anything except through our choice. This includes the most difficult life experiences such as ill health, poverty, slavery, addiction, jealousy, fear, betrayal, and abandonment. They can all be changed, corrected or removed. It only requires the will and the belief that it can be done. People have reversed the ravages of terminal cancer, some adults have grown new teeth, and some have grown new limbs. *Nothing* is impossible because we are co-creators with God; therefore destiny is not fated because it can be changed; and fate is not possible, for it cannot be changed. It is only a matter of changing an adversity into a blessing, or for the unreasonable, a blessing into a misfortune.

When it's realized that spirit is the substance and the true reality of life, and that all the events and experiences we encounter are directed by the will of spirit, it can be seen that material life as we know it has no reality in itself. Material life and physical existence is directly dependent on the amorphous reality of Spirit. As such, life in this world of duality is an illusion created by spirit for the purpose of three-dimensional experiences – "life" as we call it. It is only through such experiencing that we as soul – our true selves – can undergo and develop the certain traits necessary for our spiritual growth and creativity.

If we should look closely at a human embryo, we would see the pattern of the individual it will become. It is seen in the genes and the DNA. Everything about the human to be, its strengths, weaknesses, appearance, personality, character, all the things visible and invisible of the human being are there for the reading. Our primary responsibility as soul in human life is to realize and accept our true nature – our oneness with God our creator, and claim our birthright, that which is already ours, waiting for us to claim and use. God's gifts are available to us now. We don't have to wait for some arbitrary event or condition to happen first. We don't have to get to heaven before it occurs. We can manifest these gifts now, even if we may be living in a state of self-created hell. Nothing is forbidden to us. We are already children of Father/Mother God, and what God is we are too.

Should a person accept something in life that may turn out to be undesirable or destructive, it is still the result of choice and is subject to change. As a thing is created, so can it be re-created. Fate is not truth; it is illusion. It is an ill-defined substance, having strength or power only as we lend it. We are destined from birth to be the captains of our lives and masters of our destinies, directed by the Light and Love that is our true nature. It is our destiny to live as slaves only if we have so chosen; it is not our destiny to live controlled by things unaffected by free will. We are born in freedom and have the right and the obligation to determine for ourselves what we want to be and how we will express it. The right and the ability and the freedom to change according to our wishes are available to all for it is the essence of spirit. All it requires is faith, trust and pure intent.

# 22

# MISUNDERSTANDINGS

There are many things among the dogma and doctrines of the Church that are not in full accordance with the spirit of truth as Jesus taught it. Many of them are man-made, meant to assure allegiance to the Church and a continued fear of its authority. At the worst they are blatant conjurations of lies and deceits; at their best they are confusing, misrepresentations of truth. Among the many things promulgated by the Church as truth, but which are the opposite, and not fully covered in other chapters of this book, are the following:

## SIN

To put it in a few words, there is no such thing as sin as it is taught by religion. Sin is not an evil act, or blasphemy, or any number of other things that require forgiveness if we are to be saved from hell. Sin is only a mistake, a temporary separation from God created by us and sustained only as long as we hold on to it. Sin is not to be forgiven because there is nothing to forgive. And that includes self-forgiveness. If we hold on to guilt or shame for something we consider sinful, then we hold on to the effects of self-condemnation. Should we feel that forgiveness is necessary and go to God for it, we will find that there's nothing to forgive. How can He forgive something that never happened? We should be elated in knowing that He does not reproach us for our errors, pardoning us long before they are committed. He has given assurance of forgiveness, if you wish to call it that, which is automatic, and he gives it gladly without condition or punishment, or threats of punishment.

The problem we have with religion is that it promotes sin by treating it as something that demands judgment and punishment. Since God does not judge, the Church believes it must do so in His place because the entire structure of Christian theology is based on the concept of sin. Jesus never judged. Look it up and you will find not a single instance where he did. You no doubt recall when he told the crowd waiting to stone the harlot, "Let him among you who is without sin, cast the first stone." He did not judge, it wasn't necessary, and neither did the crowd, because in their hearts they believed they were as guilty of error as she was.

Sin and its consequences are conjurations of religion, invented by the Church to make its members beholden to it for their salvation. So it was necessary to create a system of judgment, punishment and absolution to sustain its power. They operate on fear and they are sustained by fear. It cannot be that God judges, because fear is the opposite of love, and love is what God is. God wills that no man shall perish, and that includes history's worst offenders of morality, degradation and sadism. It stands to reason then that salvation is ours even before we are born. All are promised eternal life! It may take longer for such souls to return to God, but return they will! That is God's will, and it cannot be denied. In spite of our mistakes, our detours, our errors and destructive impulses, our unstoppable destiny is to return to our true home.

## THE WRATH OF GOD

This hardly needs discussion, because every paragraph in this book extols God's love for man. How could it be possible for God who is all love ever be wrathful with us? He can't and He isn't. This needs explanation only because it seems that there is hardly a church anywhere that doesn't allude to the wrath of God. Theology wraps its arms around the concept and builds a structure of faith and worship around it. How sad. Over the centuries religion has pounded in our minds the belief that God is something other that what He is. Man has been brainwashed to erroneously believe that God is judgmental, revengeful, angry, jealous – all the negative attributes of man himself. It might be said that we attribute to God, what we don't wish to acknowledge of ourselves. Such erroneous concepts of God are reasonable, because if man conceived a religion based on fear and punishment, would not then God have to reflect those traits? What we have created of God is the mirror image of ourselves transposed into a likeness of what we believe God to be. Don't we have to do that? We must if we are to establish and maintain our religious beliefs as we have done, beliefs that are based not on truth and the true teachings of Jesus, but on lies and hypocrisy. Would we not then have to create a God that would support our misrepresentations of truth? Yes, it seems so, and it is obvious that when you look at our theologies, that that is exactly what we have done.

## HELL

There is hell, but there is not *a* hell. Hell is a condition or situation; *a* hell is a place. The place called hell is located in the bowels of the earth, it is said, where there is fire and brimstone, or intense blackness and no light, with evil and pain forever. It is ruled by a sadistic monster that enjoys feasting on the souls of the condemned, gorging himself on the sinful desires and actions of what was flesh. It is a monster called Lucifer that never did and does not now exist as such; Lucifer the monster is nonexistent; such an evil spirit is a creation of thought, a conjuration of man-mind based not on reality of Biblical scripture but on misinterpretations and representations of fear created by man.

A condition of hell is self-imposed and experienced in our lives according to what we believe and accept as truth. Those who do experience it live in a perpetual state of fear and self-inflicted pain. It could be experienced as jealously, hate, envy, self-judgment, failure, abandonment, or any number of things. They do not realize the truth of their situation, that it is self-created and can be exchanged at will, for a life of peace and love. They will remain in their hellish condition only as long as they wish to continue their self-condemnation and self-punishment. They will be released when they can see themselves as God sees them in both their godliness and in their debasement, accepting themselves *as they are* with love and forgiveness, and harboring no guilt or shame.

Hell is an illusion. For those who accept its reality, whether alive in a physical body, or a seeming eternity in Hades following their death, they will in fact suffer as though it is real. They have determined its reality and all that they associate with it. In their illusions they will feel all the pangs and pain of hell because it lives in their imaginations. But hell, whether it's in our minds or in the bowels of the earth is temporary for it is based on non-reality or illusion; it is a living nightmare that lasts only as long as credence is given to it. But as in a dream, the self-condemned will eventually awaken from it. Even those who experience the virtual reality of *a* hell after death will at some time leave their prison of pain when they get to the understanding that God did not put them there, nor has He deserted them, and that there are better things than what they are experiencing.

All during their time in hell, they are never alone, for their spirit guides are with them. Among the guides are some who they knew and loved in material life. They are always whispering to the prisoner even though they may not be heard, encouraging him or her to see that there is hope and that all is not as it may seem. God wills that no man shall perish. Help and love will always be with the self-condemned regardless of how evil or self-centered his actions may have been in his lifetime. When he is ready, he himself will break his chains of illusion when he sees there is hope, and the truth that where he is and what he is experiencing may not be permanent. That understanding breeds expectation and it is the key to unlock his prison of hopelessness and defeat, and he can leave hell *whenever he wishes.* For some it may be only a very brief time, but for those who were deeply embedded in hate and evil during their earthly life, it may seem like eternity. But they too will be released from their hate and anger when they accept the love that is offered them.

Proof that a virtual hell is real in the minds of people, is found in the testimonies of those who have had near-death experiences, but came back to life in full recall of what occurred to them while dead. A few had an experience they could only describe as hell in all its horror, pain and hopelessness. They returned to life, changed people.

## SATAN, THE DEVIL, AND OTHER EVILS OF THE MIND

These entities of evil are illusions – only figments of our imagination. They're real only as we clothe them with respectability, and live only as long as we accept their illusion as reality. All the things that plague mankind and excused as acts of Satan or the Devil are wrongly identified, for they are not creations of evil creatures. They are manifestations of our own thinking, perpetrated by us. They are not God-created expressions of evil, which they would have to be if they were real and not just illusions.

All things that ever were, are now, and ever will be are God's creations, including good and evil, the substantial and the insubstantial, and that includes every expression of feeling, desire, emotion, and action. They were all created by God for us to use if we choose to, but they were not all used by Him. The manifestation of evil and its use, is created by us and used by us for our spiritual growth; if and how it is used is our responsibility and our opportunity to express ourselves in whatever manner we choose. It is all part of the necessary expression of the duality of our lives. We are not required to express, or be evil, and God certainly does not require it. But it is available for our use. It's all around us, but so is love and compassion. It's all part of the necessary expression of the duality of our lives and free will. It's all a part of our freedom to choose what we wish and to be what we wish.

God has given us the freedom to be ourselves, but the Church has restricted that freedom by binding us to an edifice of material expressions negating our God-given free will. Instead of exploring our inner natures, which is the reality that is truly us, we have been restricted by accepting a pseudo reality of illusion based on lies, and fashioning our lives and our worship on a religious foundation of restriction and fear. This we have done throughout history, both recorded and unrecorded that extends back millennia. We are responsible for our actions and thoughts, and can't excuse them by transferring the blame for destructive impulses and actions onto someone or something else. In the words of Shakespeare, "The fault, dear Brutus, is not in our stars but in ourselves…."

These creations of dark and destruction are self-created. They are in truth, figments of our imagination. "The Devil made me do it," is a common attempt to escape self-responsibility for our errors – especially the big ones that society doesn't sanction. The Devil and Satan are merely personifications of our own mental and emotional images. They exist because we create them; they live because we continue to feed them with our acceptance of illusions. They will cease to exist, unable to influence us any longer when we know the truth and accept their existence as illusion – as creations of our overactive imaginations. They are like lucid dream characters that will disappear when we accept them for what they reveal to us about ourselves. To rid ourselves of their influence, which are only thought creations, we have only to accept them, be grateful for the learning experience, and send them back to God, where their energy will be reused for further creations.

# RESIST NOT EVIL

Jesus stated that we should not resist evil. Does that make sense? It doesn't to most people because we are taught to fight evil tooth and nail, using all our energy to defeat it, and to never give up our fight to conquer it. In the urgent words of many cheerleaders: *Fight, fight, fight to victory!* That's great for a football team, but it doesn't work in our attempts to rid ourselves of real or supposed evils because we would only be fighting ghosts. Why? Because what you resist persists. You're fighting your own imaginations – change the image and victory can be yours. What you look at disappears. It ceases to hold you to its illusion. Does an image have substance? No. Recognize the image as an illusion with no substance, then release it, and seize the victory.

Note that nothing can be permanently removed using will power only. All that does is to securely bind us to the very thing we're trying to get rid off. Why? Because it's an attachment, a glue that keeps our attention on the very thing we want to void. We think of victory in the sense of overcoming. It can't be done that way; it can only be achieved by acceptance! *Resist not evil, accept it.* Once it is accepted, we can see it for what it is, and we have to only understand what it is and detach ourselves from it. You can't detach from something as long as your attention is spent resisting it. Victory can be achieved only by removing the emotional ties that are attached to results. It is best done by putting your attention on the now, with no concern for what is in the past, or what you would like in the future. Just be – be in the now and remove the tension and stress that comes from resisting something that is based on guilt, shame, or on an unknown future. Too often the future is based on fear rather than love. What we imagine, we create. Forget the results, be the process and live in the Now.

The past is over and gone; the future is not yet, unknown and without substance. So how can either of these affect us if we

165

do not accept them in our reality of the now? The harder we resist, the stronger the tie becomes. Victory can be achieved only when we detach ourselves emotionally from our self-created images of evil and accept our responsibility for their activity in our lives. They are mental conjurations, self-created and maintained. And just as we have created them, we can undo and recreate them, and become productive not destructive. Victory is not attained by overcoming; it is achieved by acceptance with gratitude for the lessons learned, and then released. Acceptance, gratitude and release are the triune of victory.

## GIVING

It is not necessary to discuss giving when it is considered in the light of tithing or special donations. Every Sunday school teaches that. What should be stressed is that giving is misunderstood. The Church says to give and then you will receive. But it fails to mention that you can't give what you don't have. The point to be made is that before you can give to another or to a cause, you must first give to yourself. This can be considered selfish, but it is not, not when you consider that you must have it to give it; you must be love to give love. To give anything, you must first be it, so give to yourself first that you may be able to give to others. In this light you must always take care of yourself first. If you wish to counsel others you must know what you're talking about; to provide spiritual enrichment and understanding you will have to have already achieved at least a degree of that; to share wisdom you have to have wisdom – you must develop your spirit, your love, your compassion – those spiritual qualities of yourself, first. If you don't, you will find you don't have much to offer to the world, or what you do have may not be worth the giving. Give of what you have, no matter how much or how little it may be. It is the intent that God loves and blesses; it is the quality not the quantity of a gift that is blessed. Consider the widow's mite – she gave all she had with love and was blessed above those who gave much but with hardened hearts.

The Golden Rule says, *Do unto others, that which you would have them do unto you.* But in the way the sentence is constructed, it fails to emphasize the fact that what you do to others you do to yourself, and what you fail to do for others, you fail to do for yourself. So there is a boomerang effect – what you throw out will come back, positively or negatively. So when you give to others, you give to yourself – but you must give to yourself first, in order to share what you have. Therefore, as long as your intent is pure, it is not selfish to take care of yourself first. Indeed, it is necessary.

## GRACE

In Christian theology grace is often erroneously confused with mercy. It is considered to be a state of being favored by God. In this misunderstanding, grace is conditional, given to a few, and then under certain circumstances. This understanding of grace is false and misleading. It is often described as unmerited love or forgiveness; it is that, but more than that. It is a state of living love, protected and made productive by the support of God; it is God's active participation in all our affairs of life. Grace is a doorway of change under the guidance and direction of Divine Order offering a transformation for the greater. It holds the highest possible outcome of future potential. Grace will only occur after we detach ourselves from ego and when we are willing to release what is no longer of benefit to us.

Grace as an aspect of love is unconditional, given freely to all, and it does not require a special indulgence or reprieve before it is offered. But to receive it, our minds must be emptied of opinion, freed of conditions and expectations, and freed from attachments to programs. We must be free from what was and what we may think is best, open to new possibilities and new opportunities. Grace enhances possibilities, creating opportunities for new potentials to occur. But it does not manifest without help; it requires our participation by giving us the opportunity of choice.

Grace occurs under Divine Order, under its guidance and direction. It occurs when the individual is sufficiently detached from ego, open and free to receive the new dispensation. It can occur only when we release what no longer serves us in our journey of soul, providing space for the presence of grace to manifest. Forgiveness of others and self is essential for the action of grace. Nothing can be accomplished when any form of pain or injury is held on to. It must be released with pure intent and no longer be a part of you before opening a passageway to new opportunities and expansion.

Grace is a doorway of change that holds the highest possible outcome and future potential for the person concerned. Grace never detracts or diminishes, it only enhances. It creates full potential for all possibilities to occur. But grace does not manifest without our help. Remember, all that is done to us and for us can be done only in agreement with our will, and it requires our participation by giving us the opportunity of choice. It is God that grants us grace; it is God that thereafter guides and protects us, wrapped in His love.

# 23

# *LUCIFER*

Lucifer is real, and he exists in hell. But he is and is not what we have been led to believe. That needs clarification because he is not a *fallen* angel. He is not evil: he is a beloved son of God that will one day be reunited with his Father/Mother, and with all that is good.

The common conception of Lucifer is that He led a revolt of angels, lost and was kicked out of heaven, sent to Hell, and there to live forever. Religion typically supports this concept by a false interpretation of Isaiah 14:12-15 that indicates that Lucifer tried to usurp God and take control of all creation. Verse twelve is the only one in the entire Bible that directly uses the name "Lucifer." It is written:

*Vs. 12: How art thou fallen from heaven, O Lucifer, son of the morning! How art thou cut down to the ground, which didst weaken the nations!*

*Vs. 13: For thou hast said in thine heart, I will ascend into heaven, I will exalt my throne above the stars of God: I will sit also upon the mount of the congregation, in the sides of the north:*

*Vs. 14: I will ascend above the heights of the clouds; I will be like the most High.*

*Vs. 15: Yet thou shalt be brought down to hell, to the sides of the pit.*

From these verses, the religions have interpreted it to mean that Lucifer wanted to be God, and was expelled to the nether regions of hell. There he was to remain as punishment for all eternity, free to trap as many souls as he could, and hold them as prisoners subject to all the horrors of pain and torture that he could conceive. But this is not entirely true. Lucifer was an archangel, and he did become the epitome of evil residing in the hell that he supposedly created. But here the truth takes a different turn from what is believed and accepted as true. Five things need to be considered:

1. In vs. 16, Lucifer is referred to as a man. *"... Is this the **man** that made the earth to tremble, that did shake kingdoms"*

2. The name Lucifer is the name used to describe the King of Babylon.

3. It is written that Lucifer wanted to *ascend* into heaven. If he was already in heaven, he could not ascend, he could only descend. Lucifer states that he would then be *like* the most high. If it is true as religion claims, that he engaged in a battle with God in an attempt to replace God, then the verse would not use the term "like", but rather it would emphasize that he wanted to usurp God's power and become greater than Him.

4. In vs. 9 it is written: *Hell from beneath is moved for thee to meet thee at thy coming. Vs.* 15 states that Lucifer would be *brought down to hell, to the sides of the pit.* In these two verses it is made clear that hell existed before Lucifer was brought down, yet religion accepts the belief that hell was created by Lucifer when he fell.

5. The entirety of Chapter 14 refers to the king of Babylon and how he ravaged the lands and laid to waste all that was good in his kingdom.

It is obvious that the Babylonian king had visions of grandeur and power. Not content to merely subjugate the nations, he also wanted to sit at the hand of God as an equal or greater. Putting verse 12 in context with the rest of the chapter, it is obvious that the name Lucifer refers to the king of Babylon.

Lucifer never engaged God in a battle for supremacy, so he never lost and was never expelled from heaven. Furthermore it is not stated anywhere in the Bible that he was. It is a conjuration of mistaken interpretation. What religion has come to accept as the truth of Lucifer, was promulgated from the early non-canonical writings, words of mouth, and hearsays of early writers and theologians having no basis in fact or empirical evidence. In spite of this, it is yet allowed through sloppy reasoning and lazy theology to flourish in Christian thought, without attempts to correct the common misconception. Little or nothing is done to correct the fallacy.

Consider this: *Lucifer volunteered to leave heaven and to establish Hell out of his love for God, and in service to Him!*

We are able to appreciate life because we have experienced death; we can appreciate a full belly because we have experienced hunger. If we are to appreciate beauty we have to experience ugliness. We cannot know the elation of success until we have known failure. We can't appreciate the good until we experience the bad. God is no different. God is a wholeness in Itself, knowing all things, creator of all things – He is the Source of all that is, ever was, and ever will be. Yet He is incomplete.

Because of His perfection, He is not able to appreciate what He is. He cannot experience ugliness because He is beauty; hate or fear because He is love; weakness because He is power. The list could go on and maybe never cover all His attributes. He is not able to fully appreciate His perfection because he has nothing with which to compare it. He is unable to appreciate His distinctions as the epitome of life and love. He is unable to appreciate His light because He has never known darkness.

God realized his deficiency and determined to experience these polar opposites so as to appreciate Himself and His perfected qualities. The only way it could be done was to vicariously experience the opposites of his attributes through the experiences of other souls. But all His angels were of the same qualities and limitations as Himself, and they could not therefore provide the experiences necessary for His enlightenment and appreciation of His reality.

A system had to be devised to give a number of angels the opportunity to experience the duality of good and evil. Because we are heart-cells of God, one with Him in our reality, God would then be able to experience through us the things He is not able to experience directly. Through us He is able to know and appreciate all that He is in His fullness.

The system He devised was a world where polarities existed, where opposites fought, where all experiences good and bad were available for the choosing. A world of duality was created for His angels who volunteered for the experiment, entering flesh bodies of material substance, living and dying, loving and hating, creating and destroying, believing and denying, and throughout all their lifetimes forgetful and unaware of their divine heritage. They experienced all there is to experience, living life to its fullness, but in the process forgetting they are children of God and separating themselves from their heritage of all that God is, settling for the less, accepting the inferior, believing only in what they experience, half alive, incomplete, yet all the while feeling something inside themselves of discontent, emptiness and a yearning for something that was no longer a part of their awareness.

The truth of Lucifer is that he voluntarily left paradise to create the world of duality envisaged by God for our benefit – a world of anti-love and separation from Him – *this he did in agreement with God.* And he has been very successful. He was not expelled; he volunteered and left paradise on his own volition to fulfill a necessary task with the blessing of God. God has never forsaken him; He loves Lucifer as His own, just as He loves us. In an expression of the greatest love possible, Lucifer created a shadow world for us, a world of illusion where our only reality is illusion, which we mistake for reality expressed in our separation from the Only One. He made for us a world of duality, of good and bad, of God and Satan, and created a world of anti-life and anti-love. He created for us a pseudo-reality, a duality of love and fear, giving us the choice to experiment with all the things of positives and negatives – to immerse ourselves in the duality of life.

For us to be able to experience this, Lucifer provided a condition where love may not be. It is a world of illusion, a shadow world of dim light, a world virtually void of the light of truth. He has blocked the light of God with his shadow, causing us to believe that the shadows we see are the reality of life, causing us to believe that what we think we image is all there is. That is the illusion we live in – one of good and evil, of God and Satan. In our illusion, we do not realize its falseness. The duality includes death, which can only be illusion, because in God, life is eternal, and as our soul is a cell of God, we too are eternal, knowing no death, only life.

As it has been explained in a previous chapter, if we were to ever become co-creators and one with God, it would require that we become a complete whole, a gestalt – an irreducible whole, balanced in every aspect of expression just as God is. We would need to experience the yin and the yang within us – the positive and negative aspects of every thing in God's creation. This includes good and evil, male and female, light and dark, weakness and strength, and all the untold numbers of opposite polarities.

If we were to have a dual nature within us, a world of illusion and duality would have to be created, and then our souls could be subjected to the opposite polarities of existence. It was necessary to believe ourselves as separate from God, no longer one with Him, and experience the illusion of separation, of anti-life, and that of anti-love. To do this, a separated existence had to be created in order to experience a lack of love – darkness, which is the opposite of the light of God. In time, we would learn to balance our dual nature and no longer be positive or negative in divided dualities; we would be positive *and* negative in a wholeness, complete in a oneness with God.

Lucifer committed the ultimate sacrifice when he separated himself from the love of God and established anti-love. Ironically, he became the nemesis of evil because of his great love. It is a sacrifice beyond measure, for he has been immersed in the illusion of evil for so long, he has forgotten his divinity and accepts his creations of illusion as the only reality. He lives in a perpetual darkness void of living-light and love. But God has not forgotten him, nor should we. God has promised that no man shall perish and this includes Lucifer and all the fallen angels, which are us. As we are being led into the realization of our false existence in duality, and as we are beginning to see the light of truth, we are balancing and harmonizing our duality and becoming once again, one with God. That is also Lucifer's destiny, but he is so immersed in the duality he created, that he needs all our love and understanding to enable him to be reminded of the truth of his oneness with God. By seeing his selfless service as a sacrifice in love for us, and by loving him and giving him our light and love, he will then begin to realize his divinity and turn back to the light of his and our Father/Mother.

The time is now upon us for all of mankind to be lifted up out of illusion into the reality of God's love. Everything created in and by Lucifer; all that exists in the world of shadows can be lifted up as well. It is hard to imagine the extent of his sacrifice for us. He gave up all love for our benefit, and accepted evil and separation from the love of God as its replacement. He has lived for eons of time in that condition. We must not let Lucifer die forever to love by leaving him behind as we return to love.

# 24

# CREATIVE EVOLUTION

There are two fundamental doctrines of how life originated and developed: they are creation and evolution. The creationists claim that God created the universe, the earth, and all that is in six days. This includes all life and the first humans, Adam and Eve. The other theory is that life evolved from the one-celled amoeba or some such, which was created by a happy coincidence of the right stuff getting together at the right time in the right way, and in time dividing and multiplying endlessly into increasingly complex forms, culminating in the supreme achievement – us. This is the theory of evolution that is based on the theories of Darwin and is accepted by the majority of the scientific community. It is in its simplicity, a creation of life by chance without first cause or intelligent direction.

The staunch proponents of these opposing theories of evolution and creationism have long been at odds, each believing that intelligent creation and natural selection are incompatible and have no correlative function or relationship except in opposition. But lately, both camps have been rethinking their entrenched positions, realizing that they may not be entirely accurate in their basic premises.

What has long been accepted as irreconcilable positions by the extremists, are being found to be opposite ends of the same pole, different but not independent of the other. It was recognized that what had seemed to be incompatible polarities, were in reality complementary, just as it is with a magnetic pole. Rather than being at odds with each other, these polar opposites are actually terminal qualities of the same thing, where one end is positive and the other end is negative. It may be said that life is such a pole with two ends, one end creates and the other end perfects; one without the other would be ineffective and non-operative.

Evolutionists are coming to understand that there has to be a *First Cause* - a creative intelligence responsible for the conception of all forms of creation with its breathtaking variety and complexity. Creationists, in light of the irrefutability of recent discoveries of paleontology that prove a steady rate of evolutionary development, are being led to an understanding of *evolving perfection*. The opposing sides are finding that there is greater concomitance than there is opposition and that each is central to the understanding and wholeness of the other.

When God creates an entity, He also establishes the pattern for its continuing development. It is being accepted that conception without change is a dead end, and evolution without first cause is impossible. One without the other is nonsensical, illogical, and self-canceling.

For consideration, take the premise that creation came into existence by desire and thought, which is the First Cause, and that from this initial desire and thought, a rational movement of energy was created that has manifested in the many and varied life forms the world has known. The effect of this is an ongoing and never-ending process of change, from the lower to the higher, from the lesser to the greater, resulting in increasing perfection and expression. In all, it is a considered evolvement into greater and more complex life forms, physically and mentally, including creative functioning.

The lifeblood of creation is love. But the order and the structure of the universe and all of God's creations, including God Himself is change. If life were created already perfect, there would be no room and no need for change. But that isn't so and paleontology proves it because change is the lifeblood of evolving perfection. Whether it's stars or man, whether it's man-made or God-made, change is persistent and necessary. It is the order and structure of the universe and all of God's creations – including God Himself.

It is commonly thought that God is a constant – many thinking that He is the only constant in all creation, and that is correct only to a point. God is constant in His totality and in His wholeness of love, but what He manifests through desire and thought is changeable. It is so because God gave man free will to create or destroy as we see fit, and in necessity to support and protect our free will, God will change things in accordance with our changing will, needs and desires. God is constant in love, but only in love. In that He is never changing, always reliable, always available because He is love. Love is God, and love is all there is, and if love is changeable, then love could not be, and God would not be, and we would certainly not be here to even consider the possibility.

What man may see for the future, or you might say, predictions of coming events, is based on the logical outcome or evolution of a thing as long as it persists in the same causative pattern that existed at the time the prediction is made. Any change of that pattern, would result in an amendment, even an abortion of the predicted event – the result of a change in desire or will of an individual or of a collective consciousness.

God gave man free will – the freedom to choose. In this is the freedom to create and recreate – to change what has already been established. A person's life is composed of the pattern and details of what he or she has created, and they can recreate or change it as they see fit. In the larger view, God created the world, and man set about to recreate things – often destructively, often unknowingly, sometimes with good intentions, sometimes in selfishness, and sometimes in misuse of power. Sometimes the creative instrument is war, and sometimes it is the accumulated energies of subjective substances radiated by groups of people with like-kind energies such as anger, revenge, and hate manifesting in destruction. But man has just as often created and manifested positive, uplifting, constructive examples of good, the creative instrument of which is love, having even greater power with manifestations of what is for the highest and best for all concerned.

The subjective elements have great power when used with pure intent, and they can create, or change anything that seems inevitable, whether good or bad, such as war or peace, famine or plenty, Armageddon or paradise, and personal things such as joy or depression, abundance or poverty.

Because our material world is one of duality – of polar opposites, nothing could exist without its complement. There is no darkness without light, no positives without negatives, no time without space, no love without fear, no life without death, and no death without life. Neither is there birth without development, or life without change. Life is a natural and inevitable process of change. Whether the birth is material or spiritual, it requires growth – another word for evolution that leads to perfection.

But what happens to the created entity between its birth and its death? Will it be a time of dynamism or astaticism? Whether the birth is a material or spiritual incarnation, it must evolve in a continuous growth toward perfection – evolution. Not even a radical fundamentalist would insist that one who is "born-again" is born in perfection. The simple fact exists that no one is born perfect, whether physically or spiritually and this includes Jesus. Didn't he say of himself: "Came I into the world to learn obedience?" Therefore there must be an evolution in one's spiritual and material life if growth to perfection is to occur. Life is the accumulating expressions of change, and change is an act of living. Everything either evolves or regresses – if it's a life of astaticism it is not growth but death, for without change there is no growth and no life.

Everything evolves. It begins with birth, the original cause, then nurtured in development, matures in expressions, and finally translates with death and rebirth in the creation of new life and new beginnings. It is the order of the universe, and finds expression in cycles of birth, evolution, death, and rebirth. It is never ending. Because life is constant; it changes form, but never ends. As it has been said, there is only one constant in life, and it is change – the pattern and the structure of life.

This cyclic process can be seen in the changing seasons: spring (birth), summer (maturation), fall (harvesting), and winter (regeneration); it is seen in seeds sprouting, fructifying, and regenerating; it is evident in the lives of animals and man, finding expression in the process of birthing, maturing, dying and new life; it is seen in the cosmic utterances of galaxies that are constantly changing with the birth from cosmic dust into the brilliance of untold beacons of light, and their final decay into supernovas, white giants and black holes – the expression of deaths and births of new stars that encompass the framework and content of their whirling, galactic forms. Life is everywhere changing and ever evolving into greater expressions of beauty and purpose, filling the vast scope of time and space.

There is no evolution without creation, or original cause, and there is no creation without evolution. God planned this duality for the benefit of soul's struggle for truth and understanding – wisdom if you will, and for the opportunities to mature in the exercising of free will, to make mistakes, to learn from them, to re-create, and co-create. Once on the pathway of truth, soul will return to its original home step by step with its will becoming one with the Creator's, and receive the inheritance that is its birthright as a co-creator with God.

There are those among us who need proof of this correlative function. There is ample proof everywhere of *evolving perfection,* or evolution, and there is also a growing acceptance among evolutionists of a *first cause,* which is basically a doctrine of Creationism, in which everything that is was created all in a moment. The only real difference is in the use of terminology. But is there evidence anywhere that can show the skeptic that these two aspects of life are not only mutually compatible but equally necessary for its vital functioning? Yes, there is. One example of this union of complementary qualities of creation and development is the fruit tree.

Let's look at some of them, both the hard-shelled and the soft skinned fruits. There are nut trees of all sizes, shapes and heights, serving the needs of propagation and food for man and animals in superb efficiency. They can be huge, and though nuts may fall from the top of tall trees, they are not damaged and remain edible. Soft fruit trees are not as generously expressed in height for a purpose. They are seen to be short, maybe squatty, with their fruit laden branches often brushing the ground where their ripe fruit can be picked and eaten before falling only to be broken and mashed, quickly rotting and inhabited by crawling critters.

Why is it that soft-fruit trees are low to the ground? If the only purpose for the fruit is for the propagation of the species, it wouldn't make any difference what height the tree is, for when the fruit falls and is broken by the hard earth, it is still food for the animals. If it's only for propagation, then case closed, for the seeds would still be scattered when the animals defecate what they had eaten. But if it's for more than the preservation of the species, it would be reasonable to assume that there is an intelligent purpose behind its specific and superb architecture.

But what force of nature, creation or evolution directed the development of the soft fruit tree in such an efficient manner that its fruit is available for man's food while still in an edible condition? It is evident that soft-fruit trees hug the ground for the sole purpose of providing delicious fruit ready to eat for man's benefit. The question remains: are these specific fruit trees a creation or a happening – or both? If both, there must be an

*Intelligent Operant* behind their unique design and function.

What directed the development of a peach tree for example in such a splendid example of orderly purpose? Was it merely a fortuitous series of accidents? Or more likely, was it the result of an intelligent interaction of creation *and* evolution? The next time an apple, a pear or fig tree is approached and seen laden with fruit, ripe and luscious, still hanging on the branches waiting to be picked and eaten with its juice running down one's chin, think about it: what made it this way? Are fruit trees the result of creation in an instant; or of a laborious and fortuitous series of unplanned changes? Or are they the creation by purpose and pattern? And is there a Supreme Intelligence behind it all? The next time you near a peach tree with its fruit laden arms reaching out to you, think about it: was it planned or accidental?

25

# PRAYER

It is sincerely believed that everyone has prayed at sometime in their life. Even an atheist will utter some form of prayer when huddled in the meager protection of a foxhole on a battlefield and the shells are falling all around him. But prayer is not always understood. The simplest definition of prayer is communication – a conversation with God. But as it is practiced, it is almost always a one-way monologue. It is not communication when one talks but doesn't listen. It must be a dialogue, and that requires both talking and listening. It can be said that praying is talking to God, and meditation is listening when He talks. Both are necessary if true communion is to be achieved.

How should one pray? Should we relax and let the conversation flow easily, as it would with a friend, or should we exercise caution and stay within certain guidelines of respect and worship, being careful of what we say, and how we say it, afraid that we may say something God may not like to hear, or in a manner He has not approved? Should we address Him as God, or Father, or Mother, or Holy Spirit, or Almighty God, or Universal Mind, or Grand Creator... or even Daddyo? How should we talk to Him? Or do we have to talk? Does it really make a difference? Silence can be a most effective prayer when one's heart is focused in good intentions.

It doesn't matter whether you believe in God or not. Nor does it matter if you approach him in love or in fear. It does matter though that you are honest and sincere. Unfortunately misconceptions have taken root. In the belief that there are correct and incorrect ways of praying, ineffective prayers have resulted.

So how should we pray? What do we do? Do we stand, sit, follow a ritual, use beads or prayer wheels? Should we be on our knees with hands clasped, maybe gazing reverently upward when we talk to God? It is believed by the different religions, that our prayers should follow certain procedures, and in fear of offending God, we are cautioned that great care must be exercised in what and in how we say what is on our minds.

Typical of many Christian theologians, R.C. Sproul, founder of Ligonier Ministries, believes that prayer has several requisites. He outlines what to him is the proper way to address God.

1. "Approach God with sincerity. Empty and insincere phrases are a mockery to Him... It is an offense against God"

*(Wrong: Fear of offending Him creates timidity and inequality. Approach Him with respect but as an equal – remember, we are His children, only undeveloped.)*

2. "Approach God with reverence. We must always remember to whom we are speaking... to speak to Him as we might speak with our earthly friends, is to treat Him with contempt and familiarity."

*(Nonsense: reverence is good, but friendship is better, and honesty is best. Respect and informality in an established friendship is desirable, as long as it doesn't stand in the way of meaningful communication. To fear, is to create separation; love Him without fear.)*

3. "Approach God in humility. Not only must remember who He is, but we must also remember who we are. We are His adopted children. We are also sinful creatures. He invites us to come boldly before Him, but never arrogantly."

*(Wrong again: We are not adopted, **we are his children**, born of His spirit, born in love, not in sin, and as such we cannot be sinful. To accept anything else is to create more fear, greater separation and subservience.)*

With such restrictions as espoused by Sproul, it makes it virtually impossible to approach God with confidence rather than fear. He doesn't want us to grovel before Him. He wants us to approach Him upright, fearless, sincere and relaxed. How can one truly and willingly open his heart and bare his soul in honesty and humility when every word must be carefully guarded and carefully thought out before utterance? It makes it difficult to approach God in love – how can we love another when there is a sword over our head hanging by a thin thread frayed by fear?

When prayer is approached in the manner that Sproul says is required, it is reduced to formalities void of heartfelt feelings of emotions and love, becoming mere repetition of meaningless phrases and words without effect or meaning. Feelings should be expressed, for they are the language of the soul, and to shunt them aside is to cut off the open communication of soul with our awareness and thus with God.

We have been conditioned to pray using unnatural phrases that do not roll trippingly off one's tongue. We tend to use the words and phrasing that we hear in church, which we clumsily use because we are not accustomed to speak in the language that priests and preachers tend to use, those of Elizabethan English – the language of Shakespeare. That language was fine for Romeo, King Lear and the students of religion in today's seminaries, but not for the average person unaccustomed to speaking in that manner. There are too many thees, and thous, and begets and begats, thys and yeas and untos, and hasts and doests. As a result praying becomes a chore for many people, making it difficult to open up in a sense of freedom and easy expression of one's feelings and innermost thoughts. It becomes an activity of the mind, rather than of the heart, by being always careful to use the same words and phrases that our preachers use.

Do we really believe that God would be offended if the words of the street are used in moments of opening our hearts to Him? Who invented words? Who designed language? Why would he be offended if we use the language he invented for us to use? It is the intent behind our words that make them effective or ineffective – they are neither good nor bad, they are just words until we let them flow from our hearts, minds and emotions. If they express our intent, then they are effective and acceptable.

God doesn't care how we pray. It does not require lengthy phrases of praise, or explanations, or an hour or more in prayerful postures to get His attention. "God, help me!" is a prayer of power, absolute sincerity and humility, said in three short but meaningful words that certainly don't need a formalized petition or description to express a need. He hears, He knows, and He responds! God wants only sincerity and pure intent, and if appropriate, should it include humor and laughter, even better.

There is another prayer of only two words that expresses what is in the heart, and which puts a smile on God's face when they are said. They are, "Thank You." Nothing else needs to be said; those two words express everything.

Traditionally, prayer may involve one or more postures such as kneeling, touching the floor with the head, head bowed, head raised, hands with palms together, or clasped in one's lap; all are meant as signs of respect to God, Allah, Holy Spirit, or the one God of other names. That is well for it can show the implied sincerity of the one who prays. But certain postures are not necessary. Prayers may be offered in any position, at any location, or at any time. One may kneel or lie prone in bed, maybe while driving a car or sitting on the potty, doing dishes or any number of other mundane activities. Outer shows of piety are not necessary, for God knows the intent of the heart. It is the pure intent of the petitioner that God hears.

When one talks to God, you can be assured that He hears. He hears what is spoken or thought, whether in English, in Greek, or in aboriginal languages. He hears what cannot be heard with outer ears – hearing what is not said. He hears the intent – the murmurs of the heart and soul. He hears the unsounded pain, the silent joy, the unspoken needs and the heartfelt gratitudes. He hears the songs of silence whether spoken in peace or fear, in hope or desperation. He hears all these and answers in love.

God is our friend and He wants us to think of Him that way. He knows what we are much better than we know ourselves. He wants us to enjoy life and to be our natural selves when we talk to him, saying what comes naturally, speaking in the languages of life. We should express ourselves in prayer as we would to a lover or a friend, and speak in words of feeling, affection and honesty, in confidentiality, of confession and open admissions of mistakes and needs. Open our selves and let Him see us as we should see ourselves. Use honest words that express honest feelings. If slang words fit the occasion, then use them. If you're at ease using the language of the saints, whatever that may be, or the phrasing of a poet, or the vernacular of the streets to express a point, use them. God will not be offended; how can He be? He would not have invented the words in the first place were it not his intention that they be used – they will not be offensive. Do we really believe that God can be offended?!

Prayer is simply attuning oneself to the presence of God. There is no set or prescribed time to express your needs or feelings. The proper time is in the now. Pray first thing in the morning, before meals, when retiring at night, before asking the boss for a raise, for courage in a fearful situation. Pray when you feel like it, in words, song, thoughts or feelings. Make your life a living prayer. In other words, prayer should be an ever-constant expression of the joys and pains of life.

When one lives in a sense of joy and love, prayers won't need to be expressed in words, or even in thoughts. They could be expressed in the language of the soul, which are feelings. Let your feelings speak for you when moved by compassion and words are inadequate. Let your cup runneth over with tears in moments of heartfelt love or sorrow. Pray whenever the spirit moves you. Pray in times of need and in times of plenty, in times of discomfort and in times of joy, at times of gain and times of loss. Pray when lazing in the shady protection of a leafy tree on a warm day, or when strolling on a lonely path in a secluded glen. Pray in heartfelt joy and exaltation when you reach the peak of a mountain and you can see forever. Prayers are feelings – the soul reaching out to touch the hem of God's cloak of love and protection. Prayer is simply conversing with Him – communing with Him in need or sharing, in respect and in unity of love.

There are many types of prayer. There are prayers of gratitude, prayers of petitions or needs, prayers of expressions of love and joy, and prayers of selfishness. In his book, Conversations With God, book 1, Neale Donald Walsch quotes God as saying: *"The correct prayer is therefore never a prayer of supplication, but a prayer of gratitude.* When you thank God in advance for that which you choose to experience in your reality, you, in effect, acknowledge that it is there...*in effect.* Thankfulness is thus the most powerful statement to God – an affirmation that even before you ask, He has answered. Therefore never supplicate, *Appreciate.*"

Kryon through his channel Lee Carroll adds to this, these words: *The prayer that is most effective is this: "Dear God, show me what it is I need to know." And then, when you receive it, understand that it's perfect for you. Don't make up your mind in advance who you are, why you're here, what you should be doing and what must be the next step. This approach is so limiting! Consider that a grander plan is known by your higher self, and that's the goal – something that you can't know or see but can reach!*

If you will notice, the above prayers reveal humility and shows that you are open to the guidance and will of God, no matter what comes from it, and no matter how far off it is from what you wanted or expected. It involves a surrender of your little will to that of your higher will.

There is no proper time to express your feelings to God, or to call on Him in your need. The proper time is now, and then, or whenever. In other words, prayer should be an ever-constant expression of living love. It doesn't need to be expressed in words, or even in thoughts. Prayer would be living in the presence of God in constant communion through feelings, sharing in a free give and take without conditions to life itself. When leaving the house on a rainy, wind-swept day, greet it with a song in your heart; or when falling snow blankets the ground and the driveway needs shoveling, feel a prayer of gratitude for the serene beauty that surrounds you; or when the green leaves are turning colors with varied shades of reds, oranges, and yellows creating a multihued blush of color in the fall, breathe deeply at these times and say, "Oh, God! What a beautiful day!" Learn to see God in everything, in every condition, and show gratitude – maybe in words, always in feelings. Either way, you are ever in a state of prayer and communion with God. Words aren't necessary.

# 26

# MEDITATION

Prayer and meditation are usually thought of as separate things – two distinct means of communication with God, one of words spoken, and one of words silent. Prayer and meditation are interrelated in the giving and receiving, in the talking and in the listening. It can be easily understood that these are both necessary parts of meaningful communication with anyone, and even so with God. Simply said, prayer is talking to God and meditation is listening to Him. Communication cannot take place if one is only talking and not listening. It is plain and simple, conversation with God.

When prayer is properly exercised it should include moments of silence. It's giving God a chance to answer us, which is necessary if we are to have true communion with Him. We must learn to listen if we are to hear what he has to say. Pure meditation is just being at one with the stillness, hearing without sound or seeing with inner vision. But it does involve thought, which is essential if there is to be meaningful reception.

It is not understood that prayer is best considered as a conversation with God. Some of us have become pretty good at talking to Him, it may be better said talking *at* Him, even though it may seem to be unproductive, but few there are who understand what it means to listen to Him. We talk wanting a response but don't really believe that we're going to get one, simply because we're not aware that we can. We're not taught to engage in a two-way conversation; or even that it's possible. Instead we have been conditioned that if we do hear Him, we react with disbelief and doubt, skeptical that it was really God talking to us. We will hear when our minds are shut off from the cacophony of rumbling thoughts, when our mind is free to roam without constriction or restriction, daydreaming if you will, and open to the voiceless words of silence.

Christians are accustomed to believe that, except for a privileged elite, God stopped conversing with man 2000 years ago. But they're wrong. God speaks to every man, woman and child in every corner of every land – always! He has never ceased talking to us. The belief system of the Catholic Church in a trickle down affect, has infected the theologies of all Christian churches: Protestants, Mormons and other sects as well. The problem is not God's that we don't hear Him, but ours in that we have been conditioned to keep our doors closed to Him. He knocks but we don't open up. He speaks to us in many ways, in moments of inspiration, in feelings or intuition, and in countless other ways, including meditation, but we keep our doors tightly closed to Him.

We are not told that it is possible to hear God, and that it is our natural, inborn right to converse with Him. And even if some of the clergy believe that we have that right, they fail to teach us how to do it. We are therefore stuck in no-man's land, caught in the midst of our battle of good and evil with only unqualified teachers. Forbidden by the inhibiting misconceptions of truth of the Church's own making, they either can't or won't help us. That's due to their obedience to the rules that won't let them, or because of their ignorance of meditation, which they may not practice themselves, and don't know how to teach, or even how to do it.

What is involved in meditation? Essentially, it is nothing but listening with a receptive mind. We listen by attuning ourselves to the stillness of silence. It is simply quieting our thoughts, stilling our minds of the extraneous thoughts and images that run across our minds like a montage of disorganized scenes on a movie screen. We enter the silence becoming one with it, and in the stillness of thought, hear the still small voice of

God that may present itself in feelings, music, visions, thoughts, and even audible speech in words without sound. Meditation is the sound of silence. There are as many ways to meditate, as there are reasons for it. And one is not better than another. Most accepted methods are quite formal requiring certain postures, certain breathing techniques, and certain affirmations. Other suggested ways are to visualize scenes of beauty: one is to visualize a black screen and concentrate on its nothingness; others use certain chants, or mantras. Some require certain postures, scents, perhaps inspirational music or environmental arrangements. A person may focus on the flame of a burning candle or concentrate on a word or phrase such as *love,* or perhaps a mantra such as, *Be still and know that I am God.* All of these approaches have been proven to be successful for some, but not all of them for everyone. It is necessary for each person to find and use the one that is best for them. But whatever method is used it is most rewarding to just be in the presence of spirit and bask in God's peace and love in total awareness of silence.

When Edgar D. Mitchell, an astronaut who walked on the moon was interviewed by A. Robert Smith, Editor of Venture Inward, about his practice of meditation, he replied that meditation is the honored and time-tested technique for experiencing the mystical. "I'm convinced," he said, "that it causes the brain to move to a more grounded, relaxed, lower energy state, what I would like to call and hope is true, a ground-state resonance with a zero-point field. A mystic would say, being in tune with the Godhead. In the Hindu and Buddhist tradition, it is oneness with the All-that-is."

He was asked if he used any particular kind of meditation and replied: "It doesn't have a particular name. It's just what works for me. I use many techniques – focusing, placing my attention on breathing. Sometimes if I'm really agitated I have to go to a mantra to calm down. But, I'm finding in the deeper states, just focusing on breathing and then stop focusing at all –

just becoming aware. Pure, basic awareness. Watching what's happening in the mind and allowing it to be doing nothing except being aware. The act of focusing on breathing or on a mantra or something else is short of being in a state of simple, pure awareness where your self is totally lost and just disappears. I call that ground-state awareness." He added that everybody could do this as a way of expanding one's consciousness.

Meditation is a silencing of the mind, but when one first starts to practice meditation, there may be a lot of static. Daily practice is for the experience of *being*. And as one learns to quiet the mind, the static decreases until the message comes through clearly like a finely tuned radio. It is found that regular, periodic meditations are best for it promotes spiritual integration with the conscious mind.

It is good to start the day with a moment of quiet contemplation or meditation, for it sets the tone for the day and stays with you. It is also good to precede a meditation with prayer for it helps to attune one to the silence that is to follow. But it is not necessary; effective meditation can occur when suddenly caught in an unexpected inspiration or need, or simply caught up in the peace of a moment.

Meditation doesn't have to be long; 5 – 20 minutes once or twice a day is enough. Reduce or eliminate as much extraneous noise as possible, but what is still there will soon melt away and be unnoticed. When something does interrupt you, including the monkeys of the mind – intrusive thoughts, just accept whatever comes and release it. Don't try to resist it for if you do, it will only hang on and invite its unwanted friends to join in. Pretty soon, you will have a group of chattering monkeys darting in and out of your awareness with thoughts of distraction – not very conducive to a state of pure, elemental awareness.

It needs to be stressed that meditation is not a process of sitting in a corner in a dark room waiting to hear a still, small voice. Meditation should be a daily, ongoing process, just as prayer should be. Where the essence of God is ever present, whispering its presence in a soft voice wherever we are, or whatever we may be doing. It can be experienced in the leisurely rhythm of a stroll when there is time as Mac Davis sings, to stop and smell the roses. It can give us time to see, really see possibly for the first time, the inner depth and beauty of the world around us, a world usually obscured by surface appearances, insensitivity, and impatience.

Any activity can be a form of meditation when it is performed with an attitude of gratitude, with a mind untroubled by the noises of life always around you – washing the car, doing dishes, building something.

Walking without purpose, free of the frets and disturbances of the day, is an especially rewarding form of meditation, for as in any process that gets you out of yourself, it allows time to see beyond the surface of life, seeing into its essence. It gives you the leisure to savor beauty all around you and discover that God is in all things. One has only to look beyond impressions and attitudes to find Him. It is only necessary to surrender oneself to the silence and peace that enfold you to realize that we are a part of it – an indispensable part, for there is unity in all things, and all things are one in God. He is not only the creator of all things, His essence is in all things. When we look with clear vision, we will see Him where He is – there and there and there... in the beautiful and in the ugly, in the saintly and in the profane.

When we walk in the quietude of nature, we are able to calm inner storms. We are able to hear the many voices of creation whispering in the rhythm of rustling leaves, in the rhapsodic melodies of birds, and the sighs of gentle winds as they swish across our path, whispering, whispering, all is well... love is with you, and the agitated spirit within is soothed and finds serenity in nature's sanctuary. These gifts of nature with the assurance that all is well, can be received when we let spirit come in while our mind is quiet and reflective of the unfolding scene... and open to the murmurs of peace.

During such moments of stillness, whether in the raucous rhythm of the city, the harmonious solitude of nature, while sitting serenely in a chair or cross-legged on the floor, we have opportunities to go within into the solitude of our own natures where we may obtain understanding, and discover the reality and beauty of our own soul. We may learn of our strengths and weaknesses and be enriched by the glories of our reality surrounding us of which we are a part. We will be in the midst of love.

By never underestimating the power of the grand creativity of love, never losing sight that love is able to do all things, and never losing our trust in love, we will always have love with us to lift us up when we stumble, encourage us when we are discouraged, and give us peace in our times of trouble. Love is a buoy in an angry sea. When we open ourselves to it, we will be blessed. Peaceful moments of meditation can be our lifesaver, holding us up in the arms of God's presence.

# 27

# GUILT AND SHAME

Our culture is ridden with guilt. We feel guilty over things we do, and things we don't do. We feel guilty regarding our mistakes, and we sometimes feel guilt over the mistakes of others. We're permeated with guilt, and the greatest producer of guilt is religion. It's religion because it's the foundation of our culture; it determines our values and forms our beliefs and attitudes, our perspectives and our judgments. It sets the framework in which we live, telling us what to think, what to do, and how to do it. And the churches threaten us with punishment to some degree if we fail to follow their rules and guidelines. The churches' insistence on holding us responsible for every little infraction of their rules and regulations feed us a steady diet of guilt, and with it shame.

We feel that when we err, we have offended the church, and worse yet, not just the church, we have also offended God. And we believe that if the church disapproves of us, then God certainly does also. We are put on the defensive and feel guilt and shame, which is accompanied with fear of abandonment by the church and by God. Our safety and our sense of well-being, of acceptance and approval lie in our fearful obedience to the requirements imposed on us against our will – imposed by the church!

The insidious fear generated by the false representations of truth and threats of punishment by our churches have become ingrained in us forming an underlying burden of guilt. Fear of failure permeates society, affecting everything we think, say, do, and create. In the very process of living, mistakes are made and will be made, failures will occur and we will feel guilt or shame, and we will continue to err and create more guilt, more shame, and we will stay on this merry-go-round of guilt or shame until the music stops! But the calliope won't stop until it runs out of steam; not until we realize that there is no reason to feel guilty about anything and quit feeding it with the fuel it needs. Guilt is not a weakness, unless you let it become one. For a day, okay. But then let it go. Guilt is not a required responsibility, but it can easily become one. We must acknowledge our mistakes and accept our responsibilities for them, but once accepted, they must be released.

In the book, "Love Without Conditions," by Paul Ferrini, he quotes Jesus: *"Those who feel guilty, see a guilty world, and the guilty world will be punished and so will you... Guilt is the root of all suffering."* When these thoughts persist, they will bring us down and we won't be released from our guilt until we are punished. So we hang on to guilt until we are whipped or chastised in some way, believing that is the only way we can absolve our pain. If our punishment doesn't come to us from an outside source, we'll punish ourselves. We don't realize that the very process of guilt is punishment in itself, for what does it bring to us except shame, fear, and separation? Ferrini continues with another quote from Jesus: *"Self-forgiveness is necessary. Without self-forgiveness, there is no release from guilt."*

Just about everything we do or don't do is related to guilt in some way, starting the moment the innocence of children is corrupted, then carried through with the correctional disapproval of parents and teachers, the negative critiques of employers and others of influence and power, and the spats with those we love. We create guilt over something we have done or have failed to do. In the belief that what was done was wrong we subconsciously hold ourselves accountable. So we judge and remonstrate against ourselves and assign punishment, which can be many things, but the most devastating of punishments, and the most common to all, is the burden of guilt and shame. It is the worst of many because it doesn't end; it hangs on like a leach sucking the life-blood of well-being and confidence out of us, infecting the things we do and feel, often lasting a lifetime.

When guilt is carried to its extreme it can produce all sorts of social encumbrances, accusations and separations, and also mental and emotional problems. It can result in alcoholism, substance abuse, sexual depravity, cruelty against animals and people, self-flagellation of all sorts, anger and violence. Every one of these reproduces more guilt and can become self-perpetuating with increasingly severe and destructive effects on others and on oneself.

Failure generates guilt, guilt produces fear, and fear spawns failure, generating a cycle of guilt and shame that repeats itself without end. It holds us back by timidity, by an unwillingness to take a chance, by fear of abandonment, by fearing to stride ahead in confidence and certainty of approval by self or by others, and of not being ourselves free of a hidden reservoir of guilt. Guilt creates a fear that causes hesitancy in uninhibited self-expression, restraining our exploration of life, of reaching out for all the opportunities that are presented to us, to grow and expand our abilities and talents.

Guilt is produced when we feel we have done something wrong. It is that little nagging voice calling attention to our shame or fear, and it doesn't have to be something big such as doing something physically damaging to another person. It can be the simple, little unimportant things such as oversleeping, for not doing our best, for taking that last piece of pie, for being late to an appointment; or of course it could be the result of more important things such as lying, deception, dishonesty, or selfishness. And there are the major things such as deliberately harming another person physically or emotionally – murder perhaps, or slander, destroying reputations and lives. And there are even vicarious feelings of guilt when we hold ourselves responsible for something another person did, even though we could have done nothing to alter or prevent it. An example would be: "If only I had said no, instead of giving permission." "Why am I the only survivor – why did I live when others died?" "Why am I so prosperous when Sally and John are so much more deserving and have less?"

Guilt plays upon the feelings and emotions. We seem to want to make ourselves guilty just to keep us in the game of life's illusions and delusions. In a way, it gives us a strange sense of importance by believing that we are so significant that we could have delayed or prevented a situation from happening when we weren't directly involved or responsible for it. A feeling of deficiency or inadequacy in the material or emotional realms of life generate guilt and it occurs when we feel we should have done something and did nothing, or if we did what we shouldn't have done. Shame on the other hand will occur because our action or inaction violated what we consider appropriate behavior according to the standards of society or culture. It has little effect on someone who is confident of his place in life, and who lives according to his personal standards of what is proper or improper.

The more one gains in understanding and wisdom, the fewer opportunities there are to feel guilt or shame. That's because it's realized that there is nothing to feel guilty about. Everything that happens is for a purpose – there are no such things as accidents.

Shakespeare has said: "All the world's a stage, and all the men and women merely players." We're all in the same game of life; in every incident, and for everyone who plays their part, there is something to benefit each and every one. There are lessons to be learned by all involved, whether it's learned by the director or the actor, by the pitcher or the catcher, or by the doer or the doee. When that is realized, what one does or fails to do, does not necessarily carry with it the stigma of having done something wrong. Things will often occur without volition or purposeful intent, or without being caused by oneself or someone else. They may happen with no one's knowledge or agreement, seemingly by accident, yet they always happen according to plan including what has been set in action by karma, or in the meeting of what you or others have sown that involve you in some manner. These things are to be accepted as they happen with gratitude and without guilt or shame, for they are opportunities for us as soul, to learn from the mistakes or situations that everyone meets in life. That is what soul is doing here on this planet earth. That's what life is about – to experience, to learn, to grow, to develop, to express, to forgive, to love, and to be – just be; to be what we are in all our glory as children of Father/Mother God.

Life is a process of experimentation and adjustment. When one is really with life, there is no place for guilt. Life is an ongoing process of expression, and carries with it the certainty of failure at some time or another. Mistakes will be made and they will be corrected. Be grateful for the experience, learn from it, and go on – but don't feel guilt or shame over a mistake. Recognize the error, if that's what it was, determine how it could be done differently, release it and send it back to God. Don't hang on to it, for if you do, it will be nothing but a heavy weight – a millstone about your neck. In time when more guilts are added, the weight will eventually pull you down emotionally and physically.

An ally of guilt is fear. Separately they are uncomfortable and disruptive; but together? ....Watch out, for they can be destructive to health and well-being. They create worry, keeping us from being ourselves when we weigh in advance the outcome of something that hasn't yet happened, and often will not happen. Worry is a thought pattern, and thoughts are creative – what you think, you will manifest. Fear, worry, guilt and shame restrict our relationships, causing us to be a non-assertive good guy, the nice lady, always pleasing others but not oneself. Or it can create the opposite, a person of ill intent, over-riding any concern for others, overly assertive, selfish, with little or no concern for others – a "me first" attitude, always trying to prove yourself to yourself.

This can cause the loss of spontaneous expressions of life – joy, laughter, even companionship if carried to the extreme. We become afraid of ourselves, disrespectful of our abilities and accomplishments. We worry about things that with the right attitude would disappear in the evening fog of illusion. Without detachment, without release, they create fear. We must learn to be ourselves without guilt or apologies and with gracious acceptance of what we are and of what happens, then learn from it and go on. God will never punish us. He doesn't need to for we do that to ourselves, and that's stupid because nothing can be gained from self-punishment or condemnation, except discomfort, shame and guilt.

Let's look at the church and its role in all this self reproach. These things together with all the threats of punishments and fear generated by the church may not be apparent, but they are real in the indoctrinated delusion that God is a vengeful God, and He will get you if you don't watch out. So when something occurs in your life and you have the feeling that the church is no longer supporting you, you feel abandoned. Since the church is in a sense, the material representative of God in your life, you feel that God has abandoned you also, and if God can't be trusted and relied on, what else is there? At that point you may abandon hope, and ask: What did I do to cause this to befall me?

Feelings of abandonment can arise with divorce, death of a loved one, or betrayal by a friend or associate; there are threats of "I don't love you anymore;" and there is the loss of respect for someone you trusted, and even the loss of self-respect when you have let yourself down. These are feelings that are often defended by finding someone else responsible for a situation or condition you're in. With these attitudes, one will actually create *more* conditions of abandonment. In reality it is an aura of self-generated guilt and inadequacy of the individual that feeds upon itself, creating a cycle of more situations of abandonment, which creates more opportunities of doubt and fear, which creates more guilt, which creates more occasions of abandonment, which....

So many of the things we do create feelings of guilt. Through our maturing years of indoctrination and conditioning of what is right and what is wrong, our thoughts are affected and they inhibit free, spontaneous expression, nagging us with doubt and worry: Is it okay? Is it right? What will others think? Will I be punished? Fear generates failure, which creates guilt and shame. But there is nothing beyond our control, for we are the creators of all that we are, and of all that happens to us whether we realize it or not. When we recognize and accept this truth, we will be able to create anew everything in our life to make of it what we will.

When we can blame the failure on something beyond our control, it keeps us feeling safe in a pocket of illusion, protected from feelings of being looked down on by others, or by oneself. On the other hand, it is easy to blame oneself for things not of one's doing, and to feel shame for something we are innocent of. In both cases there can be a pervading sense of guilt, which if not checked will hang on, decreasing a sense of self-worth and respect. Carried to the extreme it can seriously damage one's performance and participation in life and in one's relationships with people.

Shame likewise is insidious, often hidden and unrecognized yet able to influence opinions and actions, often resulting in self-denigration. It creates an aura of unworthiness, of inequality and a sense of inadequacy. Not wishing to experience blame, rejection or hostility for something even minor, we tend to pull away from other people setting up a pattern of isolation and guilt. Criticisms and accusations made by a parent, teacher, spouse or friend, if accepted on a level of personal attack, especially by a young child, may have negative results that can reverberate throughout an entire life.

Everything we are, everything we succeed at or fail at, are created by our thoughts and attitudes. They are what we think of ourselves: our desires, hopes, fears, strengths and weaknesses. Though often unrecognized yet still creative, they are the molds of that which we use to form intent, to manifest what we harbor in our beliefs. But as we create, so can we undo what we have created; we can re-create any and all things. If repeated situations of abandonment occur for example, the fault is in our selves because we permit them to rebirth.

*The fault, dear Brutus, is not in our stars,*

*But in ourselves, that we are underlings.*

Shakespeare

# 28

# TEN COMMITMENTS

Moses led the enslaved Hebrews out of bondage in Egypt, into a life of discipline and obedience. It required a 40 year journey full of difficulties, rebellion, fear and loss of faith. But eventually the journey ended when they crossed the Jordan into the Promised Land. They brought with them the Ten Commandments that God gave to Moses on Mt. Sinai.

The reason it took 40 years before the crossing was realized, was because it was necessary to first cleanse the tribe of old attitudes, and conditions of fear and allegiance to other gods. It was necessary to remove the old concepts of multiple gods so that the new generation could mature in the acceptance of One God. To accomplish this, the older generation had to first pass away to make way for a new generation open to new ideas, understandings and acceptance of one God. That couldn't be done in a brief journey of a few days. It took 40 years for it to be accomplished.

Moses brought Law to the Hebrews. Its effect was to give unity and communal responsibility to their lives. It gave them a sense of purpose and belonging in a system of justice, law and order that had been lacking. The Law gave them a guideline of personal and communal conduct to follow, with the assurance that if the Law was obeyed, then salvation and happiness could be theirs. The Law created a more civil society and peaceful relationships between men, and peace when the law was obediently followed. It helped to know that a judgmental God was watching all their activities, ready to punish any infractions.

But in time, the interpretation and application of the Law grew out of proportion and exceeded its intent. The priests and rabbis weren't satisfied with what Moses gave them. In their finite reasoning they created stifling provisos and procedures of worship and obedience that ballooned over time to become hundreds of rules, limitations and requirements, all in attempts to secure compliance and strict obedience to the commandments. Instead of a guideline of ten, that if obeyed would create a relationship with God that would assure salvation, it became a noose of a thousand knots. Their religion became one of impossible laws governing and restricting everything they did from eating to worshiping, prescribing in exact detail how to live their faith on a day by day, minute by minute program of obedience. The difficulty of living up to such restrictive requirements became over time almost impossible to obey.

It is believed by the Jews and Christians that God gave Moses ten commandments, a list of rules and regulations that everyone must follow in strict obedience. Failure to do this would pretty well result in spiritual condemnation and could result in an eternity of punishment. There were ten items of conduct, or commandments on this list, graven in stone, to be carried in the Ark of the Covenant wherever the Hebrews moved. It was to be with them for all time. The acceptance of the Ten Commandments as rules of conduct and belief has been with mankind ever since, forming the basis of secular law and religious conduct in the Christian religion as well as in the Hebrew. There are positive results when the commandments are followed in good intent and obedience. But there are also negative effects because the demand of obedience negates the right to exercise the free will that God gave to each of us. It is this gift that enables us to freely navigate our journey home to God. By imposing rules and regulations of conduct on us, it restricts our choice of what courses in life we shall follow, to change directions when it is best for us to do so and tack with the changing winds and currents when it is necessary to maintain our chosen direction.

We must come to God in freedom and on our own volition, because we want to, not because we must in order to be saved from hell. Our motive should be one of love, not fear. If God commands us to do or be what He wants of us, then there could be no creative freedom. That He would never do.

But God never gave Moses Ten Commandments! He gave him an everlasting promise, and *Ten Commitments*. In "Conversations With God," book 1, by Neale Donald Walsch, God states:

> "Who would I command? Myself? And why would such commandments be required? Whatever I want, is. *N'est ce pas?* How is it therefore necessary to command anyone?

> "And, if I did issue commandments, would they not be automatically kept? How could I wish something to be so, so badly that I would command it – and then sit by and watch it not be so?

> "What kind of a king would do that? What kind of a ruler?

> "And yet I tell you this: I am neither a king nor a ruler. I am simply – and awesomely – the Creator. Yet the Creator does not rule, but merely creates, creates – and keeps on creating.

> "And the word of God was not a commandment but a divine covenant. These then are the TEN COMMITMENTS. You shall *know* that you have taken the path to God, and you shall know that you have *found* God, for there will be these signs, these indications, these *changes* in you."

And then He lists the ten thou shalts, or the Ten Commandments. The intent has been misunderstood for they are not things that must be obeyed, but expressed, things that will be observed in those who are living in the spirit of the commitments. They are not things that must be obeyed, but things to be. They are the results of a life of intent that renews our oneness with God.

In the above quote, God uses the term divine *covenant*. It is good to understand what that means. There is a common misunderstanding that the word covenant is synonymous with contract. They are not the same. A contract is an agreement between two or more individuals, in which each agrees to perform certain tasks, and meet certain conditions for the contract to remain viable. Should either party fault on his responsibility, the contract is void, and the responsible one is held accountable. A covenant in the legal sense is also a binding agreement, but biblically, it is God's promise to the human race. It does not require a *mutual* agreement by which man can be held accountable. Refer to Genesis 9: 8-17, where God tells Noah of His covenant with all of men, whereby He gives His promise to never again flood the earth, and establishes the rainbow as a token of His promise. In a covenant, God promises certain things based on our willingness to also do certain things. If we do, God will fulfill His promise; if we don't do our part, then He will withdraw, but He will not punish. We are not bound to fulfill our end of an agreement; if that were so, it would also negate our free will.

We must remember that God demands nothing of us, for if He were to require obedience to His will, it would destroy our free will – the cornerstone of our mission in life – our reason for being. God wants nothing of us except for us to use our free will to develop our ability as co-creators with Him. And this requires freedom to make mistakes – to lie, cheat, steal, murder even, and all without God's judgment or punishment. This does not mean that we should do these things; it means only that we have the freedom to do them, if we so choose. Should we choose to experience any of the negative things, we must be ready to receive in like kind what we have chosen to experience. It is in this way that we learn to balance our positive and negative polarities. Through this process of experimentation and adjustment in life after life, we will balance our duality, and reduce the polarity to one of complete harmony and moderation in everything. We will then be like God – to know ourselves as God. We will then be living love.

God states though, that what we sow we shall reap. So whatever we do, we will be held responsible and have to pick the fruit of our plantings in order to attain the desired quality or understanding we are developing. This however is never for punishment; it is to give us opportunities to see our mistakes as mistakes or errors of judgment, and to correct them. It is God's love in action; it is His mercy in application. He does not punish; He forgives and He loves. In forgiveness, there is mercy, and should we attain the desired change, the meeting of what we have sown may not be necessary. Karma is not fated and immutable; but it is destined and therefore changeable.

# 29

# GOOD INTENTIONS

It is taught that the road to hell is paved with good intentions. It is still believed in our present day that regardless of what we try or what we hope to do, good intentions are never enough. Christian religions say we must have results; we must make it to the finish line without blemish and free of sin. And what we *intend* to achieve is unimportant for God requires total and complete compliance with His demands – results! No matter how sincere we are, if we don't succeed, then we have failed. Furthermore, if we fail, there is no second chance because we have only one life in which to make it or break it.

And they say, no matter how sincere our intentions, or how hard we try to be obedient to God's will, no matter that we sweat blood and tears in failed attempts to conquer an addiction for example, such as drugs, sex, or gambling, if we don't succeed we will be punished. It sounds hopeless, but as a sop to sinners, of which we all are, they say, in a manner to cement our allegiance to the Church, salvation was promulgated by the Church and attained by way of penance and absolution.

That's what we are told, and that's wrong.

The Church pays only lip service to mercy and grace, because to receive God's beneficence we have to meet certain conditions of forgiveness, and they are those that are established by the Church. In their view, God's grace is unwarranted mercy and forgiveness – *and* it is conditional. But grace isn't conditional, it's free and available to everyone, and it doesn't need an intermediary of the Church to obtain it. And it doesn't have any conditions attached to it except for intent. But that is not adequately understood or applied.

Under these circumstances, it's easy to believe that God discriminates, and sometimes grants His favors in special dispensations for special reasons for certain people. It is also easy to believe that mercy and grace are acts that require a conscious appeal whether by ourselves or through the intervention of the Church. But God may grant His favors with or without our request. If He sees that grace is warranted and is for the highest and best for all concerned, He may give it and we may not even be aware of it at the time. It is given in a manner, and in a moment, that is often without notice of intervention. We may see a change, but we may not attribute it to an act of Spirit.

Grace is not a sometimes thing depending almost on the whim of God. Grace is an always thing, because God sees what is in our heart. He knows our intent. What we say, what we try to do, whether we succeed greatly or fail mightily, perhaps failing to love without condition, or maybe harbor anger, unable to forgive, all our efforts can count in our favor – *if we try; if the intent is pure.* The intent to set a goal, to want, to desire, to attempt, to try, is as pleasing in His eyes as success is in ours.

Good intention coupled with passion, is the motivator, the life-blood of any new thing: a new venture, idea, desire or program. It is the power source of creation. Intention is the prime mover; it feeds, propels, sustains and encourages. Without intent nothing can be accomplished. With pure intent the world is our oyster.

There are various levels of intention ranging from the whimsical to the pure. We all have the ability to create, but the quality of the creation is determined by and limited to the degree of intent. Pure intent – the highest and the noblest, is capable of creating a new life, a new medical breakthrough, even a new world. But it is also able to create mundane successes; for example: an improved drive on the golf course, an improved posture, or an improved job performance. Pure intent is unlimited potential in every field of endeavor and expression; it is harbored in the heart in unfailing dedication, desire and expectation.

With such possibilities of success and attainment whether material or spiritual, it is sad that we have been taught such a lie that we believe good intentions by themselves are a road to hell and let it negatively affect our desires and aspirations. Good intentions do not lead one to hell or to failure, quite the opposite. Good intentions are not the road to hell; they are the roadways to success and to heaven.

Before you judge another, try to determine his sincerity, his intent. What he intended may or may not be what you see. Being human and subject to the frailties of humanity – prejudices, biases, angers, opinions, affections, misunderstandings, and plain and simple mistakes, can make what is intended, appear to come out opposite to what is desired. Then the person's actions and motives can be easily misinterpreted and wrongly judged.

We have all experienced being unfairly judged by someone who fails to honor our good intentions. So look beyond the act, past what is seen, then what may seem to be inconsiderate or destructive behavior or criticism may be merely false impressions of good intentions. In other words, don't judge another; we don't know their intentions; we see only the results, whether they were what we thought they wanted to express or not. And forgive those who fail to understand and appreciate our intentions – and do not judge them for their failure, if it is that. For again, we don't know what is in their heart, or what their intentions are in criticizing or putting down our personal intentions. Their intentions may be only to help, without realizing that it may be doing the opposite of what they want to do.

But keep always in mind that God is not blind; He sees all and He knows all, including what is in your heart. That and that alone is the measure of love in action. Always follow the lead of your heart-feelings, for your feelings are the language of your soul. It's pretty smart; it knows what is best for you.

# 30

# DEATH: WHY WE RESIST IT

It goes without saying that life blooms with our first breath, but it's also acknowledged that death is life's inseparable companion. Whether one lives or dies is not the issue; rather it's how one lives his life, and that is determined largely by attitude, and on where the primary emphasis is placed – on life or death. Some live longer than others, some shorter; some live lives of joy and love, others of pain and fear. For some heaven is on earth, for others earth is a living hell – it largely depends on attitude.

A recent column in the Buffalo News written by *The God Squad*, was headlined, "Life Beats Death Any Day," and it proceeded to offer advice to a family whose aging uncle wanted to die. His life was over; he had been confined to a nursing home for seven to eight years; he had lost his spirit and the will to live. He was alone and had nothing to live for. That happens quite often, but what kind of life is that? He wanted his family to pray to God to let him die. What should one do in such a case?

The advice was: *"Do everything possible to keep him alive, to help him find some reason, any reason, to live... sure, winter is coming to the world, and sometimes winter comes to souls, as well, but remember that at the end of every winter is a new spring."*

Such advice is based on fear – fear of death. It is not the voice of reason; it is the voice of ignorance, the voice of doubt. It is fear that what they profess to believe of life after death may not be true. They put greater value on physical life than they do on spiritual life.

Many would consider the advice given as sound, but was it the best advice? How do we know it would be best to fight to keep him alive? Who tells us that – the Church? Parents? Hospital?, or the one that wants to die. How do they know? No one does except God, God and the one who is ready to die. Note that the dying man didn't ask to be put to death; he didn't ask for doctor-assisted suicide. He simply wanted God to let him die in peace because there was nothing left for him to live for in his physical condition.

The advice as given was well intentioned, but wrong nevertheless. It was offered as the wisdom of God, but was it? Was it the *will* of God? Does God want us to suffer needlessly to avoid what is our fate just to delay the inevitable? The advice seemed to be without real understanding of what life and death are, especially death. It can only be reasoned that if God wants us to hang on to life in spite of unbearable pain or the hopelessness of a condition that is terminal, He would have to be uncaring, even callous. Can anyone believe that God willfully wants us to prolong pain and the dying process just to gain a few more hours of a life embedded in loneliness and hopelessness with no hope or expectation of anything better? Is that a God of love? What are a few more hours or days in a flesh body when a condition is terminal and death is inevitable, especially when compared to the infinite number of days in heaven that awaits the spirit body?

Is God so unfeeling that he wants us to live as long as possible in spite of terrible conditions? Do a few extra days of misery appeal to God? Of what value are a few more days of joylessness and pain to one who is going to live on forever following death.

The minister should have said in his response, "Grant him his wish. Ask God to let him die, but with the stipulation to do so only if it is for the highest and the best for ALL concerned" – that includes the dying person, the family and loved ones, and everyone that is affected by the death. That puts the whole thing in God's hands where it belongs.

Ironically, God does not determine the death of an individual. That is determined by our soul, using the gift of free-will that we are created with. But too often the natural order of things is interfered with when well-intended people do everything they can to prolong the life of someone, using prayer and the courts, when it would be better to step back and let the natural course of events proceed without interference.

It has to be asked, and a forthright answer needs to be given: what is there about life that is so great that it is worth keeping a person in a straight jacket of inactivity and helplessness, and often unceasing pain with nothing to look forward to but another day, another week, another month, another year of the same thing, until in desperation, the body says enough!, and the soul departs for a better place of peace, and joy!

For the man that asked to be allowed to die, prolonging his life would only offer unrelenting boredom – and for what reason; for what purpose? In response to the minister's reply: "Do everything possible to keep him alive," ask yourself, why? In all things, the answers lie within. It is only necessary to enter the silence and seek the source of knowledge and truth. It's there and it's available to all. Books, teachers, guides are not necessary, for truth lies within the heart and soul of every living being.

Go within to the source of truth – your own higher self and listen to the reasonable voice of God – our intuition that speaks to you in feelings – the language of the soul. Listen to your own soul, follow it and you can't go wrong. Don't assume God's will, for it's more than likely not God's at all, nor is it the individual's will that wants to continue a life for no purpose – it could just be you that wants it. Then ask again of yourself, why? For another seven or eight years of regret and helplessness for a person you love? Is that selfless love? Does God – a God of love, mercy, and compassion, really want us to hang on to such a life regardless of what it does to the ill person or to his survivors. Heaven awaits; in selfless love let him or her go if that is their wish.

So who was right – the patient, or the minister who advised the man's family to fight death? Why should he fight? Why should the family encourage him to fight? They fight because neither he nor the family knows what death really is; they resist death mostly because of fear – fear of the unknown; lack of faith; lack of trust. Christians, in spite of professing that they believe in heaven and how wonderful it will be when they get there, are actually afraid of stepping across the line. This, in spite of their avowed belief of life after death, and in a heaven of peace and love that awaits them in paradise. They simply don't have the faith they like to think they have. Christians as a whole, laymen and clergy alike, don't seem to believe a word of what they profess to believe. If they did, why would they all be so afraid of the inevitable?

What compels us to resist death so strongly? It seems that in spite of our professed belief in life after death, we are nevertheless a death-obsessed religion rather than life-oriented – we truly don't believe what we so glibly say we believe. We're death-obsessed because we don't believe deep down inside us, that there is life after death. Our religion does not stress, or go into meaningful discussions of what occurs at death, and what follows it. That's because our shepherds – the teachers, ministers and clergy... don't know! Why are we so afraid of dying? It's simple: we doubt – we don't believe what we say we believe, or we don't trust what we say we believe. We are mistaught by clerics that don't know themselves. We are all, truly ignorant of the truth. And because of ignorance we doubt, and doubt creates fear. Because we fear, we resist death, and we will fight to the last breath to prevent the inevitable. Because we don't know, we are even afraid of talking about it when death approaches.

What right do we have to tell another, "You can't die. We don't want you to die." Who are we thinking of when we say that, the dying person or ourselves? Who has that right? Only the one that's dying and God have that right, and no one else. The man didn't do anything wrong in his request to be let to die. He only

218

wanted God to let him die in peace and reap the rewards of heaven that he believed was awaiting him.

Such advice as that given to the family, which was meant to encourage their uncle to fight death, is not always for the best, because there are times when it is better for all concerned to quit fighting death and welcome it. Often, death is resisted by the survivors for personal reasons – they are afraid not for the dying person but too often for themselves – they don't want to be left alone, or maybe they are emotionally dependent on the dying one, or fearful of losing someone very near and dear to them. There can be any number of reasons. But how often is it concern for the one dying? They are fearful because they fear their own death; a fear that is based on misconceptions of what death is.

It is time for Christians to examine what they say they believe. If they do believe in life after death, then it should be accepted without fear and resistance when its time arrives. When there is no purpose in prolonging life, there should be no reason to resist death. There are some good reasons to fight for life when there is hope of change or recovery; there are equally good reasons to accept death with peace and gratitude when it's time. Some examples are: cancer with unremitting and incurable pain; or when one is in a coma or vegetative state unable to communicate, with signs of meaningful life absent, existing only with a feeding tube and persistent bed sores. Or simply when one is old and feeble, tired and lonely, and all they want is peace and joy again in their life that awaits them upon their transition from their life of flesh to a life of spirit and unbounded freedom. Do we put that person's needs ahead of our misconceptions and our fear of death, which are based on the misunderstood and mistaught ideas of our religions?

Do we resist death because there is a chance of recovery, or because in our fear we consider life to be the better of two evils? The known is always more comforting than the unknown. As unpleasant as life may be, it is still more acceptable because we know it; it is ours, whereas the future is still shrouded in ignorance. Who are we to try to prevent another person's passing when there is no purpose to prolong it? Are we God?

When death is inevitable and when the time is right, death should not be resisted, but welcomed; it should not be mourned, but celebrated; it should be greeted not with tears for the departed, but with joy for their departure to a new world of joy, beauty, peace and love that is unimaginable by material standards. Mourning is good for the survivors, but it does nothing for the departed. For the deceased there should be a celebration.

Death is not an ending, but a beginning. It is a transition of a soul from physical life to a life of spirit in astounding freedom and unimagined peace and beauty. Let's turn the words of the God Squad into a question and ask: Does life really beat death any day?

So cheer for life; but cheer also for death, for death is a continuation of life. It is a graduation to a higher school of learning and accomplishment. When the time comes, let the dying go. Resisting their death only prolongs their agony of spirit and suffering. That is not what you want. That is not what God wants. Let them go in peace, and celebrate!

# 31

# *SEX AND HOMOSEXUALITY*

Sex in American culture is a tangle of confusion. The historical religious attitude toward sex is that its primary purpose is for procreation, with some churches going so far as to say it's the only reason for sex and that any other use of it is sinful. Hedonists claim that sex is for pleasure first and foremost. Spiritually minded people will say that it is the highest expression of love men and women are capable of attaining. Some people use it with selfish reasons without concern for anybody other then themselves. Others are more concerned with pleasing their sexual partner than themselves. And there are those like-minded people who make love to please both themselves and their partner.

If people would rank the value of sex, according to conditioned beliefs, Christians would likely put procreation first on the list, the second would be for its spiritual benefits, and lastly it would be for pleasure. But they would be wrong. In the eyes of God, the greatest value would be for pleasure; second would be for an uplifting spiritual expression between two people, and procreation would rank as third in importance.

With a lifetime of conditioning behind each of us, it is difficult if not impossible for many people to believe that God really wants us to enjoy life. There are churches for example that believe that laughter and dancing are sinful and lead one to hell. They are wrong because God does not judge and there is no sin. He places no restrictions on what we do or how we do it, leaving it up to us to decide what's best for ourselves and for others. Sex is pleasurable, and God wants us to enjoy it free from worry and fear of sinning.

During the 1960's era of the Flower Children, a major change occurred in American mores and values. It was marked with what appeared to be a revolt of sexual libertines, free of restraints and sexual taboos. It was an era of experimentation and freedom of love making without restraint or conditions. In many ways it was an open expression of their God-given natures in freedom to follow their inner feelings of love with unrestricted expression. It caused a lot of societal tut-tutting, but that was not necessarily a bad thing because a closed window was opened to us all for greater and natural understandings of love, sex, and self. It was a swing of the pendulum away from the restraints of our puritan heritage with all its sexual taboos and fears. It was a breath of fresh air, allowing us to explore our God-given right of self-determination and expression.

As in all things when there is a new venture, a new era of exploration, there are excesses. But overall, the upsurge of sexual freedom was a good thing. Was it any worse than the puritanical attitudes toward sex, where the word "s-e-x" had to be spelled even in a family setting, and any open discussion of sex between people was met with disdain and disapproval? Any word associated with the "privates" and normal bodily functions were never spoken aloud, if at all. Silly names were substituted to avoid saying the actual name. Pregnancy was hidden from children, and sometimes even from adults. Teachers had to take a leave of absence when they became pregnant. Sex was considered so dirty and shameful that many married couples never bared their bodies to each other. Lovemaking was often done in the dark and under the covers. With the lights off, it was virtually impossible to see each other's naked body. Puritanism colored every aspect of society and culture, creating a very abnormal restriction of natural expressions of individuality, not only in sex, but also infecting all of life with its warped concept of right and wrong, and its ungodly restrictions of the simple pleasures and joy of living.

Life often follows extremes like the swing of a pendulum. In regards to sex it swung to the extreme of puritism, then it swung back to the opposite extreme of sexual libertinism where we have been experiencing free-swinging sex with little restraint and often with little or no regard for the sensibilities of others. That may not necessarily be an all-bad thing because it forces consideration of the proper role of sex in our lives. There is now a final movement away from the extremes. The pendulum has swung about as far to the right of sexual liberty without restraint as it can.

It has swung both directions, touching both extremes, away from the severity of guilt and shame, and across to the excesses of unrestricted pleasure without discretion and good sense. But now, it is returning to its nexus, the balance point between the extremes; with occasional jerks of libertinism to remain with little further movement to one side or the other. It will come to rest, balanced in a harmonious expression of responsibility, love and pleasure.

Religion is still hung up on sex, still believing that it should be for procreation primarily. But that attitude is slowly changing with the recognition that sex can be Godly when performed in the way of godliness, and still be pleasurable. But that is only a beginning – there is still a lingering attitude of guilt and shame in the nagging feeling that sexual pleasures are not godly. When in fact, sex is one of the greatest gifts God has given to man. A revolt of sexual freedom and expression is continuing, bringing sex out of the closet and into open acceptance of its rightful place in our human nature – our innate sexuality. It is being accepted as our right to enjoy sex with little or no restriction as long as it doesn't interfere with the rights and sensibilities of others. In that, it is right and good, and well within the intention of God. There is no such thing as too much sex, but there is too much of a *need* for sex. God suggests that we should enjoy everything and need nothing – especially needing people, because needing someone is the fastest way to kill a relationship.

In the book *Conversations With God,* God was asked how we might best express the thing called sexual energy.
God replied:
*"Lovingly. Openly. Playfully. Joyfully.*
*Outrageously. Passionately. Sacredly. Romantically.*

*Humorously. Spontaneously. Touchingly. Creatively.*
*Unabashedly. Sensually.*

*And of course frequently.*

*"The good news is that it's all right to love sex. It's all right to love yourself. In fact it's mandatory.*
*What does not serve you is to become addicted to sex (or anything else). But it is "okay" to fall in love with it!*
*So choose sex – all the sex you can get. Yet do not choose sex instead of love, but as a celebration of it.*

But how we should deal with the incredible experience of sexuality? In words of beauty and power, God answered:

*"Not with shame, that's for sure and not with guilt, and not with fear.*
*For shame is not virtue, and guilt is not goodness, and fear is not honor.*
*And not with lust, for lust is not passion; and not with abandon, for abandon is not freedom; and not with aggressiveness, for aggressiveness is not eagerness.*
*And obviously not with ideas of control or power or domination, for these have nothing to do with love."*

The sexual act is perhaps the greatest expression of love, and it should be engaged in freely and spontaneously in total joy. God makes no judgment on any personal expression; what we do is our choice with God's blessings because that is the freedom He gave us in order to become co-creators with Him. God created sex for our use and pleasure, and He has no intention of spoiling our enjoyment of it by sitting in judgment of what we do, or how we wish to express it. We have a choice of whether to honor or abuse sex. If honored, it creates sacredness in itself, with love and joy at its center. Although nothing is good or bad in itself, its effects can be either to our disadvantage or to our advantage for rapid spiritual growth. But the choice is ours to make without fear of censure or judgment. The only choice we have really, is shall we engage in sex with gratitude and pleasure, or with guilt and shame. The choice is ours.

### REGARDING HOMOSEXUALITY

If one is to understand sex and its role in our lives, it is necessary to see sex as a divine gift that God has lovingly given us for our pleasure. It is not restricted in any form or manner by God; only man sees sex as something it should not be, something immoral, bad, evil, unnatural; something that must be tightly controlled by society and our culture. If there was a list of such no – no's, homosexuality and lesbianism would be at the top of the list; but that would be only the confused noises of prejudice and ignorance.

To understand this is simple: to begin with, soul is androgynous, neither male nor female, but both in balance. Soul in its essence is one as Father/Mother God is one, balanced in all aspects of positive and negative attributes. Only in materiality does this unity divide into a duality of numerous polarities of positive and negative, including the duality of male and female expressions.

God created earth to be a total learning environment for soul to experience all forms of duality. In its journey in materiality, it embodies a physical body in an illusion of reality. It can be said that life is but a soul's dream. In this experience, soul does not engage in anything that would be construed as good, bad, or evil in the eyes of God; no more than we could be considered guilty of sin in a dream of immoral activities.

225

Our purpose on earth is to learn to harmonize our polarities of opposites such as male and female. This can be done only in successive rebirths in human physicality. It is therefore necessary that in order to eventually harmonize and balance one's sexuality of male or female, soul must experience lives of each sex. Only in births as male and female in different lifetimes is it possible to acquire the necessary understanding and acceptance, or appreciation of the values and importance of what we refer to as the opposite sex.

In our duality, the polarities of cultures and religions come to battle with the duality of our sexual natures. After reincarnating as a female in many lifetimes for example, the soul can become unbalanced with a preponderance of negative attributes, becoming ineffectual, weak, passive, and so on. Conversely, a soul in male incarnations can become unbalanced with masculine attributes and become overly aggressive, too assertive, and power-mad.

When that happens, it becomes necessary for a soul if unbalanced in female qualities, to rebalance its lopsided negativity with the opposite masculine qualities such as assertiveness and strength. The soul will then reincarnate in a male body and begin to balance its female qualities with the male qualities. But herein is a problem, at least as far as society and culture measure it, in that the soul carries with it in its new male body, heavily influencing characteristics of the female qualities of its past lives. The male then is buffeted by expressions of these female attributes, influences, mannerisms and desires – including sexual preferences. Thus it is that that person is labeled queer, fagot, fruit or other equally offensive names.

There is nothing a person can do to change inborn sexual inclinations or desires, only time and one or more successive rebirths will resolve the conflict of inner and outer modalities – emotion vs. physicality. But it is possible when once resolved, for that soul in successive incarnations to become unbalanced again, this time in male attributes.

When this happens, the soul will need to reincarnate in a female body after a succession of lives as a man, and this time it may affect masculine mannerisms, desires and characteristics. It will also be labeled by society and called derogatory names such as dike, butch and others even more reprehensible. But here again, as in both cases, the soul expression follows the pattern of Father/Mother God, which was established by His/Her will for our spiritual benefit enabling us to become one as He/She is one, balanced in a unity of wholeness, harmonized with balanced polarities of male-female attributes.

It must be understood that this balancing mechanism is all designed and promoted by God. It cannot therefore be considered against His will, for God not only made it possible for that soul to experience life in what could be a heavily influenced and unbalanced identity, but also approves the choice. How then can it be considered unnatural, or a sin?

The underlying foundation of all this is love – God love. Such love is without condition or judgment, and without condemnation or condescension. It is full acceptance of the condition and the men and women affecting this difficult transition of polarities from male to female, or from the female to male. Every single individual on the face of the earth, has at one or more times throughout their many incarnations in physical bodies, gone through this transition and have only gained as a result.

It is in our own best interests to accept homosexuals and lesbians without thought of judgment, and with unconditional love, accepting them as we would accept people with different colored hair as a natural condition of birth. The end result of what can be a difficult learning process, is a soul-being that is equally balanced in all its attributes and attitudes in a harmonization of opposite polarities, being neither male nor female but both in one, as God is both in one. The man or woman would then have all the beneficial qualities of both the male and the female, expressing itself in harmony, joy, peace, universal love and freedom. This is the goal. The purpose of life in flesh bodies is to become one as God is one and thus one with Him/Her in love and creativity.

To be gay, whether male or female, is an expression of love. It is a choice for soul's growth. Such individuals should not be considered as outcasts of society, but as children of God who are in their current expressions of individuality, growing ever closer to God, their Mother/Father, becoming of like kind, balanced in harmony, love and sexuality in oneness with God. You've done it; I've done it; ministers, priests; politicians, parents, macho men and parasitic women have done it. We ever have and ever will continue to do it until we, one by one, have balanced ourselves in equal expressions of male and female characteristics. Such men and women should not be excised or ridiculed, but applauded for their courageous decisions to regain their balanced polarity of male/female attributes.

## 32

# FAITH AND DOUBT

St. Paul stated that *faith is the substance of things hoped for; the evidence of things not seen.* The American Heritage dictionary defines faith as *confident belief in the truth, value, or trustworthiness of a person, idea, or thing.* In both definitions there is an element of trust, a reliance not on mind or mental acuity, but on an inner acceptance of truth and a reliance on spirit. Note that in these definitions, faith is accepted as a quality, not a condition. They exclude knowledge as a criterion of faith that needs no rational or mental understanding for its validity. They define faith as an attitude, an acceptance of a supposed reality that does not need empirical proof or material evidence of its existence. Its proof will not be in the now but in the manifestation of what is believed; a proof that is not yet, but is yet to be. In its essence such faith is blind. Faith in such definitions has the ability to create, but it lacks the full power of creativity because it doesn't encompass its full potential.

There is a third definition that came to the author during a meditation, one that more clearly defines the full meaning of the word, faith. It stated: *Faith for the most part is sanguinary, equating knowing with feeling.* Webster defines sanguine as hopeful, cheerful, confident and optimistic, so then by adding knowing to feeling, one can get a lively and meaningful understanding of what faith can be and truly is. To put it all together, it can be said that *Faith for the most part is hopeful, cheerful, confident, and optimistic, and equates knowing with feeling.*

Most, or all religions regard faith as hope mingled with a feeling of a thing's existence. Feeling is good, but by itself, it is inadequate. If faith is to be a power in one's arsenal of life there must also be a knowing of a things existence before it can be seen or felt. The two must exist together with feeling and knowing united in a powerful and inseparable gestalt. Knowledge is the recognition of a thing that is, or a thing that is relative to a past expression or experience; but that is not enough. Knowing is the acceptance of a reality that is alive and viable with strength, which is realized before it is manifested in physical reality. Knowledge is of the mind and by itself it is nothing but a mental activity in an empty framework of bits and pieces lacking unity and strength; feeling without knowing and understanding is only emotion without power. Separately, they lack authority, but when feeling is combined with knowing, you have the power of creation – the ability to create what you will. It is said that faith can move mountains, and that is fact! But it requires more than simple belief or blind faith. It is a knowing and a certainty of success without hesitancy or doubt; it is the visualization and acceptance of the reality of a creation before its manifestation.

We glibly use the term faith without real understanding of what faith is, or without a realization of its power. It is accepted as a belief without conviction or understanding; a faith built on hope and wishes, but not on substantive reality. Such faith is powerless. It is so weak that any challenge of adversity or danger can quickly destroy it. Religion is prone to advise us to just have faith when they don't know what else to say. Ask the clergy what faith is, and you will get either the above definition of St. Paul's, or an attempt to explain away their lack of knowledge. Ask them how to get faith, and they tell you to pray, but they won't tell you what or where it is or how to find it. Ask them how to restore a dying faith, and they will say you must have faith. But they will be unable to tell you how to save it, or how to get it if you don't have it.

Almost all religions advise that knowledge is available, but it is always located somewhere outside us. The answers to our questions they say are in books; in the words of advice written or oral. They may say, read this book, or talk to Pastor Henry, or Father Joe, or pray to God that is up there, or somewhere out there, or maybe even beside you, but they don't say go within. They don't know that all knowledge is contained in the higher mind of each and every individual and is available to all who seek it.

In 2 Corinthians, 6:16 it is said: *"Ye are the temple of the living God; as God has said, I WILL DWELL IN THEM, AND WALK IN THEM; AND I WILL BE THEIR GOD, AND THEY SHALL BE MY PEOPLE."* The temple of God is within, and if God were in us, wouldn't it be obvious that his knowledge and wisdom are within us also? Isn't it evident that all that is stored in the temple within is available to everyone? And if that is so, then isn't it possible to go within into our own minds and hearts to find what we seek? There are few who understand this, and many of them are mostly unaware of how to go within to get it. For those that do, the knowledge and wisdom they gain will create a faith that will withstand all adversity, all difficulties and all attacks upon their persons and their trust in God. They will then have the faith of a mustard seed that when planted and nourished, will not just move mountains, but *create them.*

Sometime the supplicant when praying, is unable to put into words what is felt, but that isn't necessary because words aren't all that important to God; He reads the language of the soul, which is feelings and *intent.* God knows your intent, and doesn't need to be told in certain words or phrases what is desired or needed. Pure intent will give you what you seek. Intent is the power of creation.

Faith is in our hearts and is unique to the individual. We are God's creations and in turn, we are the creators of all that we are and will be. Our creative ability is based on faith – faith in God and in ourselves, knowing that God is within us, and one with us. It is faith, but it is also trust – trust in God and in our divinity; it is the knowing and feeling that all will be done for the highest and the best for all concerned.

There is a polar aspect of faith that together with faith comprises a duality of opposites; the other pole is doubt. Doubt is decried by many as the work of the devil that is doing his best to destroy the faith that we may have, or to prevent us from gaining faith when it is lacking. The devil in any case is not a single entity of evil; it is oneself, found in the faulty attitudes and opinions that cause disbelief in themselves or in God and His activity in our lives.

The advocates of faulty self-judgment are too often people of religion and their respective churches. This is most noticeable in the Catholic Church that purportedly strives to build faith in God, but they surreptitiously accomplish the opposite – sometimes unknowingly, sometimes purposefully. They strive to make the people believe that only what they teach is God's truth and that it is only through them that truth can be attained. They want control, but that cannot be achieved until they first cause their followers to lose faith in themselves, thereby creating a dependency on the Mother Church. They use doubt as a means of attaining that control. If people did not doubt, they would more likely exercise their power to be themselves free of outside influence or religious persuasion.

Doubt is the opposite of faith and together they form the dual nature of the positives and negatives of belief. But doubt is not always a bad thing. Doubt can destroy effort or faith, but it can also be a catalyst for constructive change. We are so used to thinking of doubt in a negative way that it is difficult to understand that doubt can be constructive. Contrary to prevalent belief, it can be a blessing that comes in through the back door, for it prompts us to look at a situation in a new light. It encourages us to look at ourselves or at a problem with clearer vision, and to seek answers and new directions. It compels us to re-examine long held beliefs and to see them from new perspectives. We will start to wonder, then to question, then to seek answers, and finally strive to find new solutions and new directions. Doubt can be a builder when it is seen as a constructive element in our lives. We would be wise to accept doubt as a blessing when it occurs, and use it to build new foundations and new solutions, using it as a springboard to faith. Atheism is usually thought of as a ticket to hell – a guaranteed one-way ticket with no return. But like everything else in our lives, atheism is only an experience from which we learn and grow. It is nothing but a form of doubt, albeit an extreme form. It is not insurmountable; it is not a sin, nor is it unforgivable. Atheism may delay one's spiritual growth and development, but it does not and cannot prevent it, because God will not allow *anything* to prevent one's eventual return to Him and their true home.

Taken together, faith and doubt are or can be, an unstoppable force for spiritual growth and creativity. Whether it is or not will depend on the purity of one's desires and intentions. As in all things, what we are, what we achieve, what we will to be, is in our hands. As God says: *"Know ye not that ye are Gods?"*

# 33

# FORGIVENESS AND GRACE

Forgiveness is simple, yet difficult. You can say the words, "I forgive you" and think you mean it, but deep in the hidden recesses of the subconscious mind there may be a residual anger, or an unrecognized determination to not forgive. If so, it will hang on like a leech and won't let go – and that applies to forgiving oneself as well as to the forgiving of others. In either case there can be resentment, or a wish to strike back in some way.

Words in themselves are meaningless unless accompanied with pure intent. Within the heart lies the truth of sincerity and forgiveness; but there can also be found the lies embedded in insincerity. Forgiveness must come from the heart; else it is meaningless tripe meant either to placate another person, or to hide the truth of one's feelings, even from oneself. Forgiveness is without meaning and valueless to anyone if there is not a pure intent to go with it. If the anger or hostility, or emotional reactions are not released along with the words of forgiveness, the cause creating the need to forgive will hang on and become an ingrained part of the person – a millstone around one's neck. In such a case, it is not the one that is to be forgiven that suffers, it is the person who withholds the unconditional love that would accompany the act of forgiving. The two are inseparable. Love without forgiveness, or forgiveness without love free of conditions, is meaningless and without any value whatsoever. It is a cause of distress and dis-ease.

Some will say that if you haven't forgotten, you haven't forgiven. But is it possible to wipe from our memory something that caused injury or some sort? To be truly forgotten, there would need to be a total erasure of the incident from our memories. It's a nice thought, but not wholly practical, for should one be harmed by another person emotionally, physically, or any other way, and the act is totally deleted from recall, it would remove the safeguard of recall and the protection that would come with it.

Although things are never totally forgotten, they can be managed and controlled. It is not the eradication of memory that is purposed. The intention should be to set it aside, giving or paying it no thought, or giving no further attention to it once it is forgiven. There will always remain however, a cellular memory of the injury and it will lie in wait for unexpected recall. It is the hanging on to an injury through deliberate and unnecessary recall that creates the impossibility of true forgiveness. What should be done is to separate oneself emotionally from the incident or situation that was the cause of the hurt. One would thereby detach oneself from the injury as though it never happened, yet still be capable of bringing it to awareness should similar conditions arise.

The value of forgiving is for the forgiver, not the forgiven.

The greatest harm that occurs with non-forgiveness is the harm that is done to oneself. When we do not forgive and refuse to release grievances, we create a poison that pervades every cell and tissue of the mind and body. Unforgiveness along with guilt and shame are three of the greatest destroyers of peace and well being there is, and that includes the physical, mental, emotional and spiritual attributes of man. The harm one can do to oneself is, over time, tantamount to self-destruction. It won't occur in a moment, but a little at a time when pieces of self-respect, selfless love, friendship and such will be chipped off from our mental, emotional and spiritual bodies. Eventually our armor of inviolability will be removed, opening us to assaults on our tranquility and harmony.

It is to be understood that when we are unable, or when we refuse to forgive, we are in effect judging. Whether it is judging another person or a condition, our judgment will boomerang on us. It is a direct response in the creation of a new condition or karma, with an immediate or future reaping of what we have sown. The one that is judged is not harmed by our attitude, although it invariably creates a barrier between two people, one that the other person may not even be aware of, yet still feel. The lack of forgiveness is to hold judgment, and when we do, we separate ourselves from the one we judge, thus creating a separation in the wholeness of love that we should all have with one another and with God. To forgive is to give oneself a gift of God's grace.

When Jesus came, he brought not only the great gift of universal love and forgiveness, but also grace. Grace means you can simply turn around and re-decide the moment of creation and accept the love you have within. The moment of creation is the act of choosing what shall next be experienced, creating a new paradigm of opportunity and expression. Emmanuel says: "Grace is the fabric of God's consciousness. It is eternal love. Everything is grace."

Grace is often described as unmerited love or forgiveness. It is that, and more than that. It is divine love, given freely and unconditionally; it is the state of living love, protected and made productive by the favor of God; and it is God's guidance in all our affairs of life.

Grace is a doorway of change under the guidance and direction of Divine order offering a transformation for the greater. It holds the highest possible outcome of future potential. Grace will only occur when we are willing to release what is no longer of benefit to us, and after we detach ourselves from ego. Our minds must be emptied of opinion, freed of conditions and expectations and from attachments to opinions and expectations, free from what was and open to new possibilities and new opportunities. Grace enhances possibilities, creating full potential for new possibilities to occur.

Forgiveness is essential in the act of creation. Nothing new can be accomplished when any form of pain or injury is held on to. It must be released to no longer be a part of you, opening a passageway to new opportunities and expansion.

# 34

# MARRIAGE

In human associations, there lie fundamental needs of self-expression. This applies equally to the most intimate relationship of marriage. It is considered to be the consummate bond between two people who have entered into a contract of love, promising to care for and honor each other for the rest of their lives. The vows of marriage are usually expressed in sincerity and good will, with every intention of fidelity to one another.

Regardless of intent, there is an innate problem in many marriages because it typically involves a need for security of one type or another; it may be emotional, financial, social, or any number of other needs. It is often prompted by fear, unrecognized but real, and becomes a primary factor in a relationship's difficulties. It's because any deviation of behavior from what one or both have expected creates suspicion and casts doubt on the integrity of the other, creating a sense of unreliability and uncertainty. Such marriages are based on needs, surrounded with conditions and expectations, and are self-oriented. It is the opposite of unconditional love, or love without conditions, expectations or demands. When one person deviates from what was expected, fear and suspicion create a wedge of doubt and loss of faith in the other's sincerity and reliability. Much of it is prompted by uncertainty of self-worth and feelings of abandonment.

When a relationship becomes subject to demands and requirements, it would likely result in the denigration of one or both partners. Such things do not promote freedom of expression and personal development for either person, and certainly not happiness. Instead, it tends to separate by creating anger and hostility, indifference and unwillingness to cooperate, resentment and isolation, hardly the things that either one wants. The effort to make the other person fulfill one's expectations and conditions will only push the other person away creating a rift, a separation that will be increasingly more difficult to repair in the fulfillment of their vows. When such a situation occurs and there is little or no chance of reconciliation, or no willingness to correct such attitudes, divorce could, or maybe should be a natural result.

Unfortunately, marriages based on hope and illusions are usually not successful and divorce usually results with a great deal of pain for all concerned. But if the two people have put the other person's needs and interests, not necessarily ahead of their own, but in the proper perspective, and do it without fear of loss or failure, but with encouragement for their partner to develop their unique characteristics with the freedom to be themselves, their relationship could not only survive, but flourish.

If a divorce or separation did come, the separation would likely be amicable without accusations of unfairness or mistreatment, emotional or otherwise. Both could likely remain friends and supportive of each other. Contrary to what most believe, in the end, divorce could be beneficial for both. There is nothing wrong with divorce as long as it is done in what is the highest and best for all concerned.

The cause of divorce is often the difficulty or even the refusal to let the other person be themselves. The cause of pain in a divorce is most often caused by an inability to let go, so often aggravated by fear of abandonment. Its root cause often rests in a person's poor sense of self – an ingrained feeling of unworthiness and failure. Misunderstandings, attachments, anger and spite only worsen an already difficult situation, pushed over the edge by a refusal to let the other person be what they are meant to be.

But before divorce is seriously considered, there should be an honest self-evaluation of what is really desired and needed. If honesty prevails, it can promote cooperation and respect for each other by encouraging pursuit of individual interests and development. Failure to accomplish an evaluation of expectations and commitments, which could lead to greater respect and cooperation, would only result in dissatisfaction and frustration, and eventually unhappiness and separation. When commitment to marriage vows interferes with or prevents one or the other's personal growth, and there is no possibility of adjustment or compromise, it is time to affect a separation. There are times when divorce is best. Whether it would be of benefit to both partners would depend on attitudes and needs.

It should be considered that personal development is the essential purpose of every person's mission in life. Self-development is primary in any association, and if blocks are put in place to hinder or stop that growth, it is usually advisable for each to go their own way and let the other be what they choose to be, whether it's a partnership in business or one in marriage.

Life is a process of experimentation and adjustment; it is a process of change that can result in growth; it is natural and should be expected and encouraged. A major element that contributes to difficulties in marriage often results from what should be desirable – individual growth, and it should be acknowledged as a normal process of life. Instead, we often hear the complaint, "You've changed. You're not the same person you were when we were married." Although it's usually said disparagingly, it can be an unintentional compliment when the change is accepted in the context of a normal function of life. People should change because it's the only way they can grow. They should explore their inner selves for the truth of what they are and grow into it. They should not be regulated by the fears or needs of another person, which would inhibit their own development. The problems in relationships arise when change and growth are seen as a threat to expectations. And it would be if there were not acceptance, even cooperation and encouragement for the other person to pursue his or her individual interests.

Without growth, material or spiritual, the person is not going anywhere with his life, stuck in a rut and will go out the same door he or she came in. So what was the purpose of being born if there is no change in attitudes, desires, activities, expectations or accomplishments? From the standpoint of spiritual growth, this would refer to the inner person – their concepts of beliefs, values, and spiritual factors in their life.

Difficulties in an intimate relationship arise from an unwillingness to give each other the freedom to be themselves, including spiritual and material expressions. But the gift must be given with respect and encouragement to explore and develop personal interests and needs that differ from earlier expectations.

Unfortunately, marriages are usually entered into tagged with the baggage of conditions and expectations. The result can only be unhappiness because it's impossible to live according to the expectations and demands of another person. They are deadly enemies to compatibility and happiness and will in time destroy a meaningful relationship. Unless pre-marital attitudes of expectations and demands are changed, the relationship can deteriorate into meanness and unhappiness. When one goes along with the demands of another person against their own will, there will be a deadening of desires and interests. Growth stops and freezes in its tracks, and so does respect and love.

A look at the typical marriage vow will reveal a contract that is built on promises and commitments, but are there any that include promises of freedom and respect for the individuality of each other? And are there any that include commitments to help the other person develop and mature according to their unique interests?

If love is true and without conditions or selfish expectations, it will carry with it a desire to let the other person grow according to their individual bent. This can mean a willingness to step aside when necessary, giving the partner freedom and encouragement to explore, develop and become a person different than the one they thought they had married. Naturally this could create problems, perhaps a separation or even a divorce. If so, then let be what must be, and let each depart in peace and friendship.

In any marriage, changes in one or both are going to happen and adjustments must occur. It would not be possible to remain as they were. Marriage can be a major avenue of growth, and if there is to be growth, there has to be change with each person exploring their personal avenues of desires and potentials. Freedom must be given each to the other, with the allowance and encouragement for each to be themselves. This freedom and its opportunities must be shared equally without conditions or expectations. This is not entirely selfless, for when freedom is given to another, it is given to oneself as well.

Marriage must not be based on obligations; it must be based on freedom and respect. A successful marriage is built on an ongoing, daily refreshing of the demonstration of love that is unlimited, eternal and free. It is a daily recommitment to a promise of consideration and appreciation for the uniqueness of each other. Change will occur and it can either be welcomed and encouraged, or feared and resisted. Changes are based on ever-changing interests and needs involving continual choice, and should be acknowledged as part and parcel of life, and never to be feared. Should the marriage be founded on obligations and requirements to be and do things not in accord with the best interests of the other person, without the allowance to just be themselves, it will come to be resented. But if the marriage commitment is offered in unconditional love, without obligations and expectations, there will be no resentment, only appreciation and peace.

You cannot love another while seeking to control them, nor can they love while being controlled. Only by wanting what is best for them can you give them the freedom to be themselves, and only in this way can you ever have a marriage of mutual respect and a sharing of the deepest love. Human love is an extension of spiritual love, wherein Love is All. Love is life, unlimited, eternal, free, and this is what marriage should express.

Growth is change. Therefore, to be held in abject obedience to a promise or commitment, with little or no opportunity of change, is to inhibit, even stop growth. One must have the freedom to change and develop as one chooses. Restricting this may be acting against the best interests of the marriage itself. We experience life through living it, and that requires movement from one condition to another. It means tasting the bitter with the sweet, and it entails successes and failures. In any marriage there must be change if there is to be increased love and respect for each other.

Respect is essential in a marriage, but to put respect for others first and respect for ourselves second, can destroy personal integrity, and result in mediocrity in one form or another. One's love and loyalty must be to oneself first. Shakespeare said it well in *Hamlet*: "This above all: to thine own self be true, and it must follow, as the night the day, thou canst not then be false to any man." If a change causes a negative response in another that they may consider betrayal or abandonment, it still must be, because we owe it to ourselves to be true to ourselves first and foremost. If we refuse to accept change, or to promote our own growth, we go against our best interests and betray ourselves, defeating the very reason we chose to be born in the first place. In a quote from *Conversations With God* by Neale Donald Walsch, God says, *"Betrayal of yourself in order not to betray another is betrayal nonetheless. It is the highest betrayal."* So it reduces to what we should obey: our truth and our personal integrity, or capitulate to the demands and conditions of another, which can only result in stunted emotional and spiritual growth.

# 35

# CREATIVITY AND CO-CREATION

To create is to bring into material manifestation something that already exists in the spiritual realm. It is a realm where time is not and space doesn't exist. Time and space are expressions of our world of duality, where everything has its opposite. This gives mankind the opportunity to experience all things of positives and negatives, such as good and evil, where nothing is real except in our dreamlike condition of illusions.

This makes sense when it is understood that everything that exists in our present experience, exists also in the past and in the future simultaneously. Everything was, is, and always will be, for the past/present/future is an eternal now. In this sense, time is non-existent. Time, space, and our sense of material reality are illusions with no substance and exist as our reality only as we give credence to them, and only as long as we accept them as our reality. It is necessary to do that if we are to express our dual nature in this world of duality, which is a world of the real and the unreal, a world of truth and illusion. Time therefore, becomes a means to an end, enabling us to relate to events, and these events to other events, situations, or conditions.

Time is essential if we are to experience duality, for as we move through space, we move also through time. Science now postulates that space and time are one, and if an object moves fast enough, time for that object will cease to exist and so will space, so the concept of no-time is supported by science. Time and space are aspects of our material reality, which in truth is nothing but illusion. Therefore, all things that we create are already existent because there is no past or future; what we think of as of the past is actually of the now.

To realize anything in our lives, whether material or immaterial – whether substantial or ephemeral, or things of deceit or truth, they must be willfully created by thought. To create merely means to manifest, or bring into our pseudo reality, that which is already existent in another realm of life and awaits our summons. We are not originators; we are generators or facilitators of that which already is, bringing into sensibility that which is hidden from our perceptions. But understand, what we bring into our reality from the spirit realm, exists only as insubstantial matter in that realm and it requires a process of intent and creation to manifest it. Not everyone can do it; yet everyone is able to do it. Creativity is a natural part of our being that lies dormant because of ignorance and unbelief, but it can be developed, and when understood, it's extremely simple.

The great creators, inventors, artists and writers of history were "inspired" with visions or insightful moments: Newton, when the apple fell on his head "discovered," or developed the concept of gravity; Einstein received visions of his theories in his dreams; Michelangelo could "see" the finished sculpture in a block of marble and only had to chip away excess material to reveal the form within, like removing the flesh of a peach to reveal the seed within. Faraday, Robert Louis Stevenson, Beethoven, Archimedes, Edison and countless thousands of others created new things that have changed the world. They created objects of form and beauty that dazzle the emotions and uplift our spirits. They received their inspiration not while diligently and painstakingly digging out new ideas or concepts, but in moments of quiet and stillness while meditating, in daydreams and nightdreams, perhaps in visions or sudden intuitive inspirations and insights, even while soaking in a tub of warm bath water, as did Archimedes. The creation of new concepts came not from mental activity, but through intuitive revelations and insights while the mind was quiet and reflective, while they were "out of their mind." As Einstein said, "Imagination is more important that knowledge."

The effort expended to manifest their inspired ideas came when they had to translate the idea into material reality. That's when the blood, sweat and tears scenario enters the picture, occurring not at the conception of an idea but in its development and maturation. It is as Edison said of creativity, "Genius is 1% inspiration and 99% perspiration."

What is not understood is that everyone is capable of creating something; some of magnificent works of art, others of new inventions that can shake the world, and from some a more efficient potato masher, or a prettier flower arrangement. Everyone has this ability, but it is not used because we have been taught that we are not able. But we are able for the fact remains that we are truly sons of God. Since we are that, and we are, then it rests that as inheritors of all that God is, there is nothing that is beyond our ability to create. Nothing is beyond us if we believe and understand how simple the process of creation is, and if we cooperate as a co-creator with God. As He has stated, if we have the faith of a mustard seed, we can move mountains – but we are not limited to just moving a mountain, we can create one if we choose to.

God says: *Know ye not, that ye are Gods,* and also, *The temple of God is within?* We are one with God and we are at once the creators of what we are and of what we experience, but also the re-creator that can change or alter what there is in ourselves and in our lives that may no longer serve our needs. We are not unwilling recipients of fated events or conditions of personality, or physicality, subjected to past conditions, to the whims of an unjust or uncaring God, or to the capriciousness of natural events beyond our control. Remember: we are soul – the individuated spirit of God! We are the creators with God of our lives and of all that we are or wish to be. In this is our liberty from bondage to unwanted conditions, and the freedom to choose whatever we wish for ourselves, and to manifest that in our lives when and as we will; we are subjected to no one or anything outside of ourselves unless we permit it, or will it.

There are three tools to creation: desire, thought, and word. In the beginning God desired, then He thought upon His desire, then He spoke and brought it forth. By His word, or in the speaking, He created the universe and all that is in it. In such is revealed the process of creation. Jesus believed it and said to Lazarus, "Come forth," and the dead man arose and walked out of his tomb.

Creation is not limited to God only. As He created man in His image, we have equal power and ability. Unfortunately, we do not use it as He intended for us because rather than being taught how to become one with Him as co-creators, we have been taught by misled theology and clergy that we are not equal to God, and to presume equality or anything near it, is blasphemous. So we cower in fear of doing anything that may displease God, and refuse to acknowledge our inherent divinity and our ability and right to create as we wish or desire. We have been enslaved to mediocrity and by religion, unable or unwilling to change for the better. But that is changing. We are in a new age – the New Millennium, where God expects us to be masters of our lives, subject to nothing else unless we let it be.

Thoughts are builders, and what you think about, what you place your attention on will manifest in your life. Thought can change sadness into joy, poverty into plenty, and doubt into faith or faith into doubt – it can work both ways. Thoughts can heal, and they can destroy; it all depends on intent. In other words you can think your way to health and new realities. But creation by thinking is time consuming. There is a quicker way, creating in a moment anything you wish simply by knowing it to be so, and declaring it to be so. It is not a state of becoming; it is a state of being, of being in the now where our past, present and future are simultaneous. It is the declaration of *"I Am"* – the most powerful creative force in all of God's creations.

The process of thinking a thing into reality, will delay its manifestation because thinking takes time. And while thinking, all sorts of negative things could surface that might convince you that it isn't for you, or that it won't occur, denying what would manifest with faith. The *I Am* procedure is instantaneous, because it is a declaration of what is right now. It is a state of being that is creative, calling forth what already exists: *"Lazarus, come forth."*

People at one time or another in their lives, wallow in a slough of doubt and disbelief, without understanding or awareness of their divinity, or of faith in their innate ability of creation. The problem basically, is one of ignorance rather than stupidity; it is the unawareness of their birthright as children of God and co-creators with Him.

"I am not creative"... "I'm a dunce"... "I'm incapable of doing anything original" ... "I'm unable to change anything. I'm stuck with what I am and with what I've got" – all typical attitudes. And those who hold them learn to live with them, unaware that they have created their lives as they are and have the power to change or re-create them anew. Their lives bear out their beliefs, unable to do for themselves, stuck in a neverland of inadequacy and insufficiency – all because they have long accepted the lie that they didn't have the right stuff. Their self-assessment is not based on truth, but on false doctrines and failed attempts, and these usually rest on the indoctrination of misleading and false understandings of parents, and the conditioning of teachers and religion. It has been said, the child is the father of the man. So thoughts of inadequacy, inability and negative personal evaluations embedded in a child's mind, find expression in the adult mind, and manifest in the manner that one's beliefs direct them, for thoughts are the builders. What the mind holds as truth, manifests in concord, constructing for good or bad all there is in one's life.

Everyone is at the exact place in life where they have put themselves. Their thoughts lay the foundations of their lives, and if they are negative, by holding on to these evaluations, layer upon layer of doubt and inadequacy build up, reinforcing their attitudes, manifesting in their lives at every turn in the road, becoming rigid, unbending and unchanging. But everything can be changed and reconstructed to conform to new ideas, new beliefs and desires.

Change is a process of experimentation and adjustment, the warp and woof of life's tapestry. Without change there can be no life for there would be no growth. Opportunities to change constantly appear, but they are too often unrecognized and not seized as occasions that can alter the direction lives have taken. Breakdowns, malfunctions, disappointments, failures and a prevailing status quo become unwelcome companions. What you are, you have chosen to be; what you choose to be, you can will to become. Your life is yours to create as you intend. What you don't like, change it! What you do like, create it!

# 36

# I AM AND CO-CREATION

There is nothing in our lives that cannot be altered to some degree or other, or even completely changed with different conceptual experiences. We are not locked into anything – including karma, or the reaping of what we have sown. It is to be remembered that nothing is frozen or buried in concrete never to be forgiven, never to be forgotten, never to be escaped, never to be removed or remodeled, whether it is attitudes, actions or things.

Karma is simply opportunities given to us to re-evaluate our thoughts, actions and desires – to correct mistakes, create new life patterns, to learn from our experiences, to grow and to realign ourselves with our true mission in life. Therefore it is not something that is punishment, nor is it anything that has to be met, no matter how grievous or damaging it has been to ourselves or to others. We are given the chance to learn, to grow, to develop our better and higher selves, and to create new conditions and experiences – the opportunities to live in joy and peace. This is grace – the chance to turn around, to change, readjust, recreate, and proceed on a different path. A path free of negative conditions, one open and receptive to love with the ultimate goal of returning home to God. Life is a process of creation and re-creation affording everyone the chance to make their lives ones of peace, abundance, and prosperity, or they can be lives of desperation and poverty, whatever one may choose to experience.

So, if we don't like what we are or what we have; if we want a life of abundance instead of near poverty; should we desire a better home, car, or lifestyle; if we desire love and friends in our life instead of loneliness, we can create it. Whatever we desire: better health, abundance, authority, love, prosperity, success – material or spiritual; all are in our power to create. Nothing holds us back from enjoying what we want in life, except ourselves. We are our own worst enemy. In the words of Pogo, the comic strip possum, "We have met the enemy and it is us."

God doesn't withhold from us, conditions don't withhold, people don't, and governments don't; only we do. Conversely, God, conditions, people and government cannot create for us what we want in our lives. We are the creators; they are facilitators only, subject to our co-creations. Our ability to create – our power as co-creators with God are what conceives and generates our wishes. Our success rests on intent. Intent is the divine tool of creation. It is the energy of the New Age, a catalyst of divine energy, and one of the keys to personal co-creation.

Some mistakenly believe that God creates our happiness for us, and our wealth, our peace, success and the other things we want. But He doesn't; we do. We create what we are, what we experience and what we have through our intent. But we create with God. We declare our intent, and God as our co-creator manifests it for us. The purer the intent, the purer is its manifestation and the sooner it develops. It requires teamwork and belief in God and in ourselves. If we lack this we can accomplish little, and then only through hard, laborious effort.

Wants, desires, wishes, hopes and dreams don't have the ability to create, or to fulfill our needs. They don't have the power. They are merely the first steps in attainment, which is the recognition of a desire or a need. In the actual creation of a thing, the first thing is desire, followed with thought, then the spoken word, which is the act of manifesting our desire – the creation of what is wanted. In the beginning God spoke and the word acted: "Let there be light"… "Let there be firmament"… "Let the waters be divided"… His word created all that is. His word created everything, and we as co-creators, create with Him all that is in our lives. The Word is the tool of creation. It is the creator. The

Word is: **I AM.**

Desire, thought, and word together constitute the process of creation: desire is the catalyst – the mover and shaker; thoughts are things – the substance of desires; the word is thought expressed or manifested. Deeds and actions are words in movement. From this, life proceeds out of your intent for it. Desire is the incubator, thought is creative; word is productive. Together they conceive and give birth to things of desire. But behind these is the great power of pure intent. But care must be taken for if desire is impure, what you fear will manifest – a creation of your own making. Fear clouds the vision of desire and hinders its pure manifestation. Thoughts alone are constructs of the mind – made up creations without guarantees of truth or veracity, and subject to error and inadequacy.

Feelings on the other hand, being the language of the soul, cannot give anything false or untrue. They are real and we should trust them and follow them without questioning for they are pure soul guidance. But a word of caution is necessary: it is possible to be misled by the mind, for it can counterfeit feelings, having you believe that they are the voice of the soul. Care must be taken here, and caution exercised, being certain that it is soul speaking, not some errant thought or desire of your mind. What you think, you will create, and once it is created, it will exist forever. Before creating anything, be it objective or subjective, to assure the purity of the manifested thing, it is necessary to ask God beforehand for guidance and protection.

The greater the intent, the stronger the belief and the more certain one is for what is desired or wanted, the greater is the certainty that it will manifest. God's covenant with us is that He will always and forever grant us our heart's desires. We are made in His image, and in that, we are *all* that He is, *co-creators* with equal power, and we are thus able to manifest the beliefs of our hearts.

Everything that can be conceived can be created by thought and word. Some things require mastery of the process before they can manifest, but all things are attainable by everyone. Walk on water? You bet; Heal the sick? Of course. Raise the dead? Some do and you can also. Healing yourself of infectious disease or physical or mental impairments? Yes. All are possible and are being done by countless thousands around the world. Success depends on purity of intent and the strength of belief. It requires persistent and constant application of focus. In that is your power. The actual manifestation could take anywhere from a few nano-seconds to years – all depending on intent and belief – and personal mastery. The closer you get to masterhood, the interval between conception and manifestation shortens. A master can speak and immediately manifest the intent such as Jesus did when he raised the dead and healed the sick. Always remember that we are children of God just as Jesus was, and what he did, we are able to do also – and he told us that! *Thomas, do you believe?* "I don't know; show me proof." *Peter, do you doubt?* "Yes, help me, I'm sinking". That's why you are where you are – lack of belief, lack of faith and trust in God's word.

Creativity comes to us from God – His power, light and love. He *always* grants us our heart's desires. But how many of us believe it? Few do because we don't see immediate results of our attempt to manifest a desire, so we think failure, or disappointment and reinforce our unbelief. But the fact remains, *God always answers **every** prayer!* And not the way He might think would be best for you, unless you stipulate it. He answers it in the exact way it was requested. The problem is not that He doesn't answer our prayer; the problem is that we have asked amiss because of our ignorance. We must be specific in our request because the Universal Mind hears not just what is said, but our sponsoring thoughts also. This includes not only what is intended or desired, but what is feared – our doubts and disbelief. For example: You pray: "I want a new car," or "I need more money," and the creative powers will enhance your wanting, or your needing, and you will keep on wanting and needing without getting your desire.

The word "I" is the catalyst of creation. It calls forth the Great I Am, and whatever follows the "I" is produced. *I want* gives you the wanting. *I feel* gives you the feeling. I Am is the most powerful creative statement in all of creation. Whatever follows the words "I Am" propels the desires or experiences into activity and manifests them. Whatever you think, whatever you say after "I Am," sets into motion those experiences, calls them forth and brings them to you, becoming material reality. So be careful of what you call for and how you say it. Say, "I have a new car, or I have enough money," rather than, "I want."

It is necessary to stop wanting and start having. Instead of saying, "I want prosperity," say, "I am prosperous," or if you can't believe it, say instead, "Prosperity is coming my way." Say it in a way that you can believe what you're saying is fact. You must believe what you are saying or else failure is certain. Intent and belief are equally necessary. To say that you are prosperous while you are struggling for enough money to keep the wolf away from the door, requires an act of faith. But knowing that the desired thing is already in existence in the spiritual realm and merely awaits the proper command coupled with belief, will manifest it in the material realm.

Affirmations are extremely powerful when they are repeated over and again, but only when they are believed as fact. The greatest affirmation is gratitude, thanking God in advance for the manifestation of a desire or need. For example: "Thank you God for bringing me prosperity in my life." It is the idea or thought, spoken and acted upon that brings success. Know it to be so, declare it to be so, and you make it so.

"I Am" declarations, whether positive or negative, are statements of being, of fact – not hoping, not wishing, not wanting, but being in the reality of the intent. I Am is a shortcut to a state of being, and beingness is the fastest method of creation. Creation can be more than a process by which things develop step by step; it can be an awareness of what has already occurred, of what already is and coupled with grateful acceptance.

Hence you thank God in advance of the manifestation. It is an understanding of creation, an awareness of what is, of what has always been and always will be. Creation then is the calling forth of what already is in the spiritual realm. So there's nothing original about it. And even the most doubtful person can "create" his desires with this understanding. All it takes is intent and belief.

To be successful at creating, it is necessary to be consistent, choosing the same thing with constant affirmation of the choice. Don't keep changing your mind, or showing hesitancy or doubt. Consistency is power. When you don't receive what you intended, it is due to one of several things: disbelief or doubt; indecision of what you want; uncertainty of what is best for you; a need for a guarantee that your choice will be the best for you; and finally, the changing of your mind. For guidance and answers, listen to your feelings; follow them and honor them for they are your truth.

But the greatest cause of failure is sponsoring thoughts. These may be spoken or unspoken thoughts, attitudes, feelings or words that accompany your intent. You may intend to receive money to pay your mortgage, but unconsciously append a thought to it that would negate your intent, such as "I have $1500.00 for my new car, *but where's it coming from?*" Or, "I will get that promotion, *but Mary will probably get it.*" "I will win the lottery. *Fat chance.*" These are the reality of intent and they are what are operative. It is not what you want, but what is said or felt that accompanies the declaration. Any mitigating factor such as doubt, questioning, or fear can abort the creative attempt. Our thoughts are the creators, and what we receive or don't receive is always in absolute concordance with what is said, felt or thought.

Holding the thought of creation in your mind can be strengthened by visualizing the object of your desire. Picture the result of your intent, hold it in focus, and hold the realization of its manifestation. Let's say you want a new car. Determine which car you want, believe it is yours now, and picture it in your mind.

Visualize driving it, parking it, seeing it in the safety of the garage, wash it and polish it, smell the newness of it, and be glad its yours – make it yours – thank God for it, believe and you will receive. Or perhaps visualize the conclusion of a successful transaction – see the contract lying on the table, see yourself signing it, keeping a copy and filing it away and know that it is what you wanted. Visualize the process, accept its reality, and know it's yours. Do the same thing with new curtains for the room, the achievement of a new job, promotion, rewards and recognition, or whatever. Don't do it once, or maybe twice; the power will come from two things, persistence, clarity of vision, and constancy and expectation.

The following quote is taken from *Conversations With God*, and aptly summarizes the process of creativity.

*What you think is what you get.*

*What you fear is what you will draw to you.*

*What you resist, persists.*

*What you look at disappears – giving you a chance to recreate it all over again, if you wish, or banish it forever from your experience.*

# PART THREE

# THE NEW AGE OF SPIRITUALITY

# 37

# THE WINDS OF CHANGE

There are cleansing and purifying winds sweeping the lands today, scouring and purifying the earth and our lives. The accumulated effects of twisted truths, misinformation and muddled thinking over the centuries have resulted in the enslavement of our minds to the will of man-made religions. But they are now in the process of readjustment and correction. Spirit is urging us to question long held and cherished beliefs and attitudes and start thinking for ourselves – a difficult thing to do when we have been brainwashed to believe illusion is truth. We are being encouraged to break free of our enslavement to convictions that have warped our understanding of spiritual truth, and recognize the deceptions that have held us in abject obedience for what they are – doctrines not of God, but of man. We are besieged with feelings that are forcing us to recognize the falseness of things we have long accepted as unassailable truth as being nothing but deceptions – will-o'the-wisps without substance.

It's a new wind of freedom and spiritual truth that is scouring our land. Christ has returned and has been making Its presence felt and known for some time. It has come like a thief in the night unseen by most, but heard and seen by a few who are spiritually attuned to the spirit of God. Christ is ushering in a new age of responsibility and love with new knowledge and understanding of the reality of God and our oneness with Him. We are being decontaminated of the lies and untruths of false prophets that we have been conditioned to believe are the inviolate words of God.

As in all the ages past and so in the present age, we were created free to follow the lead of our hearts and the will of our minds in the pursuit of oneness with God. We haven't been doing that because of fear of punishment by the forces of man-made religion, which is their God, the Church, should we transgress what we have been taught is sinful. The age in which we now live is the age of promise when we shall return to our true home with Mother/Father God waiting for us with loving and open arms. Like the willful son in the parable of the prodigal son, we have also made mistakes and lost our way, misled by choice and our own creations. But through it all with all its successes and failures, pains and gains, loves and losses we are beginning to accept our Godship and beginning the long walk to our true home from where we started.

People have been conditioned to assume that everything the church promotes and teaches is based on the inspired words of Jesus, when in reality most of it comes from within the hierarchical domain of the Church itself. Much of what was created in the developing years of the Church was inspired not by unassailable truth, but by the motivations and ambitions of self-serving men seeking to establish and protect their fief. Enslavement to illusion became our inheritance rather than freedom of love and truth that was promised by God. In the early four hundred years after Jesus, the growing Church subdued the minds and hearts of its members, and wrested control of its followers by creating and maintaining its authority through manipulation and the imposition of fear. That power has remained unassailable for 1600 years, and is only now being revealed for the false bastion of truth and spirit it is – a creation of its own worldly ambitions – a Tower of Babble that is crumbling.

When the mind has been conditioned to believe untruth is truth, that the Church can do no wrong, and that everything it says and does is sanctioned and approved by God, it is not hard to understand how people can be controlled in blind obedience, when even the slightest deviation from Church dogma would subject them to Divine wrath, and if severe enough, to hell. The Church has ruled by fear, and now that rule is being challenged and replaced with the love of Christ, for he has returned and is making himself known throughout the land. The winds of freedom are blowing. The freshening breeze of truth is seeping into the crevices and dark corners of our minds, cleansing and purifying with love all it touches. The rule of fear and illusion is being replaced with the love of Christ and the responsibility of the New Age. Christ has returned with Universal Love giving it freely to every one willing to receive it. It carries with it the growing understanding that much of what has long been accepted as truth is an illusion without probity, based not on the truths of God but on the self-serving definitions of man.

The promise of the New Age is upon us and it is being realized now. The change is not a sudden, overpowering transformation, but one that is being ushered in in slow and purposeful progressions of adjustment and renewal from the old to the new. It is a process of a purposeful and organized revolution orchestrated by God, accompanied with the inevitable upheavals and alterations of established beliefs and conditions that always accompany change.

When it is understood what change requires and what must occur when it comes upon us, we will no longer wonder why the world and mankind are now experiencing new fears, things unknown and not considered or concerned with in previous generations. Why there is such distress and destruction prevalent across the world today: wars, famine, pestilence, unknown and incurable diseases, mental anxieties and distress, depressions both financial and mental, earth upheavals, rampant nature determined to have its own way. All accompanied with the exposure of unbelievable acts of depravity and immorality in the political arenas of the world and within the hollowed chambers of churches – the supposedly untouchable bastions of love and purity.

263

These things now occurring in our world and in our lives are not whimsical acts of nature or of man run amok; nor are they punishments meted out to us for our sins as retribution by a vengeful God. These things are only necessary readjustments of both mankind and the earth itself, restoring all to health and to the original condition of wholeness and purity established by God when He made all that is – until man decided he could do it better and moved God aside.

The necessary cleansing and purification is seen everywhere: in the corporate offices of institutions once untouchable and respected; in politics where malfeasance of duty, corruption and disrespect for the Constitution is common and accepted with little censor by the populace; in the military and other institutions of authority where cheating and misuse of power is practiced; in education where opinion is taught as fact and teachers male and female seduce innocent children; in the police forces with bribery and dishonesty. And most reprehensible of all – in the Church, the supposed citadel of morality and probity, where the opposites of gross immorality including homosexual pedophilia is practiced and condoned without condemnation or punishment by the Church officials.

The burning fires of purifying crucibles across the land are not for punishment or aimless destruction, but for purification where the dross is burned off and nothing is left but the pure essence of God in our institutions and in our hearts and souls. In the process, nothing will be left untouched; all will be cleansed and purified.

There is always conflict in change because by its nature, it incorporates death as well as renewal. Change impregnates death with new life. With any birth there is travail and always carries with it discomfort and often severe pain, but it does not last and is soon forgotten. When change occurs it affects all of life, mental and material, man and earth. The change and the distress can be formidable and earth shaking, as we have been witnessing. We are in the midst of the change that was predicted by God, and it is affecting everything from our thoughts and desires to economics, prosperity, war and peace. We can accept it and live in peace, or we can resist it to our destruction. We can't stop it for it has already been set in motion, guided by the perfect pattern created by God in the beginning of time. But it's all to our benefit, all we have to do is to roll with the flow, knowing that God is with us and nothing can harm us if we live in faith and under His protection.

When change occurs there is always an end to the beginning. When and how it ends is determined not by God so much, as it is by those who are affected. The determining factor is our adjustment to the new spirituality which we are being gifted with, and how quickly we can throw off our old attachments to outmoded, destructive attitudes and practices, and absorb the new reality, blending with it to create a new spirituality, a new age of universal love, responsibility, peace and oneness with God.

God tells us that we shall reap what we have sown. Since we created what we are and what we are now experiencing, we should not resist what we are meeting, but accept it with gratitude in the understanding that there is growth spiritual and mental in the experience for our benefit. Once accepted without resistance, we should then release it and send it back to God. That will free us to create a new paradigm of our future. Our opportunity and responsibility to ourselves is to change or remove whatever no longer serves us well. In that freedom, is our opportunity to create or manifest in our lives what serves others and ourselves best.

# 38

# THE END TIMES

The end times that so many fear is misunderstood. It doesn't refer to the end of the world and life, but to the end of life as we have known it. The upheavals in the earth and in ourselves are the necessary readjustments of the negative energies we have created individually and collectively. We are currently experiencing the fruit of our plantings – the accumulated effects of the past thousands of years. Its purpose is for the restoration of the wholeness of the earth, and our spiritual selves so as to regain our original unity with God. The change is the turning point from the past two millennia that we are familiar and comfortable with, to the new millennium we're just entering. What lies ahead of us is a new era under the banner of responsibility and co-creativity with God. People fear this change because they don't understand. They're comfortable and complacent with what has always been constant and reliable in their lives, but now they're being shaken up and they don't like it. For those who do understand, and are united with God in faith and love, there is no room for fear.

Biblical predictions of the end times are not set in concrete. They are malleable, influenced by changing events and conditions – mostly by the spiritual qualities that are expressed in the collective thoughts and attitudes of mankind, with the most influential of them being love. Predictions are always predicated on present conditions, and they are only accurate if conditions remain as they were at the time of making them. They are never 100% accurate because all conditions are affected by man's free will, and when that will is exercised, events will change. Our thoughts and desires, our fears and emotions will all manifest and affect our future if they are allowed to persist long enough with no interference by a change of will or desire. Dire biblical predictions have changed because man has changed, becoming more spiritual, and contrary to appearance, in many ways less material. Hence, the Battle of Armageddon that has been so feared will not happen because we have recreated our future by way of increasing and expressing our developing spirituality. Therefore, what would have been, becomes what could have been, and is no longer viable. We are and experience what we individually and collectively create in our thoughts, fears and loves, and we can change and recreate them as we choose. Accordingly, there will be no final battle of Armageddon in the Valley of Megiddo; the streams will not be running blood; and one-third of mankind will not be destroyed in the world's final battle of obliteration. We have bypassed the need for it because mankind has collectively created a new energy of love that has changed the predicted course of events.

However, Armageddon in a modified form will still occur, but it will be not a singular battle on the plains in Palestine. Instead of one battle of annihilation, it will be six billion personal battles fought in the minds and hearts of each living human being all over the world. Every man woman and child is already in the process of fighting their personal battles of the forces of good against the forces of evil. In each of us, we will experience our own Armageddon, which is the war of our dual nature – the duality that is the warp and woof of all materiality: good and evil, love and fear, selfishness and selflessness – all the warring qualities of our positive and negative natures. Our battles will not be new to us, because we have been battling with our dual natures since the beginning of time. But now is the moment of truth, when each of us will engage in our personal and final battle of duality – that is the essence of Armageddon. As we each win our individual battles, we will enter the millennium as promised us, in peace and love.

It is natural when engaged in battle to believe that the battle has been won when one side has been defeated and the survivor is the victor. But such is not the case when dealing with duality. Victory will not be won with one party defeating the other. Victory can only come when neither is defeated; when there issues forth a balancing of the two in a union of complementary qualities – a balancing and harmonizing of our dual nature to become whole and complete in oneness with God. It will be a final balancing of opposing forces that have so ravaged our lands and lives – the balance that is found in Father/Mother God, and our peace and harmony not just of individuals but also of groups, families, associations, and nations.

The solving of differences has long been considered to be possible only in final battles for supremacy, but that does not bring peace. Lopsided victories are self-perpetuating root causes of distress and loss of peace. Peace can exist only if and when there is a merger of oppositions into the wholeness of unity and love.

The Armageddon that we have feared will not occur between warring nations or individuals, but between warring values and dualities within each of us. If victory should be the elimination of either the negative or positive qualities within us, there would result an imbalance that would become extreme in its manifestation, to our detriment. Either victor would become tyrannical and destructive if it were not kept in check by its opposition. In such cases, love could become conditional, demanding and controlling; zeal could become overzealous and self-righteous; charity could destroy self-initiative and self-respect. It is not necessary to suggest how evil could become increasingly destructive. It can be seen then that a balance of the opposing dualities is necessary. It could occur in an amalgamation of the two into a unity of oneness with God. We would become what God is – a wholeness, a gestalt of love that composites all qualities in a balance of power and creativity. A poor example could be one of opposing political parties. Should one achieve supreme power, gaining control of all branches of government without a counter-balance, it could be destructive to our country and our way of life. Political opposition is necessary to keep the majority party in balance and in harmony with the will of the people. Just so, it is also necessary for a parity of our dual natures.

Among the necessary changes occurring in our lives, the greatest of these are the changes occurring in the churches across the lands. Change is endemic in the religious communities of the world today. Differing sects are uniting, old differences are being erased, and commonality among men and systems of belief are increasingly recognized and stressed. Errors and weakness are being exposed; lies and deceptions and the bastardization of what Jesus taught are being revealed and reexamined for their misconceptions and lies; internal structures are being reorganized and reenergized. The sins of the fathers – our priests, bishops, evangelists, pastors and teachers of the ages and of today, are being exposed for all the world to see and weep over. Judgment is upon the church, but it is the judgment that comes with the reaping of what the church body has sown. God is not mocked.

Change is in the air and brings with it a new world order – a new spirit of universal love, responsibility, freedom and co-creativity with God. What has been going on behind the veils of darkness and self-righteousness in our churches are being exposed to the purifying light of truth. Judgment is coming to the perpetrators and is brought on not by God, but by the perpetrators themselves – the sowers of the seeds. They are picking the sour fruit of what they planted in years past.

People have been conditioned to assume that everything the church teaches and does, are the same things taught by Jesus during his ministry, when in reality the dogma and doctrines of what came to be called the Catholic Church, originated in the secret chambers of the Church-mind itself. Their contrived dogma has given the Church power to hold their congregants in strict obedience and loyalty. Its power is derived from the imposition of fear based on the threat of eternal damnation. When that is understood, it can easily be grasped how the church has been able to retain its control over the minds of it's congregations for 2000 years. But that control is eroding and steadily slipping away.

People are growing in sophistication and are no longer accepting what the Church has been feeding them carte blanche for two millennia, without seriously questioning the truth and accuracy of what they've been told. They are growing suspicious of what they see as apparent contradictions between what is heard and what is seen and felt, and are wondering what to believe, no longer certain of what truth is and what it is not. They're looking for answers, and they are not finding them in their churches.

Jesus did not establish a religion; he did not formulate Christianity. But he did show us the way to unity with our Mother/Father through his examples, and urged us to understand that what he was and did is within our ability to do and be also. Didn't Peter walk on water? He started to sink not because of inability but because of doubt. In *The Universal Gospel of Jesus the Christ,* Jesus is quoted as saying, *"My human life was wholly given to bring my will to tune with the deific will; when this was done my earth tasks all were done...All my life was for the sins of men. I lived to show the possibilities of man. What I have done, all men can do, and what I am all men shall be."*

Jesus simply called attention to the church *within* – the Temple of God. Although he said: *"Thou art Peter, and upon this rock, I will build my church,"* it was not meant to be what the church has made it to be. Peter symbolized faith, dedication, loyalty, strength and purpose. It was meant to symbolize the staunch faith and intuitive understanding that Peter exemplified, which would be the rock, or foundation of the church. It was not meant that Peter would be the first in a long line of successive bishops that would develop a religion around what they have come to erroneously believe Peter represented, and wherein the Bishop of Rome, the Pope, is considered the Christ on earth.

Jesus was not determined by men to be the Christ; he earned it through his obedience and sacrifice, but more than that, he became the Christ by the will of God. The Pope is declared the

271

Christ by the will of assembled Cardinals.

The wrong interpretation of Jesus' statement of Peter being the rock on which the Church would be built, has culminated in a lineage of clergy that have over the centuries created an institution that has abased the purity and wholeness of Jesus' example. In its claims of papal infallibility and unsupported assertion of God's under-girding support for the Church, the Church has desecrated itself. It has misused its power to ensure obedience and enslavement to false doctrines, rather than to freedom of belief and exploration of truth and true spirituality.

The religions that men have established as institutions of faith and worship mostly emphasize the human side of mankind rather than the spiritual. As a result, their philosophies stress material needs and interests, expressed in social and humanistic programs that de-emphasize the spiritual core of religion. The church has been de-spiritualized and humanized in the process.

Some individual churches have grown so large that their congregations can be numbered in the thousands. They are so huge, they sprawl across the grounds in campus-like settings of many buildings. They have programs for this and others for that, trying to cater to all the social, cultural and human needs and interests of their congregants. And that may be wonderful, and that may be good, but where in all this is the balance? Do they have programs that have as their *primary* aim the uplifting of spirit in the spiritualizing of man, of helping people to find God's presence and truth within themselves, of personalizing their relationship with God – *of becoming one with God and co-creators with Him?* Are there any churches, large or small, that mention, or yet stress such possibilities? Do they teach the Truth of God, and the pure intent of Jesus, rather than the conjured philosophies and dogma of worship and ritual formulated by men and not God?

The foundations of trust have eroded and the Church is undergoing a crisis of faith and fidelity. We hear preachers and priests at the altars, and evangelists on stage at their microphones, all praising morality and we find immorality behind the veil. We hear the preaching of humility and see vanity and arrogance of power. We see quantity over quality. Rather than using spiritual growth as an indicator of success, the size of congregations and overflowing collection plates are the measurements too often used. We hear of the benevolence of giving and see the accumulation of riches of greedy clergy and evangelists. We hear of honesty but hear false teachings and see misuse of Church funds. We are taught to respect truth, and are told lies. It's no wonder why there is a falling church membership coupled with an increased interest and participation in New Age movements. People want and need truth, and they're going within to find it. They are realizing the truth in God's promise that the truth will set them free. The time is right and it is upon us. The time is now.

# 39

# THE NEW AGE OF RESPONSIBILITY

The spiritual evolution of mankind has gone through several levels of development. The first recorded change was the dispensation of law about 4000 years ago as a response to developing human consciousness. It was implemented when Moses was selected by God to lead the Israelites out of bondage in Egypt. For forty years over 600,000 Israelites walked the desert while being subjected to a spiritual cleansing, creating a new spirituality through the shedding of old beliefs of multiple gods, and a creation of a new belief of law under one God. What was accomplished has lasted 4000 years, held together by a system of law that regulated behavior and allegiance to the One God of Moses. Its most notable feature was the Ten Commandments, on which the rule of law rested.

The second major change occurred when the rule of law gave way to universal love and forgiveness two thousand years after Moses, again prompted by the changing consciousness of mankind. Jesus was the prophet who established this new dispensation in Israel among the Jews. It spread throughout the entire Mediterranean area, eventually converting all of Europe, and finally the western world, in a new age of universal love.

The revelation of each of the dispensations was revealed and promulgated by a single person. Moses became the father of the Hebrew religion based on law, and Jesus became the progenitor of a religion based on love and forgiveness. In each case a single person established the basis of the respective belief system.

The era of law, and later of love, were dispensations of God. Both were responses to developing human consciousness. As mankind evolved, so too did the introduction of new teachings and teaching energy. The dispensations changed to meet the developing needs of mankind.

Over time, the pure intent of Jesus was distorted by the followers to become a rigid system of belief and regulations that stifled our innate right of freedom of expression and worship. Their efforts, though well meaning in some cases, were too often outright manipulations for personal gain and power. In general, they resulted in a mechanistic system of worship without spirit, void of direct communion with God. It has created in Christians a stultifying reliance on what the clergy mistakenly tells us is truth. We are discouraged from assuming any responsibility for our own spiritual understanding and growth.

But now, mankind is at a new stage in soul development where we are given the opportunity to write for ourselves the new text of spiritual enlightenment. It is a time when it is incumbent upon us to assume responsibility for our own lives and the future that will result. We are no longer beholden to the past, or to what we want the future to be; we are now in the Now, and the instructions for the Now must come from the new energy sources, where they are to be found at the core level of our new consciousness, which is our higher mind.

Mankind has reached a level of spiritual development where it is no longer necessary or desirable for us to continue to be led by another person. We are no longer sheep that need to follow a shepherd whose responsibility it is to see to our growth, and to protect and guide us in everything we do, even our thoughts. There is no freedom in that, and without freedom to choose and apply according to what we feel is best for us, which is our right to succeed or fail, thereby creating and establishing our unique individuality of expression and being, there is no way we will ever become co-creators with God. We must exercise our free will, and to do that we must be free to choose.

There must be a change in our beliefs and in the application of God's Truth, and the time for that change is upon us. We are at the beginning of a new millennium, which is the new age of responsibility. This dispensation is not brought to us fully formed by a new avatar or spiritual master, such as occurred with Moses and the Commandments, or with Jesus' teachings, crucifixion and resurrection. It is not a system ordained by God; there is no dogma and no rules and regulations. There is no plan, no program or teachings that we are to follow; there is only freedom and responsibility. There is only that which is being brought up out of our higher minds, inspired and guided by the Universal Mind, or God.

No single person is birthing this new world. No one person is responsible for this divine dispensation. We, you and I, are the avatars, the prophets of this new age. It is being brought into material reality by the collective consciousness of all mankind. Its matrix, or pattern is the composite of our collective desires and thinking. We are the progenitors of this new age, and it is we who shall determine what it will be, and it is we who are responsible for its birth and survival.

God has given us the responsibility to create this new world, using the divine power that is inherent within us – to express ourselves as the Gods and Godesses we are. All our many lives throughout the millennia have been spent learning of our divinity and how to live and create in the will of God. It is now time to learn again what we have forgotten, and to use what we have learned and to be responsible for its expression. We have written the past, and now it is time to let the past write our future. We are to forget what we have long held to be sacrosanct and begin to live in the new texts that we are beginning to write ourselves. We must go within to the new information sources that are at the core level of our new consciousness.

The age of law gave way to the age of love; and now the age of love is giving way to the age of responsibility. Whether we like it or not, it's our baby and it is up to us to mold its character, and how it shall express its maturity. But whatever, this new age is here to stay to become a world system of equality and freedom for all of mankind, based on a new era of responsibility to us and to others. It is now in the labor of its birthing. Here and there one can already see its fruits. Seeds are being planted all around the world; some are freshly planted, some are showing shoots, and some are already yielding their fruit.

We have a responsibility to society, to family and to those "not like us." Our responsibility is to let our light so shine that others can see God within us. Then they can see themselves in our light and be cooperative and honor their individuality and their free choice. We will grow to respect differences and acknowledge our right and obligation to be ourselves in whatever way we wish to express our own Godhood.

We have an equal responsibility to Earth – the land we breed on and live with – the land that gives us our nourishment, beauty, peace and plenty. The earth is alive; it is vibrant, and it has a consciousness. As the scientists of botany have proven that plants have a consciousness, it is equally a fact, although on a far grander scale, that our planet does also. We must live with it in appreciation for all its diversity and individuality; we should value it, care for it, and waste it not; we should respect it, give to it and it will give back to us.

## WE ARE RESPONSIBLE TO *NOW*

The United States was established on a firm base of responsibility to God and each other. Lincoln reaffirmed this responsibility by declaring the equality of all men and their right to be themselves in whatever manner they choose. The pioneer families established an ocean-to-ocean nation that rested firmly on a foundation of responsibility and mutual concern and tolerance. We have fought wars to preserve our individual rights of freedom and responsibility. Our nation has grown and thrived in a manner unprecedented by any other nation in the known history of the world. It is no accident. God has looked upon us with favor, not because we are a chosen people, but because of our compassion and sharing of what we have with the less fortunate. The foundation on which our nation was built is evidenced on our coins – *In God we Trust,* and in the Pledge of Allegiance: ...*One nation under God.*

Our forefathers assumed their responsibility, individually and collectively, with concern for the survival of all. Among our dispensations of responsible acts were the expressions of self-responsibility, religious tolerance for others, and personal and institutional responsibilities for society, families and groups of all ethnicities and persuasions. We were weaned as a nation of giving without conditions, a nation of sharing without expectations, of respect for individual rights, and of self-respect – all expressed in stability, strength, and unsurpassed energy. We have spiritual foundations with allegiance to a God of love and protection, expressed in a myriad of ways with religious tolerance for all.

But we are now a nation under attack – both by outside forces and by insidious forces within our borders. We are self-destructing because we have become a nation of dependents – with diminishing responsibility for the caring and nurturing of ourselves and others. Our liberty has become dependency; freedom has become license, doing as we wish, how we wish and to whom we wish in a deteriorating sense of individual or corporate and collective responsibility with little or no concern for the rights and welfare of others or ourselves. As individual responsibility has deteriorated, so also has individual freedom. We are becoming a nation of dependents, living in fear and self-defeat, unwilling to assume responsibility for our creations. In the willingness to let others assume control over us, we are losing freedom and self-respect.

Responsibility finds expression in stability, strength, energy and spirituality. It is responsibility to God, to society and family. And it is responsibility to outsiders – those who are not in our little inner circles – persons who are different from us with different outlooks, beliefs, cultures, skin color or whatever may mark them as "different."

We have a responsibility to the world and to the society in which we live and are a part of, and this includes all the varied religions of the world. We have a responsibility to those who differ from us in philosophies and worship. We should let the light within us so shine that others can see the God-self within us. Thus in His light expressing through us, they may see themselves as the Gods we all are. We should be non-judgmental and honor their individuality and their free choice – to respect differences and acknowledge the right and obligation to be themselves in whatever way they wish to express their Godhood.

We are responsible to *now,* for *now* is our life. We should live not in the past, for that is gone, over, and cannot affect us unless we let it. The future is not yet, and therefore can't affect us, unless we live it in constant expectation of what is hoped for or feared to be. The now is our reality, our only reality; all else is illusion. It is in the now that we express what we are and in which we lay the foundations of what shall be.

Our first responsibility is to ourselves – to be what we want to be and to create our reality and our future. We owe to ourselves the respect of caring for our body, the exercising of our mind, and in keeping our thoughts and desires in line with self-less love for all of God's creations. But our greatest responsibility and opportunity, is to know that *we* are Gods. Realize that the words of the Bible speak to us when it asks, *Know ye not that ye are Gods?* In this acceptance, lies our creativity and our ever-present now. In this knowing, we are all power, all abundance, all strength, all health, and all love – we are the all in all, one in ourselves and one in God. We are truly a grand creation, a grand people and a grand nation, and it is ours to take the seed of our Godhood, nurture it, protect it and make of it what we will.

This is a concept new to us, even though Jesus tried to tell us this truth. We rejected it then, and we mostly reject it now. The

Catholic Church in a trickle down effect has permeated all churches and sects with the belief that we are innately evil, based in the false teachings that we are born in original sin and unworthy to even approach God in any kind of equality. Hence we are inferior and unworthy of God's love and attention. We have been conditioned to live in fear of God who is love, afraid to express our true selves, and live by our true divine nature.

Jesus taught us through his examples and his teachings that we are his equal; if we are his equal and he is a Son of God, then so are we. Remember, it says *The temple of God is within.* He told us that we can do what he did, and as he said, even greater things. That is truth! But we don't believe it – we won't even consider it. When we accept our responsibility to our self, when we believe in our divinity, and exercise our creativity in harmony with the will of God, there is *nothing* that will be kept from us, and nothing we will be unable to accomplish. We will be all things, able to create all things; we will be love in its grandest form of selflessness without conditions – we will then be Christed and one with God. We, His prodigal children, will then be home with our Mother/Father God and receive the inheritance of power, love and creativity that is rightfully ours.

# 40

# *THE NEW CHURCH*

As mankind evolves, changes occur with or without approval, or with or without understanding of what is happening. When there is no understanding, changes will still occur but not necessarily with acceptance and often met with suspicion and intolerance. That is so in every area and every aspect of life and expression – whether in science, personal relations, human temperament or addictions, but most noticeably in religion.

There are many forms of spiritual expression in the world, ranging from primitive shamanist systems of communion with God, to the sophisticated world-wide paradigms of religious faith. Christianity is but one such form of spiritual expression among the world's major religions. Whether we believe that Christianity is truth or not; whether it is for our good and for the good of others or not; or whether we are comfortable in our belief or not, it remains our belief. It's an ingrained part of us, and we will resist any attempt to change. It's part of us because we have been conditioned to believe certain things in certain ways, and to deny it, is to deny ourselves. The illusions of what we believe are our reality.

We're always more accepting of what we are familiar with, than of something new and unknown. And it matters not whether changes come from a highly respected source of the world's sciences and politics, from theology and religion, or from within our own higher God-self.

Change is seldom welcome, but without change there can be no life, for life is growth and growth is change in a constant state of evolution from the lesser to the greater. When change is thwarted, or prohibited, apathy can set in and we become hog-tied to tired, outmoded and ineffective systems of attitudes and beliefs, even when they have not been for our good. In spite of gut-feelings that prod change, we succumb to the indolence of thoughtless loyalty to the familiar because we are ruled by fear. Fear of change is a bondage to sameness, drabness and failure in everything we are or do.

Religion has taught us, maybe conditioned is a better term, to accept and not question what we have been taught is truth. Each religion and each church within the religions, have their own and different interpretation of truth, but nevertheless, in the minds of their defenders, they each alone have THE truth. We accept the declarations of our particular church without examination or investigation, and then we base our spiritual lives on what we are told. Our structural system of attitudes, worship, spiritual understanding or misunderstandings, and our hope of salvation are all founded on something that we don't know for certain if it's truth or not. When we assume it's truth we're stuck with it, and nothing will dissuade us. We are taught to fear anything other that what we have been conditioned to accept as truth, so in our obedience to fear, we don't question.

Yet there grows within each and every one of us, at some time or another, an emptiness not understood and not questioned, and it's accepted without consideration of its import and what it could mean to us. We are complacent in our beliefs; comfortable with our mental stations in life and with our tolerance of being shepherded with all the other sheep who don't think for themselves. We await our instructions complacently on what to believe and how to express it in worship, and do our best not to question, but obey. We have mistakenly put our trust in the idea that our pastor or priest should know what they're telling us. Haven't they gone through religious training, don't they know the Bible by rote and can spout off verse after verse (often taken out of context) to support their beliefs? Yes, they're sincere, but they are also too often wrong in their basic understandings because they believe without questioning what they have been taught by others who teach what they have been taught by teachers who teach as they were taught, on down the line to the originators of their particular system of belief and worship. And the promulgators of the faiths? Where did they get their knowledge of what they say is truth? Did their beliefs originate when they might have heard the voice of God? Was what they heard, their own thoughts based on their fears, desires, or vanity? Or did they like a good writer, concoct a fable and present it as truth?

The Church, and all churches in all religions, have been very effective in planting in man their ideas of truth and what they believe man's relationship to God should be, and how we should live and conduct our lives. The Christian churches have had 2000 years of faulty leadership of their members. But in all that time they have not freed men from their ignorance of God's truth. They have rather, impounded error upon error, leading us ever deeper into false beliefs fed by fear and sustained by threats of hell and damnation. Their method of saving our souls is not effective and never will be, because it is based on lies and self-serving motives; that, plus the over-riding fact that there is nothing to be saved from!

The Church has become mired in self-serving protectionism, setting the needs of mankind aside in order to protect its quirks and privileges. But its time of supremacy over the lives of men is coming to an end. The Church cannot long survive as it is presently structured. It must give way to the new order of things, led by the responsibility of all men to care for themselves.

Belief systems throughout the world are in turmoil and are in the beginning stages of major changes. Their old ways will no longer work and will be restructured and re-energized. They may very likely remain under the same name with the same founding prophet or avatar, but not as they are currently structured. They must and will revert to the original teachings of their particular prophet without additions and embellishment. When once again in the purity of original dispensations from God, they will realize that all religions bespeak the same God, and that there is no difference in their essential relationship with God, and in this there is no essential difference between men of different faiths. Differences will disappear; harmony, mutual respect and goodwill will prevail in their discovery of unity in the one God.

The churches have always talked about the love of God, but they consistently preach a God of judgment and punishment. These systems of belief are not self-destructing as much as they are being reconstructed. They are in the process of rebuilding what they have almost destroyed – the trust of those who follow them. There may always be a need for organized religion, but the new religions will have to meet a more spiritual and discerning humanity.

People are starting to think for themselves and as they do, they realize that what they have been told, no longer satisfy the demands of the new age of responsibility. They are looking around at others, at their church, at their own established beliefs and attitudes and opinions, and they're seeing that something is not right. To quote a well used cliche, *"There's something rotten in the state of Denmark"*. They're taking their blinders off and are seeing their religion and their church with a clearer vision. No longer satisfied with the misteachings and deceits they have been fed, they're asking questions and demanding answers. They're becoming dissatisfied with their dependency on what the churches have been telling them and want to find the truth for themselves. They are beginning to feel a spark of their inner divinity, and are building a new faith on that. People are beginning to understand that they can communicate with God directly when they open themselves to Him, and realize that they are equally able to touch God's garment and to receive from Him his healing truth without needing to go through intermediaries of the Church.

The Church as it has been known for 2000 years is dying, and doing so with the blessing of God, because it has been a carrier not of truth but of truth misshapen with lies, deceits, and the misrepresentation of the words of Jesus. But all is not doom and gloom, for it is to be remembered that new life always follows death in a natural continuum of the essence of life and spirit. The demise of the Church as we know it, will rebirth in a new reality, a new structure, stronger, truer, more spiritual and vibrant than before. With the right attitudes and intentions, the Church will survive, but in a different form and with different expressions of its new role as a facilitator of God's truth, rather than as a shepherd and protector determining for its sheep what is best for them.

Catholicism is breathing hard trying to catch a second wind but with a great deal of difficulty. It is self-destructing because of its deceits and excesses, most noticeably in its immorality and arrogance. It has proved many times over that it would rather protect its vested interests and power by showing greater concern for itself, than it does for the welfare of its people. The innocence of little children has been destroyed, deliberately entrapped by the immoral licentiousness of the clergy. Their experiences have created life-long emotional trauma that has resulted from being sexually abused by "men of God," and *condoned by their Bishops.*

Ministers, evangelists, elders, bishops, cardinals and the Pope have always known what was occurring in their respective dioceses and neighborhood churches. It is impossible to believe otherwise. Protestant and Catholic Churches alike, too often turned their face away from the light of truth exposing their own internal rot, trying to hide from the world and themselves the horror that the churches have perpetrated on the children of God. The world is beginning to hold them accountable for what they teach and practice.

The Church we have known is swaying on rotting foundations. It can be saved but only if it is willing to look within and see itself as God sees it. The churches will have to remove their rose-colored glasses and the blinders from their eyes and see in truth and humility what they have become. They will have to recognize and accept that they are not the chosen of God, for there are none that are chosen; God does not have favorites. They will have to realize that what they are, and what they have been teaching are bastardized versions of what Jesus taught, promulgated not by Jesus, or by God, but by their own self-serving predecessors, nourished by the next in line, and maintained by themselves. They will question the veracity and infallibility of their respective leaders, past and present, and their ecclesiastical congresses. The Catholics will no longer accept the Pope as an infallible channel of God, or as the Christ on earth.

The belief systems all over the world are not necessarily on their way out. Instead, they're in the process of rebuilding their foundations and the trust of their followers. There will always be a need for organized religion, but it will need to change, enabling them to meet a more discerning and spiritual humanity. Although the progress is slow, there is an awakening and progress is being made.

Their change, if it is to be successful, will require a complete reorganization starting with humility and acceptance of their vulnerability. Then they will have to become like the rich man who wanted to follow Jesus, but was told that he would first have to give all he had to others. So too will the church have to divest itself of its treasures – its riches, entitlements and power that serve no other purpose than to acquire more riches and more power and grander cathedrals. It will have to go deep within and find the humility and truth of what Jesus taught, and no longer jealously guard and protect their conjured interpretations and additions to his teachings.

People are going to have to be willing to accept God in place of the Church as their personal guide and no longer consider their pastors and priests as the mouthpieces of God, from whom they have accepted without questioning what they have been told is His truth. Clergy will no longer be shepherds of flocks, but way-showers who in humility and honesty will help others grow in knowledge and understanding, showing the way to personal relationships with God. In the cliché of today, they will have to "walk their talk." But first, they will have to know themselves as God knows them in truth and humility. When they are able to love without conditions or expectations, and love and respect themselves for what they are in truth, accepting their bad with their good, then they will be qualified to assume the mantle of lightbearer for those who are seeking the truth but stumbling in the darkness of ignorance. They will be light-bearers, holding high the burning torch of truth.

# 41

# WHAT LIES AHEAD

We are increasingly aware of the inadequacies and inconsistencies in what religion teaches. Evidence is mounting that what we have been taught by the Church, is not necessarily what Jesus taught. It is being revealed that much or most of Church doctrine is based on misunderstandings and outright falsification of the original teachings of Jesus. Indeed the very foundation of Christian religion, is based on the revisionist policies of the early Church, and is being revealed at its best as mistakes, and at its worst, fabrication and willful distortion.

Proof of this abounds everywhere. It is found in the cloisters of monks, in the catacombs of religious institutions, in the vaults of libraries accessible only to theologians and scholars, and in the archives of the Vatican, available to none but a privileged few. But there is a source that is available to all who earnestly desire and seek it. It is found lying in the higher recesses of the mind, festering and impatiently awaiting its revelation.

Among the many alterations and aberrations the early church made to truth when first selecting and organizing the many books that would compose the Bible, and then following the original compilation with the rewriting of it, decisions were made to remove certain passages, and even entire books. These included the Gnostic Gospels. Some of which were the Gospels of Mary, Thomas, Judas and Enoch; and all references to reincarnation and the twelve lost years of Jesus' life. Perhaps the most eye-awakening evidence of inaccuracy is found in the Dead Sea Scrolls, found to be authentic and historically accurate, which rips apart many of the long held beliefs and assumptions regarding Jesus and his ministry.

There is proof in ancient Tibetan manuscripts that Jesus was there during his lost years undergoing further training. There are records in ancient Hindu and Persian texts that Jesus was there as well; and evidence in Egypt that he received his initiation in the Great Pyramid of Giza. These were times during which Jesus received in-depth education and instruction that trained and prepared him for the role he was born to play in the upliftment of mankind. Furthermore, in the old Toltec and Aztec Indian traditions there is evidence that their revered blonde-haired, blue-eyed God, Quetzalcoatl, may have been Jesus who is purported to have walked the Central American region at a time approximate to Jesus' years on Earth.

The truth is coming out and it's rattling the foundations of our cherished institutions. It is especially noticeable in the major Christian religions. A lot of soul searching is going on creating dis-ease and fear among the theologians and clergy, and distrust among the lay people. Something is going on, and the people are wondering what it is and why it's happening. Everything they believed in and trusted is being questioned, and they're frightened. In the many sects of Christian religion, most noticeably the Catholic Church, they are being exposed for their hypocrisy, and are being forced to regroup to reconsider long held doctrines. Bishops are beginning to display discreet opposition to the Pope – telling evidence of dissatisfaction of existing policies and practices. Revelations of lies, deceits, immorality and misuse of power for selfish purposes are exposing the rot within the hallowed halls of the gilded sanctuaries of Catholicism.

Other sects of Christian religion and their various churches are also under attack by concerned people. Recalling that they are after all, offspring of their Catholic parentage, it is no wonder that they too are being examined in the light of truth. All dogma and doctrine that Christianity has accepted as sin, original sin, hell, punishment, absolution, forgiveness and judgment have their roots in the early teachings and fabrications made by the Catholic Church. It leaves people wondering what the truth is about God and Life, and where do they fit into it. They have been conditioned to believe that God is a fearful God, full of retribution and punishment. They have little or no understanding and slight appreciation that God is love, that He does not judge nor punish, and that there is no hell. They don't understand that these things could not be if God is love. It would be impossible for Him to punish and condemn any of His children to an eternity of agony and pain, simply for errors made when learning to use the free will that He gave them and wants them to develop.

It is only through the exercise of free will that we learn to become united with God. Errors will be made, mistakes will be compounded, corrections are certain, spirituality will increase, and we, each and every one of us, will in our own time, stumble and curse, laugh and cry, as we doggedly follow the winding and tortuous path home from where we started our long journey of soul. But we will persist and we will find our way back. We are Prodigal Children, and our Mother/Father awaits us with love and open arms.

The groundswell of purification that began in the churches as a ripple in the ocean of complacency and fear, is increasing in speed and size and in its fury will soon crash upon the shores of our splintering religions. And like the Flood of Noah's time, there will be a cleansing and a restructuring of religion and the Church.

Peter Steinfels, in his book, *People Adrift: the Crisis of the Roman Catholic Church in America,* states that the choices for the Church are stark: "Irreversible decline or a thoroughgoing transformation." He states that portents of this are seen in the decline of the number of priests and nuns who are resigning in great numbers. In 1950 the ratio of priests to the number of Catholics was one in 652; in 2000 the ratio fell to one for every 1257 Catholics. The nuns in the religious orders fell by half of what they were in 1950. It is seen in the intense resistance among Catholic laypeople regarding the Papal instruction that restricts sexual union only to the acts of procreation. Another and perhaps the final denouement is the decline of the moral basis of the Church as revealed in the sexual abuse scandals of priestly pedophilia that rocked the world recently.

The Catholic Church rests on a foundation of quicksand. Its cathedral of power and legalism is being sucked under by its own weight, forcing a re-examination of intent and practices. The de-spiritualization of the Church has infected all other Christian sects as well, because their inherent structures reflect that of the parent Church. No church from the smallest to the grandest, from the neighborhood to the universal, is immune from the cleansing and purifying effects of the new age of reformation that we now live in.

The Church is like the Leaning Tower of Pisa – a structure that when built, stood tall in beauty and grace, but now in its later years is seen standing askew. Its stability is an illusion. From one perspective it still seems to stand tall, retaining its original beauty and structural integrity, but from another, it is seen to lean precariously about ready to fall. Extensive examination and reconstruction of the tower's foundation, is comparable to the Church's unstable foundation of morality and intent. In both cases, it may be too late for there is still the possibility that both may collapse of their own weight.

The theological foundation of Christianity must also be re-examined because its rationale too often rests on power, greed and misleading and self-serving doctrine. Its conjured systems of worship and faith are not of God, nor of Jesus, but of men. It will be a painful examination because the Church must dissect the core of its religious expressions without evasion or reservation, and in full acceptance of what they find. They must see what they have done to the pure teachings of Jesus, and how they have destroyed his concept of universal love, freedom, non-judgment, forgiveness, and responsibility. But most especially, how it has all but destroyed our innate freewill and oneness with God, and enslaved us to the Church. It has worked against rather than for our right and inborn ability to communicate with God on a one-to-one basis. In its place, they substituted church appointed intermediaries, or go-betweens, between God and us because in their estimation, we are not worthy to be in direct contact with God. It's ironic that the priesthood that is guilty of homosexual pedophilia, is worthy of such direct contact, whereas the rest of us are not.

The Church must see itself as God sees it in all Truth; it must accept the bitter along with the sweet, and change what must be changed if it is to survive. The Church must be restructured and strengthened to reflect the Truth of God and the purity of Jesus' message to the world. It must be cleansed and purified of its adulterated conjurations of fear and power, and be infused with the transparency of love and forgiveness if its foundation is to stabilize and the Church is to be saved. Time is of the essence, and the time is now.

Much of what has long been accepted as God's truth is being shown to be not God's truth at all, but false truth as fabricated by man in the expressions of religiosity. A new spirituality is birthing and nothing will be able to stop it. The time of transition and change is upon us; it is discomfiting and not at all to our liking, but it will not be diverted nor stopped for it is God's will that it be accomplished. It is we who must change. When we discover the truth and accept it, we will change automatically for it is to our benefit to do so, and it is then that we will realize the fulfillment of God's promise that the truth shall set us free.

Error compounds error; power feeds on power; religions perpetuate themselves in false beliefs, arrogance and self-righteousness. But no longer will the reins of power remain in the hands of the few priestly elite; it will be expressed through the hands of the many. We have been conditioned to believe ill of ourselves, to see ourselves in the shadow of the Church, with lesser light, lesser power, lesser ability, and the minutest understanding of our strength and glory. But no more! The light of God is within us, not in a church. It is God's brilliant light radiating from us that we should follow, not the shadow-light of a man-made institution. We can undo the indoctrinations and conditioning imposed upon us by religion by going within to the Source, finding there the truth of what we are and who we are. We can then establish an unbreakable communication with God our Mother/Father, never again needing someone else to tell us what to believe and how to live. Never again will we be subjected to the will of others for we will learn to exercise our own will, determining and creating for ourselves our reality and how we wish to express it. Power will continue to be exercised, but it will not be the power imposed upon us by a select few as it has been. It will be the collective, unified power of families of light, of individuals manifesting desires through co-creativity with God.

The new church will facilitate this. No longer will the clergy be shepherds but facilitators, showing us through their examples and wisdom how we can become Christed as Jesus was, and how we can become one with God in love and co-creativity as he was. They will be way-showers, not shepherds that confine us to an isolated meadow of spiritual nourishment, guarded and held there by the shepherd's dogs of doctrine. No longer will we be fed a restricted diet based on what they provide, preventing us under the banner of protection from straying away from their paddock of dogma. On our own, we will be free to explore the bountiful meadows of life that Love has provided. We shall be free to explore any and all pastures rich in resources and potentials, choosing what we believe is the best nourishment for our soul, free to become what we choose to be. In this freedom we will become one with God, and it is only in this freedom, in the uninhibited exercise of free will, that it will be possible. But first we must remove the shackles of indoctrination.

# 42

# THE DAWN OF A RISING SUN

A new age is upon us. It is the millennium as prophesied many centuries ago, the promise that mankind has long awaited in a mixture of hope and fear. It is the new age of love and peace, but it has come upon us not in expressions of love but in a rampage of terror and hate, and we don't know what to make of it. We see changes everywhere, but they are not the changes we had hoped would greet us but what we had feared as we entered the year 2000. In our limited understandings, the changes seem to be not as improvements in our material and spiritual lives, but as the destruction of what we have long revered and respected. It helps to understand that often a new edifice is sometimes built on the destroyed remnants of the old. The walls of our institutions are crumbling: social, political, religious, morals and mores are undergoing reevaluation and restructuring. Our values are in a collision course with changing realities. But on the rubble of the old, a new city and a new future will arise.

What we see is not the reality of the New Age, but the illusions of reality based on misunderstanding and fear – fear of the unknown. This new age, of which we are a part, willingly or unwillingly, is a new age of spirituality, a new era of freedom and responsibility to self and to others. We are experiencing the dawn of a rising sun that will illuminate the world in its golden rays of peace. It will enlighten not only our little cubicles of communities, cultures and institutions, but all that is, impregnating all nations and cultures with new understandings and values. Nothing and no one will be exempt from the inevitable changes.

Appearances often give a false picture of what is experienced. The shift from an age of comfortable dependency on the government and God to do for us what we are able, and should do for ourselves, brings with it a new standard of self-responsibility. It is feared, but it should not be, for it brings with it opportunities of freedom and creativity. It's a new reality in which we will each be responsible to do for ourselves what we have heretofore relied on others to do for us. We will no longer be rooted to conditions beyond our control. We will create for ourselves new lives of health, prosperity, love and peace. The world will be reborn in new understandings and acceptance of responsibility with unconditional love for all of mankind. It cannot be stopped. But before these seeds of revolution can be rooted and flower, the ground must be tilled and the weeds of resistance and complacency removed. Much of the old must first be revised, reenergized, rebuilt or destroyed. The old must prepare the way for the new.

There is great resistance to this change. Fear is building a wall of hate and denial of what must be and will be, and of what must first be implemented to expedite the needed alterations of attitudes and illusions. Nevertheless, the world will be reborn in new understandings of what responsibility really means, of what unconditional love really entails, and what respect, compassion, and non-judgment of others really holds for all peoples. Not until it is understood and applied by every individual of every religion, of every political persuasion, and of every personal, social and cultural belief, will there ever be the peace that God has promised the world.

In the past, change was oftentimes achieved only with the use of forceful persuasion, which was too often translated into coercion, often military. That has happened too many times in our world history for it to be denied. War is not pretty, and is usually inflicted on peaceful people against their will, such as what America has experienced too many times. But the wars we have fought have all been in the defense of freedom, and lately for the preservation or establishment of freedom for other people who could not do it without our help. Some examples are: Grenada, Panama, Slovakia, Kuwait, Afghanistan and Iraq. Of course this list must include the major wars: WW I, WW II, Korea and Vietnam. Vietnam may or may not have been a just war, but it was entered into with the intent of protecting our freedom from the unrelenting and feared encroachment of a spreading communism. Although the result was not what we had hoped, the intent was good.

Wars have traditionally been fought along the time-honored system of open attack and counterattack with the opposing forces in direct contact with each other. But that kind of war is no more. The new wars are unpredictable battles of insidious strikes of terrorists where there is no concern for innocent civilians including women and children, where slaughter is the desired option. Our enemy is filled with hate and has but one goal – the total obliteration of freedom and all governments and religious beliefs other than theirs. There is not one single country or nation, including Germany, Russia, France and Canada that will not eventually meet the hateful wrath of religious zealots if terrorism is not stopped. A stand has to be made, and it has been struck.

The enemy is devious and strikes unbidden, unheralded and without warning. Our greatest enemy now is the Islamic extremists. They justify their hate with the doctrinal misinterpretations of their revered Quran. There are terrorists elsewhere in varied lands, whose incentive is political such as Chechens fighting against Russia for political freedom, using terrorism as a tool of war. A terrorist does not listen to reason, for reason does not exist outside the narrow confines of their hateful ambience. This enemy cannot be fought the way WW II, the Civil War, the War of Independence, or any of the thousands of wars in the world's history have been fought. We are in a new age with new problems, new resources, where the old paradigms no longer serve us. We are in the process of re-evaluating our concepts, values and practices, and determining new strategies and programs of survival. In many ways we don't know what we're doing, mistakes are made, and we find it unacceptable, yet we must forge ahead, doing the best we can with what we have. We can only put our trust in God to guide us and protect us from enemies as well as from ourselves. We cannot stand still; the enemy won't allow us that luxury.

Little will remain the same in the new age, not as we have known it. Change is usually uncomfortable, often misunderstood, and almost always unwelcome and resisted – look at what's happening everywhere. Little is being left untouched. But look also at what the results can be, when with concerted actions of the global community, terrorism will be destroyed, and self-government and freedom will be established worldwide. The new millennium as promised by God is now in the throes of its birth.

When a child is born, it is with heavy pain for the mother, but also joy. That is the way of things. Physical births are always accompanied with pain, but once the birth is complete, the mother has no more emotional connection to the pain of the birth process; she knows only the love and the promise of a new being created through her travail.

The world's birth of the New Millennium is similar. But it will never know the peace of a new age until the umbilical cords of attachments and allegiances of past attitudes and beliefs of superiority and inferiority, of uncompromising rights and wrongs are removed, to be replaced and firmly established with beliefs and applications of universal love and forgiveness. God facilitates this change, else it would never occur. He creates new conditions, turns things upside down and inside out, creates new alternatives and sets into motion situations and conditions that would not be possible without His intervention. God is behind the world's determined response to terrorism. The goal is the complete eradication of terrorism, to be replaced with mutual respect of differences, with non-judgment and universal love without conditions for all of mankind. Only then will peace be assured.

Peace is desired by all freedom loving peoples. To achieve it they petition God, but they mistakenly pray for the end of war, whereas they should instead pray for peace. Although peace will come when there is no more war, it is often attained only through military action. That is the way of man. That has always been the way of man. But it will soon be the way no more, for we are in the process of recreating what we are, individually and collectively, and creating a new future for all men.

There are light-workers among us, people who know their true relationship with God. They know and practice their God-given rights of co-creation with Him, and they are working with Him to create a new world. And it will be accomplished not with armed warfare, nor with attitudes of anti-warfare. It is being accomplished with love. The time for peace is not yet, but the time for its coming is upon us. We are now in the process of its birth. The travail of creation and re-creation is ours to experience and it is inescapable, but through it all we will change for the better. What has so long been accepted as the natural order of things will fade away and a new order will emerge, first in the minds, hearts and souls of individual men and women, and then in the souls of nations and the world.

The world as it has been known will no longer be. A new world is aborning. We are in the forefront of a new world of new life, a new world of love and peace for all of mankind. But if it is to manifest, we must not grow faint with fear in desperate surrender to comfort, or through pacification or complacency to the illusions of false peace. It must be done with love – *it can only be done with love* – love without conditions or expectations, and never with hate. Hate is a destroyer, and it will rebound on the individual or nation who hates. That is why terrorism and hate filled pseudo religions will come to their own demise. Love knows no limits, no restrictions and no regrets, embracing all with its touch of joy and peace. And in its application, it creates a new world, a new people, born and expressed in universal love and co-creativity with God.

This book has discussed the birth of a new people, a new nation and a new world birthed and expressed in spirituality, as distinct from religion. It will be a new world encased in individual and collective responsibility for all. There will be new relationships with God based in freedom and equality, free of the conditions and obligations of formalized thought and stifling rituals and doctrines of religion which only tend to divide. It will be a new world without the borders of hate, envy and fear dividing it into little enclaves of so-called self-protectionism. The fences of isolation will fall, and we and the world will breathe and live in peace and prosperity for everyone. War will be no more; peace will prevail in a renewal of love, equality and non-judgment. That is the reality that will be, not an illusionary reality based on the misunderstood and misapplied paradigms of the past. A new world, a new church, a new age of peace, of universal love and abundance is ours to create. It has already begun. It is our responsibility to continue. It will not be done for us.

It is asked in the Bible: *Know ye not that ye are Gods?* It is to us that the question is directed. We are the Gods it speaks of; it is we that have the ability and the power to co-create with the Supreme Creator all that we desire, all that we will be, all that we love, or all that we fear – the choice is ours. The power and the ability to create are ours; all we need to do is claim and exercise our rightful heritage as sons and daughters of God, and use the power of creation that was given to us at our birth. It is we who will lay the foundations for world peace. It is we who will reap the benefits of a world of brotherly love. It is we who will usher in a new world of non-judgment, forgiveness and prosperity for all. And it is we who will bring to fruition God's promise of a millennium of peace; and in so doing we will reap the fruits, sour or sweet, of what we sow today.

# CODA

*What shall we do?*
*Shall we be a part of this New World, or shall we isolate*
*ourselves, resist change and surrender to comfort?*

*What shall we do?*
*Shall we boldly step out and claim our place by God's side, or*
*bury our minds in the thirsty sands of a barren past?*

*What shall we do?*

# About the Author

Keith Bender is the author of several books, one of which is "Ark of the Rainbow," the story of his personal quest for truth. He has written scores of articles and was the editor and publisher of "Teaching Consciousness" an international newsletter. He is a priest according to the Order of Melchizadek, and currently resides in E. Aurora, NY with "Honey" his inseparable companion, a lovable Pit Bull loved by many: feared by none.

You may reach Mr. Bender through Ozark Mountain Publishing, Inc.

## Other Books Published
## by
## Ozark Mountain Publishing, Inc.

Conversations with Nostradamus, Volume I, II, III...............by Dolores Cannon
Jesus and the Essenes.........................................................by Dolores Cannon
They Walked with Jesus......................................................by Dolores Cannon
Between Death and Life........................................ by Dolores Cannon
A Soul Remembers Hiroshima..............................................by Dolores Cannon
Keepers of the Garden.........................................................by Dolores Cannon
The Legend of Starcrash.......................................................by Dolores Cannon
The Custodians....................................................................by Dolores Cannon
The Convoluted Universe - Book One, Two, Three..............by Dolores Cannon
I Have Lived Before.......................................................by Sture Lönnerstrand
The Forgotten Woman..............................................by Arun & Sunanda Gandhi
Luck Doesn't Happen by Chance...................................by Claire Doyle Beland
Mankind - Child of the Stars...........................by Max H. Flindt & Otto Binder
The Gnostic Papers.................................................by John V. Panella
Past Life Memories As A Confederate Soldier........................by James H. Kent
Holiday in Heaven.............................................................by Aron Abrahamsen
Is Jehovah An E.T.?................................................................by Dorothy Leon
The Ultimate Dictionary of Dream Language...........................by Briceida Ryan
The Essenes - Children of the Light...............by Stuart Wilson & Joanna Prentis
Rebirth of the Oracle...................................by Justine Alessi & M. E. McMillan
Reincarnation: The View from Eternity......by O.T. Bonnett, M.D. & Greg Satre
The Divinity Factor...............................................................by Donald L. Hicks
What I Learned After Medical School ..........................by O.T. Bonnett, M.D.
Why Healing Happens....................................................by O.T. Bonnett, M.D.
A Journey Into Being...................................................by Christine Ramos, RN
Discover The Universe Within You.......................................by Mary Letorney
Worlds Beyond Death.......................................by Rev. Grant H. Pealer
Let's Get Natural With Herbs................................................by Debra Rayburn
The Enchanted Garden..........................................................by Jodi Felice
My Teachers Wear Fur Coats........................by Susan Mack & Natalia Krawetz
Seeing True.......................................................................by Ronald Chapman
Elder Gods of Antiquity.......................................................by M. Don Schorn
Children of the Stars ............................................................. by Nikki Pattillo
Angels - The Guardians of Your Destiny .............by Maiya & Geoff Gray-Cobb
Seeds of the Soul...............................................................by Maiya Gray-Cobb
For more information about any of the above titles, soon to be released titles, or
other items in our catalog, write or visit our website:

**OZARK**
MOUNTAIN
PUBLISHING

PO Box 754
Huntsville, AR 72740
www.ozarkmt.com
1-800-935-0045/479-738-2348 Wholesale Inquiries Welcome